PERSONALITY
AND POLITICS

PERSONALITY AND POLITICS

Problems of Evidence, Inference, and Conceptualization

With a new preface

FRED I. GREENSTEIN

PRINCETON UNIVERSITY PRESS

PRINCETON, NEW JERSEY

To Amy, Jessica, and Michael

Published by Princeton University Press, 41 William Street, Princeton, New Jersey 08540

In the United Kingdom: Princeton University Press, Guildford, Surrey

Preface to New Edition copyright © 1987 by Princeton University Press

Library of Congress Cataloging in Publication Data will be found on the last printed page of this book

First printing, 1969 by Markham Publishing Company
Norton edition, 1975
First Princeton Paperback printing, 1987

LCC 87-2427
ISBN 0-691-07731-2
ISBN 0-691-02260-7 (pbk.)

Clothbound editions of Princeton University Press books are printed on acid-free paper, and binding materials are chosen for strength and durability. Paperbacks, while satisfactory for personal collections, are not usually suitable for library rebinding.

Printed in the United States of America by Princeton University Press, Princeton, New Jersey

Preface to New Edition

This book addresses a ubiquitous real-world phenomenon and a controversial scholarly specialization that bear the same name: personality and politics. Because I find it compellingly evident that in some contexts and at some times the phenomenon has been highly consequential, I consider it vital that paths be cleared through the tangle of intellectual underbrush that impedes more and better inquiry. The underbrush consists of disagreements among scholars about whether personality and politics warrants study and, if so, whether it is amenable to disciplined study. Fundamental questions about how to explain human behavior in general and political behavior in particular underly these controversies. What is appropriate evidence? What kinds of inferences are plausible? What conceptual strategies are productive?

I first encountered the controversies that were to be the "data" for this 1969 book in the 1950's, as I began to chart a personal path of inquiry into political psychology. I sought perspective on the debates in political science from other disciplines in which problems of linking psychological functioning to social phenomena also arise—for example, sociology, psychology, anthropology, and history. I gained some clarity, but also encountered much the same debates. Indeed, debate seemed to be more extensive than research in some disciplines. In Chapter Two I quote the 1960 observation of sociologists David Riesman and Nathan Glazer that the culture and personality literature (an analogue to the personality and politics literature) has "more critics than practitioners."[1]

There *appears* to be less contention now. But this is largely the result of compartmentalization in the social sciences. Increasingly, scholarly discourse takes place among specialists within narrow disciplinary areas rather than throughout or across disciplines. At the same time, the volume of work on political psychology, including issues

---

[1] David Riesman and Nathan Glazer, "*The Lonely Crowd*: A Reconsideration in 1960," in Seymour M. Lipset and Leo Lowenthal, eds., *Culture and Social Character* (New York: The Free Press, 1961), p. 437.

related to personality and politics, has grown; and one kind of political psychology—the cognitive psychology of perception and misperception—has found a respected niche in a political science field, namely international relations.[2] But consensus on the overall importance of such work has not substantially increased. The journal published by the International Society of Political Psychology—a group that was formed in the 1970's—has not become obligatory reading in the several disciplines from which the society draws members, and in the official journal of the American Political Science Association, articles explicitly addressed to personality and politics or political psychology are still just as rare as they were throughout the six decades from the appearance of the first issue of the journal to the publication of this book in 1969.[3]

The claims and counter-claims that I addressed in the 1960's on the merits of studying personality and politics still have not been resolved. A historian's 1985 review of a richly documented, closely argued psychobiography of Kemal Atatürk, for example, taxed the

[2] See for example, Robert Jervis, *Perception and Misperception in International Politics* (Princeton, N.J.: Princeton University Press, 1976); Richard Ned Lebow, *Between Peace and War: The Nature of International Crisis* (Baltimore: The Johns Hopkins University Press, 1981); Deborah W. Larson, *Origins of Containment: A Psychological Explanation* (Princeton, N.J.: Princeton University Press, 1985); and Robert Jervis, Richard Ned Lebow, and Janice Gross Stein, eds., *Psychology and Deterrence* (Baltimore: The Johns Hopkins University Press, 1985). For a collection of papers addressed generally to the role of cognition in political behavior, most of which report or discuss survey research on voting and public opinion, see Richard R. Lau and David O. Sears, eds., *Political Cognition* (Hillsdale, N.J.: Lawrence Erlbaum Associates, 1986).

[3] A listing of key words in the titles of articles in the six decades of the *American Political Science Review* appears in Kenneth Janda, ed., *Cumulative Index to the American Political Science Review, Volumes 1–62: 1906–1968* (Ann Arbor, Mich.: Xerox/University Microfilms, 1969). During this period the journal published only 17 articles that included the words "psychology" or "personality" in their titles. These references were dwarfed by references to governmental institutions and political processes: "Congress" appeared in 140 titles, "political party" in 164, and so on. Since 1968, references to "psychology" and "personality" have remained rare. It should be stressed that much psychological evidence is reported in *American Political Science Review* articles, especially in articles that have appeared since survey research became a major political science research procedure in the 1950's. Typically, when they refer to "personality," political scientists do not have in mind political attitudes and preferences of the sort reported in most survey research. Much of my analysis, however, is as applicable to attitudes and preferences as to any other kind of psychological disposition. In this I follow Henry A. Murray's usage, treating "personality" as "the most comprehensive term we have in psychology." Murray, "Personality: Contemporary Viewpoints: Components of an Evolving Personological System," *International Encyclopedia of the Social Sciences*, 12 (New York: Macmillan and The Free Press, 1968), p. 9.

book's authors for employing psychological explanations of their protagonist. In the reviewer's opinion, a cultural explanation would have
been more appropriate.[4] This criticism is based on a fallacy I discuss
in Chapter Two: that of treating sociocultural background as if it
competes with psychology in explaining behavior. As is often true of
disagreements about the study of personality and politics, the dispute
about the relative merits of explaining behavior in terms of actors'
backgrounds or their psychology can be constructively resolved. The
former shape the latter; both, therefore, need to be studied as parts
of causal chains.

One of the polemical issues about the worth of studying personality
and politics is of particular interest because it can be decided straight-
forwardly in a way that directly advances strategies of inquiry. I refer
to the debate about whether actors' inner dispositions or their contemporary environments are the better predictors of their actions. The
writings that emphasize the predictive power of psychology typically
introduce qualifications to identify the kinds of situations in which
individuals with different psychological proclivities are likely to behave
the same. Similarly, writings that stress the environmental or, as it is
often put, situational determinants of behavior commonly grant that
some situations do not constrain actors to behave uniformly and thus
permit differences in personal characteristics to affect behavior. Once
each side's qualifications are noted, it becomes clear that there is
substantial agreement among seeming disputants. In Chapter Two, I
distill from the debate propositions about the circumstances under
which political analysts will find it more or less necessary to take
account of psychological dispositions and environments in order to
explain political behavior. Moreover, an overarching insight emerges:
it is essential for students of politics to heed Kurt Lewin's admonition
that behavior must be analyzed in terms of the *interaction* of individual
and situation.[5]

The most illuminating inquiries into political psychology do precisely this, identifying what in the terminology of research methods
has come to be called interaction effects—relationships in which an

---

[4] Kemal H. Karpat, "The Personality of Atatürk," *American Historical Review*, 90
(1985), 896. The book under review is Vamik D. Volkan and Norman Itzkowitz, *The
Immortal Atatürk: A Psychobiography* (Chicago: University of Chicago Press, 1984).
[5] Kurt Lewin, *Principles of Topological Psychology* (New York: McGraw-Hill,
1936), pp. 11–12.

intervening variable must be identified in order to establish the effect of an independent variable on behavior. Thus, for example, Richard Christie and Florence Geis, in their meticulously designed study of individuals with personalities that predispose them to manipulate others (Machiavellianism), find consistent relationships between the disposition to be manipulative and action consistent with that disposition—but only under certain circumstances, such as in situations in which the potential for manipulation is clearly perceivable.[6]

In a parallel program of research into the psychology of leadership, Fred Fiedler finds that environmental differences—notably, different requirements for effectiveness in various roles—are key intervening variables. Role A will elicit effective performance by personality type X, while role B suits personality type Y. In effect echoing Gordon Allport's aphorism that "the same heat that melts the butter hardens the egg,"[7] Fiedler notes that specific leadership traits do not in themselves predict leaders' performance. Because "one can be an effective leader in some situations and not in others . . . a single leadership trait or combination of traits will not enable prediction in all situations." Thus leadership needs to be studied in terms of the interaction of person and situation, since "a trait or combination of traits may well predict performance in certain situations that can be specified. . . ."[8] Alexander and Juliette George provide a perfect illustration in their observation (discussed in Chapter Three) that Woodrow Wilson's intense need for power made him highly flexible when he was seeking to gain power but obdurately rigid when he was seeking to maintain it.

In the research of Christie and Geis and of Fiedler, environmental variables intervene between psychological differences and behavior. On the other hand, in his psycho-physiological studies of the anxiety levels of soldiers in Vietnam combat, Peter Bourne finds that differences in environmental context (roles) produce different intervening

---

[6] Richard Christie and Florence L. Geis, *Studies in Machiavellianism* (New York: Academic Press, 1970).

[7] Gordon W. Allport, *Personality: A Psychological Interpretation* (New York: Holt, 1937), p. 325.

[8] Fred E. Fiedler, *Leadership* (New York: General Learning Press, 1971), p. 15. See also his "What Triggers the Person-Situation Interaction in Leadership," in David Magnusson and Norman S. Endler, eds., *Personality at the Crossroads: Current Issues in Interactional Psychology* (Hillsdale, N.J.: Lawrence Erlbaum Associates, 1977), pp. 151–63 and the sources there cited.

psychological states and therefore may have different consequences
for the behavior of individuals who do not vary systematically in underlying psychological makeup. Bourne was able to interview soldiers
at times when they were highly vulnerable to Viet Cong attack and to
obtain a medical measure of the adrenal levels in their body. Some
faced combat with anxious apprehension, others with fatalism, if not
equanimity. All of the officers fell into the first category and most of
the enlisted men into the second. But the differences in anxiety level
did not come from character traits that differentiated officers from
enlisted personnel. Rather, the officers were directly aware of how
tenuous their circumstances were, the bulk of enlisted men were not.
Among the enlisted men, however, the radio operators had the same
information as the officers and were just as anxious.[9]

A turning point in research on personality occurred in 1975,
when the first international symposium was convened on "person by
situation interaction" as a basic perspective for the analysis of behavior.
The resulting volume on "interactional psychology" and subsequent
work under the same heading provides an invaluable body of basic
research, conceptualization, and methodological innovation for applied
study of behavior in particular institutional arenas such as politics.[10]
An interactional perspective sensitizes the political analyst to assess
the effects on behavior not only of psychological predispositions and
environmental contexts but also of different kinds of psychological
predispositions.

There is a tradition in political psychology, going back at least
to Harold Lasswell's 1930 *Psychopathology and Politics*, of being
especially attentive to irrational political behavior that is deeply rooted
in the emotions and is most readily explicable in terms of the psychodynamic theories of neurosis and ego defense that stem from the
work of Freud.[11] In Chapter Four, I illustrate the problems of con-

---

[9] Peter G. Bourne, "Altered Adrenal Function in Two Combat Situations in Viet
Nam," in B. E. Eleftheriou and J. P. Scott, eds., *The Physiology of Aggression and
Defeat* (New York: Plenum, 1971), pp. 265–305. Bourne's work does not assess the
effect of emotional excitation on behavior. The extensive research on this topic is
instructively discussed in Irving L. Janis and Leon Mann, *Decision Making: A Psychological Analysis of Conflict, Choice and Commitment* (New York: The Free Press, 1977).

[10] Magnusson and Endler, eds., *Personality at the Crossroads*. For further contributions to this literature, see Lawrence A. Pervin and Michael Lewis, eds., *Perspectives
in Interactional Psychology* (New York: Plenum, 1978).

[11] Harold D. Lasswell, *Psychopathology and Politics* (1930; rpt. Chicago: University of Chicago Press, 1977).

structing political typologies by dissecting such an explanation, in this case the psychodynamic account of a type of individual who thrives in hierarchies because of ego-defensive needs. This individual has repressed impulses toward authority. Driven from consciousness, these impulses manifest themselves through a classical neurotic strategy. The individual acquires an extravagantly positive view of perceived superiors and a similarly extreme negative view of perceived inferiors.

Research on this matter soon revealed, however, that some people express themselves in typical authoritarian ways, but not out of neurotic needs. Rather, their environments have provided them with cognitive maps that portray human relationships in terms of superiors and inferiors. Moreover, different motivational bases are likely to have different consequences for behavior. An individual whose view that the alternatives are to rule or to be ruled is based fundamentally on cognition is likely to be open to a change in view if provided with new information. But new information may simply *stiffen* the views and actions of the individual who is using his views about who should dominate and who should be subordinate to shore up emotional insecurities.

Another source of contention about the merits of studying personality and politics boils down to debate not about the political relevance of psychology in general but about the levels of psychodynamic functioning that were stressed by Lasswell and in the early studies of the authoritarian personality. Here the issue is whether it is correct to assume that political behavior has psychodynamic roots and, if so, whether those roots are amenable to empirical inquiry. By thinking in interactional terms, we are encouraged to establish the motivational bases of political behavior empirically and to assess their effects, not to *assume* that one or another type of psychological disposition is politically consequential.

To clarify this volume and bring it up to date, let me offer some chapter-by-chapter afterthoughts, beginning with recapitulations of my original assertions.

Chapter One, in addition to containing an apologia for the study of personality and politics and a literature review, presents a tripartite principle for organizing the literature: single-case studies of political actors; multicase studies of types of political actors; and aggregate discussions that seek to use microdata on individuals to help to explain

macrophenomena ranging from the small group performance to interaction among polities.

I go on to introduce M. Brewster Smith's "map for the analysis
of personality and politics" in order to show the need for an interactional approach to personality and politics analysis, an approach that
encourages the analyst to examine the interplay of personality structures with attitudes and beliefs and with the past and present environmental contexts that shape personal dispositions and mediate behavior. As useful as Smith's formulation is, for some purposes it needs
expansion. Elsewhere, I have reformulated Smith's map in order to
stress the political importance of *environments-as-perceived*, as well as
"actual" external environments.[12] My reformulation also stresses that
environmental stimuli do not have independent effects on action. They
must pass through a screen of cognitive sets and processes. The latter
in turn may be influenced by underlying personality structures, such
as the individual's characteristic ways of relating to others, cognitive
style, and ego defenses.[13]   *ego adaptations.*

I also paraphrase Smith's map to emphasize that the impact of
psychology and politics on one another takes place in ongoing, historical processes. Smith's depiction, by stressing feedback, sensitizes
us to how behavior can reinforce existing relationships between individuals and their environments. Especially in studying the psychology of leadership, it is helpful to be alert to how an actor's behavior
may affect his subsequent environment. It is, for example, no accident
that President Nixon surrounded himself with the particular constellation of White House associates whose actions (and failures to act at
key times) helped lead him to the Watergate catastrophe. Pivotal aspects of his environment were of his own making.

As noted, Chapter Two explores the common ground between the
contending sides in controversies over the study of personality terms
and politics. Two of the most instructive debates concern the relative
impact of situations and personal dispositions as determinants of be-

---

[12] Fred I. Greenstein, "Personality and Politics," in Fred I. Greenstein and Nelson
W. Polsby, eds., *The Handbook of Political Science*, 2 (Reading, Mass.: Addison Wesley,
1975): 5–17.

[13] I now prefer to think of the last of these personality processes as "ego *adaptation*
and defense." For a conceptualization and empirical study that brings out the creative
as well as the neurotic consequences of psychodynamics, see George E. Vaillant,
Adaptation to Life: How the Best and Brightest Came of Age (Boston: Little, Brown,
1977).

havior and whether ego-defensive psychodynamics are consequential in everyday behavior. Each qualifies its empirical claims, and the qualifications converge, yielding propositions about when psychology in general and ego defenses in particular are most likely to be necessary in explanations of political behavior.

I would now stress that the propositions point to necessary, *not sufficient* conditions for studying political psychology. The conditions are not sufficient because the study of political psychology is itself a distinctive focus for political analysis. Political psychology should not be relegated to explaining residual behavior that cannot be accounted for in situational terms. Some analytic concerns, most notably that of assessing the development and behavior of an individual over a lifetime or career, call for comprehensive analysis of the actor in all of the circumstances he experiences.[14]

Chapter Three, on psychological analysis of individual political actors, and Chapter Four, on analysis of types of political actors, are parallel in their emphasis on the logical, if not practical, separability of the tasks of describing the surface manifestations (phenomenology), the inner psychodynamics, and the developmental history (genesis) of an individual or type. Undoubtedly, the most widely discussed contribution to these areas since 1969 is a book that combines individual and typological analysis, James David Barber's *The Presidential Character: Predicting Performance in the White House*.[15] Drawing on biographies, Barber classified twentieth-century American presidents in terms of a fourfold typology of character types. Not least among the contributions of Barber's analysis is the discussion his work has sparked about how case analyses and typologies can be persuasively documented and applied in explaining behavior. Alexander George's extended article on Barber's book is compulsory reading on this score.[16]

In discussing what makes one single-case analysis more persuasive than another, I stress the importance of making explicit the rationale for assertions about phenomenology, dynamics, and genesis of an actor's political behavior. The most persuasive of the psychobio-

---

[14] Cf. Betty Glad, "Contributions of Psychobiography," in Jeanne N. Knudson, ed., *Handbook of Political Psychology* (San Francisco: Jossey Bass, 1973), pp. 296–321.

[15] James David Barber, *The Presidential Character: Predicting Performance in the White House* (Englewood Cliffs, N.J.: Prentice-Hall, 1972, 1976, 1985).

[16] Alexander L. George, "Assessing Presidential Character," *World Politics*, 26 (1974), 234–82.

graphies published since 1969 do this. A highly selective, deliberately
diverse list of important contributions to this genre includes (in addition
to the work on Atatürk to which I have already referred), Tucker's
study of Stalin, Marvick's of Richelieu, Walter's of Australian Prime
Minister Gough Whitlam, Mack's of Lawrence of Arabia, and Hirsch's
of Frankfurter.[17]
I also note in Chapter Three that interpretations of single actors
are likely to become more persuasive if the evidence and inferences
employed are subjected to scrutiny by more than one observer, as is
done in assessing the reliability of psychological tests. There has been
some movement in this direction by single-case analysts, most notably
Steven Brown, who has applied the Q-sort procedure, which permits
quantitative comparison of different interpreters' analyses of the mul-
titude of observations that can be made on any actor.[18] But, if only
because a biographer must be immersed in great quantities of diverse
evidence over an extended period, it is unlikely that psychobiographers
will regularly employ such strict procedures for assessing reliability.

Whether or not political scientists assess the technical reliability
of the observations they make on single cases, they can attend to a
further recommendation I make in Chapter Three, that of drawing on
basic psychological research addressed to the validity of the claims
that clinical psychologists make about causal connections. The literature I cite assessing the empirical standing of clinically observed
relationships is slowly expanding. One stimulus has been epistemological analyses that undermine much of Freud's abstract theory but
open the way for empirical study of his and other clinicians' interpretations of the behavior of patients in treatment and of others in everyday
life.[19]

---

[17] Robert C. Tucker, *Stalin as Revolutionary, 1879–1919: A Study in History and
Personality* (New York: Norton, 1973); Elizabeth Wirth Marvick, *The Young Richelieu:
A Psychoanalytic Approach to Leadership* (Chicago: University of Chicago Press, 1983);
James Walter, *The Leader: A Political Biography of Gough Whitlam* (St. Lucia, Queens-
land: University of Queensland Press, 1980); John E. Mack, *A Prince of Our Disorder:
The Life of T. E. Lawrence* (Boston: Little, Brown, 1976); and H. N. Hirsch, *The Enigma
of Felix Frankfurter* (New York: Basic Books, 1981). For a valuable set of remarks on
the tasks of single-case analysis of public political actors, with comments on more and
less successful political psychobiographies, see Hirsch's "Clio on the Couch," *World
Politics*, 32 (1980), 406–24.

[18] Steven R. Brown, "Intensive Analysis in Political Research," *Political Methodology*, 1 (1974), 1–25, and his *Political Subjectivity: Applications of Q-Sort Methodology in Political Science* (New Haven, Conn.: Yale University Press, 1980).

[19] See Adolf Gruenbaum, *The Foundations of Psychoanalysis: A Philosophical*

This said, I must introduce a major qualification to the implicit proposal in Chapter Three that single-case analyses be perfected along lines that make them explicable in terms of the "covering law" principles that political scientists have in mind when they seek to falsify hypotheses. I am persuaded by J. Donald Moon's attempt to show the complementarity of the covering law explanatory modes and of the interpretative modes that prevail in the humanities.[20] The steps I suggest in Chapter Three for testing single-case assertions are heuristically desirable because they clarify single-case analyses. But the probabilistic general propositions that emerge from basic personality research are not, in principle, capable of yielding conclusive tests of explanations in individual cases.

In Chapter Four I chose to explicate the notoriously tangled authoritarian personality literature because it illuminates most of the problems that arise in formulating and applying fully developed typologies that classify actors in terms of their phenomenology, dynamics, and developmental experiences. There has been progress since the 1960's in grounding complex psychological typologies empirically.[21] Nevertheless, complex typologies are not easily constructed and documented. Therefore it can be productive to classify political actors in terms of single traits that differentiate them in illuminating ways.[22]

Both *Personality and Politics* and a later work in which Michael Lerner and I collected many of the seminal writings on the topic

Critique (Berkeley: University of California Press, 1984), and in particular the many comments on a précis of his book by psychologists, psychiatrists, and philosophers of social science in *Behavioral and Brain Sciences*, 9 (1986), 217–84, especially Robert R. Holt's remarks. See also Holt's "The Current Status of Psychoanalytic Theory," *Psychoanalytic Psychology*, 2 (1985), 289–315.

    [20] J. Donald Moon, "The Logic of Political Inquiry: A Synthesis of Opposed Perspectives," in Greenstein and Polsby, eds., *The Handbook of Political Science*, 1:131–228.

    [21] See, for example, Steven Gangestad and Mark Snyder, " 'To Carve at the Joints': On the Existence of Discrete Classes in Personality," *Psychological Review*, 92 (1985), 317–49, and Leslie C. Morey, "An Empirical Comparison of Interpersonal and DSM-III Approaches to Classification of Personality Disorders," *Psychiatry*, 48 (1985), 358–64.

    [22] See, for example, the single-trait classifications that Payne and his associates find helpful for analyzing differences in the incentives that lead varying individuals to engage in political leadership and the consequences of such differences for political action: James L. Payne, Oliver H. Woshinsky, Eric P. Veblen, William H. Coogan, and Gene E. Bigler, *The Motivations of Politicians* (Chicago: Nelson Hall, 1984).

underrepresent quantitative personality typologies, including single-trait classifications.[23] In addition to the work noted above, I have already discussed the research of Christie and Geis on Machiavellianism. Also of importance is the fruition of Herbert McClosky's long-term questionnaire studies of samples of citizens and political leaders. McClosky and his students have carefully documented the psychometric standing of McClosky's influential early reports of his findings and have assiduously winnowed their data to identify the kinds of interaction effects that often are the main links between personality and politics.[24]

Chapter Five shows the complexity of linkage between underlying psychological dispositions and the overall properties of political systems, large and small. In the area of aggregation, the post-1969 work of Alexander George and of Irving Janis on interpersonal relationships in leadership groups is of particular importance.[25] Both scholars have focused on intrinsic aspects of group interaction that, independent of personal properties, lead political decision-making processes to more or less satisfactory outcomes. Their sketches of social-psychological processes, moreover, can easily be modified to take into account the kinds of individual and typological influences on behavior that I discuss in Chapters Three and Four. In fact, in their previous work both George,

---

[23] Fred I. Greenstein and Michael Lerner, eds., *A Source Book for the Study of Personality and Politics* (Chicago: Markham, 1971).

[24] In addition to the earlier McClosky studies cited in note 30 of Chapter One, see the following other works employing the same data set: Giuseppe Di Palma and Herbert McClosky, "Personality and Conformity: The Learning of Political Attitudes," *American Political Science Review*, 64 (1970), 1054–73 (reprinted in Greenstein and Lerner, *op. cit.*, pp. 119–57); Paul M. Sniderman and Jack Citrin, "Psychological Sources of Political Belief: Self-Esteem and Isolationist Attitudes," *American Political Science Review*, 65 (1972), 401–17; Paul M. Sniderman, *Personality and Democratic Politics* (Berkeley: University of California Press, 1974); McClosky and Alida Brill, *Dimensions of Tolerance* (New York: Russell Sage Foundation, 1983); and McClosky and John Zaller, *The American Ethos* (Cambridge, Mass.: Harvard University Press, 1984). Among the many other quantitative studies of interest, see Alex Inkeles and David H. Smith, *Becoming Modern* (Cambridge, Mass.: Harvard University Press, 1974), and Stanley Rothman and S. Robert Lichter, *Roots of Radicalism* (New York: Oxford University Press, 1983).

[25] Alexander L. George, "The Case for Multiple Advocacy in Making Foreign Policy," *American Political Science Review*, 66 (1972), 751–95, with comment by I. M. Destler and rejoinder by George; idem, *Presidential Decisionmaking in Foreign Policy: The Effective Use of Information and Advice* (Denver: Westview Press, 1980). Irving L. Janis, *Victims of Groupthink* (Boston: Little, Brown, 1973), and Janis's expansion in *Groupthink* (Boston: Little, Brown, 1982).

a political scientist, and Janis, a psychologist, laid much of the ground-work for modification.[26] Interest in making inferences from data on individual dispositions to data on system states extends beyond political scientists and psychologists to anthropologists and economists, who have long sought to link micro- and macroeconomics. Within sociology, a discipline classically influenced by the Durkheimian desire to analyze social phenomena "at the social level," there is systematic movement toward establishing ways of documenting connections between social systems and the individuals who constitute them.[27]

I conclude with a point *not* made in this book, but one that has increasingly pressed itself upon me as I seek to apply these formulations to data on the relationships among American presidents and their advisers. In analyzing political processes, knowledge of the classical issues in the many existing formal literatures on psychology is no substitute for knowledge of the distinctive norms and demands of particular political institutions and processes. These elicit psychological qualities that have not always been of concern to students of psychology, unless they are informed in detail about political mores and practices. In short, there is a discrepancy between what might be called *political* psychology and political *psychology*. Thus, for example, if we conclude that Richard Nixon was deeply suspicious of the motives of other political actors, it will not do simply to describe his political behavior (or that of any other actor) in the language of clinical psychology or psychiatry.

An item of behavior that appears susceptible to a clinical explanation may be a function of the specific norms or requirements of the setting within which it occurs. An example far afield from the presidency is the reinterpretation of the research finding that American

---

[26] See, for example, George's "Some Uses of Dynamic Psychology in Political Biography: Case Materials on Woodrow Wilson," in Greenstein and Lerner, *op. cit.*, pp. 78–98, and Janis's "Decision Conflicts: A Theoretical Analysis," *Journal of Conflict Resolution*, 3 (1959), 6–27 (reprinted in Greenstein and Lerner, pp. 171–94).

[27] Paul F. Lazarsfeld, Ann K. Pasanella, and Morris Rosenberg, eds., *Continuities in the Language of Social Research* (New York: The Free Press, 1972), especially Section III. See also James R. Lincoln and Gerald Zeitz, "Organizational Properties from Aggregate Data: Separating Individuals and Structural Effects," *American Sociological Review*, 45 (1980), 391–408. For a fundamental analysis of Durkheim, including a critique of his dicta on psychology and social phenomena, see Steven Lukes, *Emile Durkheim, His Life and His Work: A Historical and Critical Study* (1973; rpt. Stanford, Calif.: Stanford University Press, 1985), pp. 10–19.

blacks exhibit paranoid "pathology" on one of the most widely used personality assessment scales. As Malcolm Gynther has pointed out, psychopathological interpretation of this finding is inappropriate: high "paranoia" scores are realistic responses to the environmental pressures faced by well-adjusted black slum dwellers.[28]

Similarly, American presidents operate in extraordinarily demanding environments that place intense pressures on them and are replete with potential pitfalls. Contrary to the theories of some reductionist psychologists, clinical paranoia is not necessary for effective leadership. Instead, such a disturbance probably is fatal in the long run for presidents and other high leaders in democracies. But a "realistic" quota of guardedness and suspicion is undoubtedly necessary for carrying out the presidential role, unless the president construes it in a highly nonactivist fashion.

The student of personality and politics, then, needs to bring two kinds of understanding to his scholarship: specific appreciation of politics and general awareness of basic psychological theory and research.[29]

Princeton, 1986

---

[28] Malcolm Gynther, "White Norms and Black MMPIs: A Prescription for Discrimination," *Psychological Bulletin*, 78 (1972), 386–402.

[29] For a fuller discussion, see my essay "Political Psychology: A Pluralistic Universe," in Knudson, ed., *Handbook of Political Psychology*, especially pp. 545–67. On the need for a political psychology that addresses psychological elements in the distinctive role requirements of political leaders, see Stanley Hoffmann, "On the Psychology of Peace and War: Critique and Agenda," *Political Psychology*, 7 (1986), 1–22.

Acknowledgements

I have been nibbling, picking at, and worrying the question of how to study personality and politics for so long that I cannot sort out all of my debts. Many people have commented on previous incarnations of this book, as well as on my efforts to think out the argument here in lectures and seminars. I simply cannot reconstruct the full list of people who have helped me at the earlier stages; but I would like to say that I continue to appreciate their efforts. The following chapters in this book are adapted with publishers' permission from the following of my previous essays:

Chapter One: "The Need for Systematic Inquiry into Personality and Politics: Introduction and Overview," *Journal of Social Issues*, 24:3 (1968), 1–14.

Chapter Two: "The Impact of Personality on Politics: An Attempt to Clear Away Underbrush," *American Political Science Review*, 61 (1967), 629–41.

Chapter Three: "Art and Science in the Political Life History: A Review of A. F. Davies' *Private Politics*," *Politics: The Journal of the Australasian Political Studies Association*, 2 (1967), 176–80.

Chapters Four and Five: "Personality and Political Socialization: The Theories of Authoritarian and Democratic Character," *Annals of the American Academy of Political and Social Science*, 361 (1965), 81–95.

Throughout: "Personality and Politics: Problems of Evidence, Inference, and Conceptualization," *American Behavioral Scientist*, 11:2 (1967), 38–53, which also appears in somewhat more polished form in Seymour Martin Lipset, ed., *Politics and the Social Sciences* (New York: Oxford University Press, 1969), 163–206.

Most of the preceding have, however, been substantially changed as a result of readers' comments, my own afterthoughts, and the requirements of assembling a book rather than a collection of essays. Much of Chapters One, Three, and Five consists of previously unpublished material, as does all of Chapter Six.

During graduate school at Yale University, my interest in personality and politics began to become something more disciplined than a diffuse general fascination with the topic. At Yale, I had the good luck to be in the seminars of three of the central writers on political psychology: Robert E. Lane, Harold D. Lasswell, and Nathan Leites. My own seminars on personality and politics, at Yale and Wesleyan Universities and at the University of Essex, have been a principal vehicle for shaping my views. What began as a drifting discussion course on disparate fragments of literature in time became an over-organized exposition on my part. The turning point between under- and over-organized seminars was in 1964–65, when I was a Fellow at the Center for Advanced Study in the Behavioral Sciences. As at graduate school, I was fortunate at the Center in finding myself together with a remarkable number of important contributors to this area of endeavor. I will mention only one of them—M. Brewster Smith. I am indebted to him for far more than the figure on page 27, which serves to organize so much of my argument. He has been a patient and extraordinarily unerring commentator on successive versions of this work; and I value his encouragement almost as much as his comments. In addition to Smith, four other readers—none of whom ought to be blamed for this book's shortcomings—went through the final manuscript: James D. Barber, Alexander George, Howard Levinthal, and Michael Parenti. The first two have given me their advice on these matters on more occasions than any of us can remember. Michael Lerner, who was kind enough to do the bibliographical essay, has also been tactfully tireless in pointing to a number of difficulties in my analysis; indeed, he finally provoked me to mitigate several of them.

I am myself aware of a number of difficulties that remain in what follows; however, I have had enough of the pale cast of thought and therefore leave the difficulties to the reader to note and hopefully resolve. I *do* want simply to mention a pair of what strike me as non-difficulties—issues (or rather terms) that will seem to some readers to be fatal omissions in a book on political psychology. Many contemporary political scientists would make abundant use of the words "role" and "culture" in writing on the matters that concern me here. They would make confident assertions about "role theory" or "political culture," perhaps even using these notions as if they had quite unambiguous referents. My failure to make much reference to "role" and "culture" is not accidental, even though I recognize that these terms have been put to good use by others. Words, in the often quoted dictum of Lewis Carroll's Humpty Dumpty, are ours to use as we choose. But it is important to make our usage clear. Mine has involved employing, as my basic raw material, categories that have reference to individual psychological dispositions, categories that refer to the environmental phenomena that impinge upon individuals, and categories that refer to individuals' actions. The terms "role" and "culture" are used in various ways by various writers. Sometimes these terms are given an inner referent, sometimes an outer referent; sometimes they are used in referring to behavior; and sometimes they are given multiple referents. I do occasionally mention this pair of terms and even briefly discuss problems in their use. In deliberately choosing not to use these terms centrally, my assumption has been that I could translate any assertions that might seem to call for the use of "role" or "culture" into the language of predisposition, environment, and response. My further assumption has been that, at least for the purposes of the present work, so translating these terms contributed both to parsimony and to clarity. The reader is the judge; but some readers will want to be warned that I have ostracized their conceptual pets.

I would like to mention several financial mentors: Wesleyan University, for sabbatical leave of one semester in 1964–65 and 1968–69, as well as occasional contributions to research expenses; the Psychoanalytic Research and Development Fund, for support of an instructive year of part-time study at New York Psychoanalytic Institute (1961–62); the Ford Foundation, for a grant administered through Wesleyan University enabling me to employ undergraduate research assistants; the Social Science Research Council, for Faculty Research Grants the summers of 1964 and 1967; the Center for Advanced Study in the Behavioral Sciences; the National Science Foundation, for a senior Postdoctoral Fellowship (1968–69); and the University of Essex, which provided me with a haven, intellectual stimulation, and clerical assistance during what proved to be a more demanding than expected period of final vision and revision before consigning the manuscript to its readers.

My wife, Barbara, having been exploited beyond reasonable expectation on other of my efforts, wisely insulated herself from the present sound and fury—until the final few weeks of manuscript preparation. At that point it became clear that, having inched painfully up the mountain for far too long, I was faltering just short of the summit. Her energetic and impeccable contributions as an editorial advisor and research assistant—several weeks of sustained effort in all—provided the necessary final boost.

June 1969   Fred I. Greenstein
University of Essex
Colchester, Essex, England

Note on Second Printing: A few editorial changes have been made in order to correct confusions, ambiguities, or misleading emphases.

Contents

Introduction

Plagues, famines, and other disasters have the grim consequence of being good business for those who attend the injured and the dead. Similarly, occasions when political actors engage in bizarre or highly distinctive behavior serve to fuel the controversial but irrepressible endeavor of studying the connections between personality and politics.

1974 provides just such an occasion. Writing shortly after the tortured, self-defeating behavior by Richard Nixon that led to his resignation as President of the United States, I must inevitably draw on topical illustrations from some of the extraordinary manifestations of political personality since this book originally appeared in 1969, notably those connected with the American presidency and high leadership in the Nixon administration in general. Moreover, this is an opportunity to refer to personality and politics literature of the post-1969 years, a task simplified by recent literature reviews, including two of my own.[1]

Interest in personality and politics has been stimulated on earlier occasions by the events of the time. During the 1930's and 1940's, the seeming incongruence of the behavior of a nation and its leaders with common-sense situational explanations provided one of the impulses for a major wave of personality and politics inquiry and speculation. I refer to the studies of the authoritarian personality, of Nazism as a mass movement, of German (and other) national characters, and (via psychobiography-from-a-distance and the work of clinical psychologists and psychiatrists who were able to interview incarcerated Nazis) of the psychological

---

[1] Fred I. Greenstein, "Political Psychology: A Pluralistic Universe," in Jeanne N. Knutson, ed., *Handbook of Political Psychology* (San Francisco: Jossey-Bass, 1973), 438–70, and my "Personality and Politics," in Fred I. Greenstein and Nelson W. Polsby, eds., *The Handbook of Political Science*, vol. 2 (Reading, Mass.: Addison-Wesley, forthcoming 1975).

characteristics of Nazi leaders. Even now, interpretations of the character of Adolf Hitler seem to be an endless preoccupation of writers on the Nazi period.[2]

President Nixon's behavior in connection with the scandals and outrages loosely symbolized by the word "Watergate" rapidly made the sometime practice of psychologizing about Nixon a major intellectual enterprise. He had been the object of psychological speculation well before he assumed the presidency, but his behavior in office, especially after re-election, made it imperative to take account of his personal qualities. Nixon's peculiarly driven personality even led him to provide the very sort of data normally unavailable to analysts of living political figures—tape recordings of his most incriminating and illuminating off-the-record encounters with his aides.

When academic students of politics fail to take into account the psychodynamic causes of the truncated Nixon presidency, they leave the field open for popular writers and investigators from other disciplines, such as psychiatry, who are not sensitized to "political realities." As an example of journalistic psychodiagnosis, consider the following peremptory conclusion by a British reporter who for many years covered Washington. Reviewing a whole series of non-psychological explanations for Watergate and finding them inadequate, Peter Jenkins wrote shortly before Nixon's resignation:

> Nixon's Presidency is the projection of his personality. Lacking any firm commitment or ideological belief, he made do with the traditional, fundamentalist values of his Middle American background which he expounded in public. The force of his destructive personality is evil, but happily his exercise of power has been inept and lacking in direction, mistaking appearance for substance, concerned more with petty vendetta than with wide-scale repression. As Haldeman lamented: "We are so (adjective deleted) square that we get caught at everything." A PR man does not have the makings of an effective tyrant. Watergate was entirely characteristic of Nixon's presidency—dishonest, disgraceful, inept.

---

[2] Much of this literature is referred to in Chapters 4 and 5. See also pp. 168–71 and 180–81 of the bibliographical note Michael Lerner contributed to this volume.

"How could it have happened?" It happened because the American people elected Nixon to be President, an unfortunate choice. But how were they to know he might be a psychopath? "Who is to blame?" Nixon's to blame—Nixon's the one.[3]

How are scholars of politics to assess such assertions? How can they become progressively better versed in dealing with these and less dramatic attempts to take the human ingredients of politics into account? Such is the concern of this book and it seems even more to the point now than when the book was originally published.

Individuals with distinctive characteristics may be notable for their political successes as well as their failures. The other most publicized figure during the Nixon years—the scholar-turned international diplomatist, Henry Kissinger—has also been the object of much psychological speculation. Kissinger's academic writings had deprecated explanations of politics in psychological terms and, although he noted that political actors themselves frequently made such explanations, he attributed this tendency to the naiveté peculiar to American foreign policy leaders.[4] Once in office, however, Kissinger was not reluctant to accept personal credit for his achievements and to attribute to his own personal qualities the many shrewd feats of diplomatic negotiation in which he was involved.

The widespread view of Kissinger's personal impact on world politics in the late 1960's and early 1970's is well summarized in the following statement by Israeli Foreign Minister Abba Eban. Eban's remarks stress Kissinger's contribution to establishing an Arab-Israeli detente, but they are representative of assertions about his performance in numerous political arenas:

> I think that Secretary Kissinger's personal role refutes the view that history is the product of impersonal forces and objective conditions in which the personal human factor doesn't matter . . . I think it does matter. I believe that the association of American prestige with Secretary

---

[3] Peter Jenkins, "Portrait of a Presidency," *New York Magazine*, June 24, 1974, p. 36.

[4] Henry A. Kissinger, "Domestic Structure and Foreign Policy," *Dædalus*, 95 (1966), 503–29.

Kissinger's skills have been crucial in creating a new climate. After all, the position after the October war is not the same as before. Instead of deadlock, there is movement; instead of rhetoric there is also negotiation, and for this I think the United States and its Secretary of State have a large amount of credit.[5]

More generally, as is noted at the outset of this book, qualities of political actors seem to be omnipresent when one examines politics closely in its immediate day-to-day details. An interesting parallel to this point can be found in a recent influential formula of "levels of analysis" in the interpretation of *collective* political phenomena, the treatment of foreign policy decision-making in Graham Allison's *Essence of Decision*.[6]

Allison refers to three approaches to the analysis of collective political behavior. The first is a mode in which nations are treated as if they were single "rational" actors after the fashion of economic-man models. As Allison points out, such models fail to provide adequate explanations of an event such as the Cuban missile crisis, because a whole series of alternative possible predictions about the missile crisis emerge when rational-actor assumptions are applied to this sequence of events. He goes on to describe a second level of analysis in which nations are treated not as units, but as collections of bureaucratic agencies. The particular routines and rivalries of these agencies then can be analyzed to explain departures from "rationality." Thus, bureaucratic disagreement between the Central Intelligence Agency and the Air Force about who should do what help explain the seemingly "irrational" delays of the United States in detecting the missiles implanted by the Soviet Union in Cuba. But Allison notes that even the bureaucratic model falls short of a satisfactory explanation.

He proposes a close and detailed case study of the actual sequence of the policy-making process, calling this the "governmental decision-making" level of political analysis. At this third

---

[5] Bernard Gwertzman, "Kissinger and the Question of 'Policy Bias'," *New York Times*, March 25, 1974.

[6] Graham Allison, *The Essence of Decision: Explaining the Cuban Missile Crisis* (Boston: Little, Brown, 1971). For an earlier statement using somewhat different terminology, see his "Conceptual Models and the Cuban Missile Crisis," *American Political Science Review*, 63 (1969), 689–718.

level, although Allison himself does not engage in psychodiagnosis, he is explicit in noting the centrality of individual actors and their personal qualities.

The core of this level of close political analysis is personality. How each man manages to stand the heat in his kitchen, each player's operating style, and the complementarity or contradiction among personalities and styles in the inner circle are irreducible pieces of the policy blend.[7]

Allison's analysis of the Cuban missile crisis does not describe more than the surface characteristics of the various protagonists in his case study. But clearly one can, and inevitably some investigators *will*, seek to introduce explicit interpretations of how actors handle the "heat in the kitchen," how this affects their operating styles, and the ways in which these influence individual and international political outcomes.

Interestingly, Allison's analysis of the logic of how the attempt to treat nations as single rational actors becomes progressively more qualified until one disaggregates the nation into bureaucratic units with distinctive goals and procedures has a direct analogy to the ways in which individuals (including both single actors and types of actors) are treated by political scientists and other behavioral scientists. As I have noted elsewhere, there is a distinct, rather reductionist sequence through which political psychology finds itself achieving currency and legitimacy.[8]

If the behavior of a political actor seems unproblematic, the tendency is to explain this behavior in terms of its "situational" determinants. Situational explanation is directly analogous to what, at the group level, Allison describes as rational-actor explanation. In effect, the situational analyst examines the external constraints surrounding political actors and explains their behavior in terms of the practicalities of how any person with a "normal" set of desired ends would operate, given such external parameters.

Much political behavior seems to lend itself to this mode of explanation, but two fatal shortcomings vitiate situational or

[7] Allison, *op cit.*, p. 166.
[8] Greenstein, "Political Psychology: A Pluralistic Universe," *op cit.*, pp. 443–45.

rational-actor analyses (whether of individuals or of collectives).
Ends vary and there is nothing in these approaches that provides
intellectual leverage to explain the variance in the goals one seeks
to maximize, given a set of external constraints. Second, given
common ends or situational constraints, political actors nevertheless vary in their behavior, as is argued at length in Chapter
Two.

  We are reminded of the endless interaction between situations
and the varying personal properties of political actors by M.
Brewster Smith's "map" for the analysis of personality and
politics. A potentially misleading aspect of the graphic depiction
of his map on page 27 is that the causal arrows point independently
from both the predispositional and the situational panels directly
to the behavioral outcome panel. But, as Allport stresses (see p.
39), human action is *never* directly caused by situations; it is
invariably mediated by psychological variables.[9] These variables
are not directly observable; they are intellectual constructs based
on observation over time of the patterning of an individual's
actions. Unobservable as they may be, such constructs are necessary to account for the ways in which different individuals vary
in response to similar situational stimuli.

  When this individual variation, in the face of more or less
comparable stimuli, is sufficiently compelling, a typical analytic
approach is to introduce rather rudimentary and uncomplicated
psychological explanations—references to the ideological differences among actors or to simple, generalized psychological traits
(introversion, extroversion, aggressiveness, etc.). These references typically are to aspects of individual psychology that the
protagonists themselves are consciously aware of or could readily
be made consciously aware of, if asked to reflect on the matter.
Stretching the analogy a bit, it strikes me that this rough-
and-ready approach of using general, nontechnical categories
and single-factor psychological explanations parallels Allison's
approach of disaggregating government into a constellation of
agencies with special operating procedures and rivalries to
account for departures from seeming rationality.

  On occasion, however, the use of trait psychology or common-

---

[9] For an attempt to reformulate Smith's map so as to evade this difficulty,
see the second essay referred to in n. 1.

sense ideological categories, and the reliance on psychological factors of which the actors themselves are reasonably aware, fare no better than the situational-rational-actor approach in yielding convincing explanations of political behavior. This is particularly true both in the case of exceptionally creative political behavior and when behavior is self-defeating, as with President Nixon's conduct in his second term. (Compare Nixon's political demise with my analysis of Woodrow Wilson's final years in office in Chapter Three.) Step-by-step through the inexorable process that led to his resignation, Nixon engaged in many acts, each of which in itself might have been susceptible to situational or rudimentary, common-sense psychological interpretation. But his overall *pattern* of action seems inexplicable in terms of his ostensible values. Thus, at least for cases like that of the end of Nixon's presidency, and cases of extraordinarily successful political performance, a third and more "clinical" level of psychological analysis, paralleling Allison's third level of group analysis, becomes necessary.

The three levels (or types) of political psychology analysis are like Allison's three levels of group behavior analysis in being *analytic* distinctions. As Allison points out, the levels are not "real." They are deliberate exercises in intellectual selective perception, and ultimately need to be merged if one seeks a holistic explanation of how an individual or collective has behaved. Failure to be holistic causes difficulties, especially if the analysis is concerned with policy problems as they manifest themselves "out there." Furthermore, from the standpoint of political psychology, not merging all three levels tends to leave psychological interpretation as a residual category and depth psychological interpretation as a residual category *within* a residual category, with the resulting danger that the lineaments of the individual actors who participate in politics are not fully taken into account.

This problem arises both in empirical research and in theoretical discussions like the one in Chapter Two. That chapter, in effect, embroiders a series of middleground propositions between the qualifications of *critics* of the personality and politics literature and the qualifications of *defenders*. Both kinds of qualifications appear to merge, forming a core of contingent propositions about the circumstances under which personality factors *must* be taken into account. A well-taken criticism of this middleground approach has been made by the psychobiographer Betty Glad[10] and by Michael Lerner, who has done a gifted depth analysis of three intensively interviewed individuals from the general population.[11] They argue that the political actor's personality should be placed in the foreground, rather than merely highlighting the incidental characteristics that inescapably impose personality analysis on any investigator.

The corrective for this shortcoming is recognizing that different investigators appropriately have different theoretical focuses. It is unsatisfactory for the analyst whose primary interest is in how the actor's personal characteristics guide the full range of his behavior simply to rely on a set of propositions about the circumstances under which "personality" affects politics. In the famous aphorism of Kluckhohn and Murray

> Every man is in certain respects
> a. like all other men,
> b. like some other men,
> c. like no other men.[12]

Particularly in analyzing event-making political leaders, the third of these facets of human nature, individuality, limits one's interest in the type of propositions advanced in Chapter Two. The biographer must treat the case under analysis comprehensively, as has been brilliantly done by the most impressive of the psychobiographers, such as George and George,[13] whose work on Wilson is extensively explicated in this volume and, more recently, by Tucker in his magisterial psychobiography of Stalin.[14]

Unfortunately, we lack adequate standards to distinguish such highly satisfactory psychobiographical performances from

---

[10] Betty Glad, "Contributions of Psychobiography," in Jeanne N. Knutson, ed., *The Handbook of Political Psychology* (San Francisco: Jossey-Bass, 1973), p. 300.

[11] Michael Lerner, "Personal Politics," unpublished, Yale doctoral dissertation, 1970.

[12] Clyde Kluckhohn and Henry A. Murray, "Personality Formation: The Determinants," in Clyde Kluckhohn and Henry A. Murray, eds., *Personality in Nature, Society and Culture* (New York: Knopf, 1953), p. 53.

[13] Alexander L. George and Juliette George, *Woodrow Wilson and Colonel House: A Personality Study* (New York: John Day, 1956); paperback edition with new preface (New York: Dover, 1964).

[14] Robert C. Tucker, *Stalin as Revolutionary, 1879–1929: A Study in History and Personality* (New York: Norton, 1973).

less satisfactory, but intellectually serious works, such as the much-
derided Freud-Bullitt work on Wilson[15] and Victor Wolfenstein's
comparative study of Lenin, Trotsky, and Gandhi.[16] The use by
Wolfenstein, a political scientist, of highly explicit psycho-dynamic
categories has been, paradoxically, the basis for criticism of his
work from within the psychoanalytic community.[17] (See my attempt in Chapter Three to show how such standards might be
perfected.) Also in the intellectually controversial category is
Bruce Mazlish's *In Search of Nixon*.[18] Various reviewers have felt
that psychoanalytic notions are merely intruded into a loosely
organized biographical analysis without being adequately tied to
the author's assertions and that they do not appear to contribute
to the substance of the author's discussion.[19]

I wrote *Personality and Politics* in a series of backward steps.
It began as a substantive review of what was known about the
subject at the time, but as I came increasingly to sense the controversial nature of this literature, that I had been reading with
more or less uncritical enthusiasm since my undergraduate years,
the book progressed inexorably towards an exercise in epistemological methodology.

The treacherousness of the terrain *Personality and Politics*
covers has been stressed by its reviewers. Most of the reviews
suggest that, if one wants a guide through the Dismal Swamp of

---

[15] Sigmund Freud and William C. Bullitt, *Thomas Woodrow Wilson,
Twenty-Eighth President of the United States: A Psychological Study* (Boston:
Houghton Mifflin, 1967).

[16] E. Victor Wolfenstein, *The Revolutionary Personality: Lenin, Trotsky,
and Gandhi* (Princeton, N. J.: Princeton University Press, 1967).

[17] Erik H. Erikson, "On the Nature of Psycho-Historical Evidence: In
Search of Gandhi," *Dædalus*, 97 (1966), 695–730; reprinted with commentaries
by a number of psychiatrists and an introduction by the editors in Fred I. Greenstein and Michael Lerner, *A Source Book For the Study of Personality and
Politics* (Chicago: Markham, 1971; now distributed by Humanities Press, At-
lantic Highlands, New Jersey). The *Source Book* collects and provides analytic
introductions to 28 basic writings in this field, many of them principal sources
relied upon in this work.

[18] Bruce Mazlish, *In Search of Nixon* (New York: Basic Books, 1972);
paperback edition with a brief new preface (Baltimore: Penguin Books, 1973).

[19] See especially Robert Coles in "Shrinking History—Part Two," *New
York Review of Books*, March 8, 1973, 25–9. Note also Coles' "Shrinking History
—Part One," *New York Review of Books*, February 22, 1973, 15–21, and Bruce
Mazlish's rejoinder and Dr. Coles' reply in the May 3, 1973, issue, 36–8. For
another fascinating, but controversial, psychological biography see Fawn M.
Brodie, *Thomas Jefferson: An Intimate History* (New York: Norton, 1974).

personality and politics, this volume is the best available Baedeker. In contemplating these reviews, however, I feel somewhat like the fabled elephant facing the conflicting diagnoses of the blind men, each of whom saw in the same pachyderm a different attribute. Not surprisingly, aspects of this book acclaimed by some reviewers were scorned by others. But most frustrating is the lack of attention given by the reviewers to some of the knottier problems I raised, probably because a number of my distinctions were too technical or cryptically stated.

On the whole, far from being blind men, the reviewers have made many observations about the main contours of the book that have helped me to think more clearly about and expand upon my formulation. Richard Merelman provides a particularly lucid and detailed precis of the *full* argument of the book. In addition to decoding my excessively telegraphic message, he also identified a number of ellipses and blind spots that I have tried to avoid in my subsequent writing on political psychology.[20]

To bring this volume up to date and to clarify some of the discussions, I will present a few afterthoughts on a chapter-by-chapter basis, beginning with a recapitulation of my original thesis in each chapter.

Chapter One, in addition to containing an apologia for the study of personality and politics and a literature review, introduces a tripartite principle for organizing the literature: single-case studies of political actors; multi-case studies of types of political actors; and aggregate discussions that seek to assemble micro-data on individuals and to use them as part of explanations of macrophenomena, ranging from the small-scale interpersonal level to the interaction among polities. The first chapter also attempts to provide a basis for a contextual approach to personality and politics analysis that avoids single-factor explanations and other attempts to reduce political behavior into a mere epiphenomenon of individual personality. For this purpose, and throughout the book, I make use of Smith's map for the study of personality and politics. I have since found it useful to paraphrase Smith's map, bringing out certain elements that are only implicit in it. This later reconstruction (referred to in note 9) focuses heavily

[20] Richard Merelman, "Review of *Personality and Politics*," *American Political Science Review*, 64 (1970), p. 919. See n. 1 for further writings.

on *environments-as-perceived*, as well as "actual" external environments as determinants of behavior. The metaphorical boxes and arrows in the revised chart are arranged so that situational stimuli must be conceived as being mediated by perceptions and conscious orientations, as well as interacted on by conscious and unconscious orientations, and affiliative reference group dispositions in order to produce behavior.

The revised map has also been re-assembled to give less impression than does Smith's depiction on page 27 of a steady state of political behavior. Smith's formulation, by stressing feedback processes, may inadvertently lead hasty readers to think of behavior as generally tending to reinforce existing patterns of relationship between individual and environment. In particular, I sought a graphic representation that emphasized how the behavior of an individual, especially a pivotally placed individual, can affect subsequent aspects of his environment. It is, after all, no accident that Nixon surrounded himself with a group of White House advisers who led him into the Watergate catastrophe. Pivotal aspects of his environment were of his own making, although not invariably. *action shapes the env't.*

Chapter Two, as noted above, explores the common ground between those who have been critical of explanations of politics in personality terms and those who have commended such efforts. After discussing some standard criticisms that probably are more the result of conceptual, than empirical, disagreements and can be dealt with more effectively by clarification of strategies of inquiry than by empirical investigation, I consider more manifestly empirical issues. On these issues, notably the familiar debates over the relative impact of situations versus personal dispositions as determinants of behavior, and over whether ego-defensive psychodynamics are consequential in everyday behavior, the contention is rarely of an either-or nature. As we have seen, my inventory of contingencies under which personality determinants of political behavior (whether ego defensive ones or not) are consequential could be a reductionist charter for leaving personality variables as residual. I think it more appropriate to regard Chapter Two inventories as indications of targets of opportunity for students of personality and politics, and targets of necessity for others. The propositions indicate circumstances under which attention to inner dispositions are *necessary*, but they do not (as Glad and Lerner make clear) delimit the *sufficient* conditions for analyzing political personality.

Chapter Three on single-case psychological analysis of individual political actors and Chapter Four on multi-case analysis of types of political actors are parallel in their emphasis on the logical, if not practical, separability of the tasks of describing the surface manifestations, the inner psychodynamics, and the developmental history of an individual or type. Undoubtedly, the major contribution to the literature in this area since 1969 is a book that overlaps the domains of single-case and typological analysis, James David Barber's *The Presidential Character: Predicting Performance in the White House.*[21] This book classifies each of the presidents from Taft through Nixon on the basis of biographical case studies informed by the four-fold typological scheme Barber has been developing over the years. Barber also embellishes his classification of political character types to include a standardized series of questions focusing on the actor's cognitive "world view" and the situational context imposed upon him. Barber's pre-1972 prediction that Nixon might well come to grief in his second term out of an emotionally based propensity to persist in unproductive courses of behavior under certain circumstances has contributed to the widespread attention this book has received. Not least among the contributions of Barber's daring analysis of recent presidents is the way his work has sparked profound debate among technical students of personality and politics about the conditions under which a properly documented typology of political personality can be grounded in satisfactory evidence and inference. Alexander George's extended article on Barber's book—a near Talmudic exercise in intellectual clarification—is compulsory reading for those who seek to elucidate the criteria for psychological diagnoses of individual actors and classifications of types of actors.[22]

---

[21] James David Barber, *The Presidential Character: Predicting Performance in the White House* (Englewood Cliffs, N. J.: Prentice-Hall, 1972).

[22] Alexander L. George, "Assessing Presidential Character," *World Politics,* 26 (1974), 234–82. See also Erwin C. Hargrove, "Presidential Personality and Revisionist Views of the Presidency," *American Journal of Political Science,* 18 (1973), 819–35; and Barber's "Strategies for Understanding Politicians," *American Journal of Political Science,* 19 (1974), 443–67. There is, sadly, a genre of exploitative and pejorative attempts to demonstrate that one or another public figure is "sick." In this category I would place most of the contributions to the

In Chapter Four the notoriously tangled authoritarian personality literature is used as a paradigmatic case for discussing the problems of political-psychology classification. This enormous body of literature has been dominated by quantitative studies using psychometric procedures that are often of dubious validity. My own reconstruction tends to hark back to the original and often forgotten theoretical issues that gave rise to the literature. Both *Personality and Politics* and a later work that collects and comments on seminal writings in the field, many of which inspired the present book,[23] have been appropriately criticized for paying little attention to quantitative studies of political psychology. Undoubtedly, my own intellectual bias is revealed in this lacunae, for I am wary of studies based on highly specialized populations who are given simplistic and artifact-ridden questionnaires that fail to reflect the complex interactions of politics—attitude formation, expression, and behavior in actual situational contexts.

Without laying claim to psychometric sophistication, I would like to note two important developments in the quantitative literature since 1969. One is the work carefully wrought over the years by Richard Christie and his associates on "Machiavellianism" as a psycho-political syndrome. Christie has gone through an extensive sequence of scale modification in seeking to establish a test for a politically relevant disposition that is independent of where one stands on the ideological spectrum—(the psychological capacity to treat other human beings as objects and thus to feel free to manipulate them.)What is especially fascinating about Christie's work is his sophisticated use of "moderator variables" to take into account the situational contingencies under which individuals exhibiting the Machiavellianism syndrome are and are not likely to behave in distinctive ways. Thus no assumption is made of the

---

special issue of *Fact* magazine, in which numerous psychiatrists were persuaded to pontificate about the psychological fitness of presidential candidate Barry Goldwater during the 1964 Presidential campaign. This episode is summarized in George's "Assessing Presidential Character." For a recent example of this genre, see Eli S. Chesen's *President Nixon's Psychiatric Profile* (New York: Wyden, 1973), a work that relies heavily on declamatory usage of psychiatric jargon, a few secondary sources and the author's observations of the televised behavior of President Nixon and those of his associates who testified before the Senate Watergate Committee.

23 Greenstein and Lerner, eds., *A Source Book for the Study of Personality and Politics.*

across-the-board significance of this psychological type, but instead, proper account is taken of the complexity of interaction between psychological and environmental determinants of behavior.[24]

Also of importance is the movement toward fruition of Herbert McClosky's long-term task of analyzing the data yielded by a rich and carefully validated instrument administered to a sample of citizens and political leaders in the late 1950's. He and his students have gradually provided careful documentation of the psychometric standing of McClosky's influential early reports of his findings. They have now extensively winnowed through their data to distinguish complex and subtle relationships that display an increasingly evident point about the connections between personality and politics—they are interactive rather than universal.[25] This has been well brought out by a number of writers on related topics—for example, McGuire on "influenceability" and Fiedler on leadership.

As McGuire puts it,

It is highly likely that personality factors will interact with various other classes of (factors)... in affecting influenceability. Hence, although we should seek the most general relationships in mapping the domain of personality-influenceability interactions, it is likely that these will tend to be interaction effects rather than condition-free main effects of personality variables.[26]

And as Fiedler puts it,

We can now quite readily see why leadership traits will not predict leadership effectiveness. If anyone can be

---

[24] Richard Christie and Florence L. Geis, *Studies in Machiavellianism* (New York: Academic Press, 1970).

[25] In addition to the earlier McClosky studies cited in note 30 of Chapter 1, see the following other works employing the same data set: Giuseppe Di Palma and Herbert McClosky, "Personality and Conformity: The Learning of Political Attitudes," *American Political Science Review*, 64 (1970), 1054–73 (reprinted in Greenstein and Lerner, *op. cit.*, pp. 119-57; Paul M. Sniderman and Jack Citrin, "Psychological Sources of Political Belief: Self-Esteem and Isolationist Attitudes," *American Politcal Science Review*, 65 (1971), 401–17; and Paul M. Sniderman, *Personality and Democratic Politics* (Berkeley: University of California Press, 1974).

[26] William J. McGuire, "Personality and Susceptibility to Social Influ-

an effective leader in some situations and not in others,
it is obvious that a single leadership trait or combination of traits may well predict performance in certain
situations that can be specified, and this is what the contingencies mode (that Fiedler presents) shows.[27]

Chapter Five shows the complexity of linkage between underlying psychological dispositions (and by inference, the genetic factors and background experiences that produce them)
and the overall properties of political systems, large and small.
In the area of aggregation, I would particularly like to commend
the post-1969 work of Alexander George[28] and Irving Janis[29] in
dealing with the interpersonal aspects of relationships among members of leadership groups. Both writers have focused on intrinsic
aspects of group interaction that, independent of personal properties, lead to more or less satisfactory outcomes from political
decision-making processes. These sketches of typical social-psychological processes are easily modified to take into account the sorts
of individual and typological influences dealt with in Chapters
Three and Four. In fact, both George, a political scientist, and
Janis, a psychologist, in their previous work have laid much of
the groundwork for doing this.[30] Nor is the interest in making inferences from data on individual dispositions to data on system
states confined to political science and psychology. This has long
been a concern of anthropologists and of economists whose efforts
to link micro- and macro-economics are legion. Moreover, within
sociology, a discipline classically influenced by the Durkheimian
desire to "analyze social phenomena at the social level," there is
now a thoughtful and rather systematic movement toward establishing the basis for documenting connections between social sys-

ence," in Edgar F. Borgatta and William W. Lambert, eds., *Handbook of Personality Theory and Research* (Chicago: Rand McNally, 1968), p. 139.

[27] Fred I. Fiedler, "Leadership," pamphlet (New York: General Learning
Press, 1971), p. 15.

[28] Alexander L. George, "The Case for Multiple Advocacy in Making
Foreign Policy," *American Political Science Review*, 66 (1972), 751–95, with
comment by I. M. Destler and rejoinder by George.

[29] Irving L. Janis, *Victims of Groupthink* (Boston: Little, Brown, 1973).

[30] See, for example, George's "Some Uses of Dynamic Psychology in
Political Biography: Case Materials on Woodrow Wilson," in Greenstein and
Lerner, *op. cit.*, pp. 78–98; and Janis's "Decision Conflicts: A Theoretical Analy-
sis," *Journal of Conflict Resolution*, 3 (1959), 6–27 (reprinted in Greenstein and
Lerner, *op. cit.*, pp. 171–94).

tems and the individuals who constitute them. The recent updating of Lazarsfeld and Rosenberg's classic *Language of Social Research*[31] shows how conscious sociologists now are of this issue.

Let me conclude with a point *not* made in this book, but one that has increasingly pressed itself upon me as I have sought to apply these formulations to data on the relationships among American presidents and their advisers. In analyzing real-world political processes, knowledge of the classical issues in the many existing formal literatures on psychology is no substitute for knowledge of aspects of psychology distinctive to the norms of particular political processes. Elsewhere I have described this as the discrepancy between what might be called *political* psychology and political *psychology*. In spite of my references to the clinical manifestations of Richard Nixon while in office, simply translating presidential behavior or that of any political actor into the language of psychology or psychiatry is far from desirable. An item of behavior that appears susceptible to a clinical classical psychological explanation may prove to be a function of the specific psychological norms or requirements of the setting within which the behavior occurs. An example far afield from the presidency is the common finding that American blacks exhibit paranoid "pathology" on one of the most widely used personality assessment scales. As Gynther has pointed out, psychopathological interpretation of these findings is wholly inappropriate precisely because high "paranoia" scores are in fact realistic responses to the environmental pressures faced by an average, well-adjusted black slum dweller.[32] Similarly American presidents operate in extraordinarily demanding environments that place a variety of pressures on them. A president cannot be as naively gentle and open as a progressive nursery school teacher. Contrary to the theories of some early reductionist psychologists, clinical paranoia is not necessary for effective leadership. Instead, such disturbances probably are fatal in the long run for presidents and other high leaders, especially in democracies. But a "realistic" quota of guardedness and suspicion is undoubtedly necessary for carrying out the presiden-

[31] Paul F. Lazarsfeld, Ann K. Pasanella, Morris Rosenberg, eds., *Continuities in the Language of Social Research* (New York: The Free Press, 1972), especially Section III.

[32] Malcolm Gynther, "White Norms and Black MMPIs: A Prescription for Discrimination," *Psychological Bulletin*, 78 (1972), 386–402.

tial role unless the president construes his responsibilities in a highly non-activist fashion.

One of the tasks, therefore, for both descriptive and prescriptive theories of personality and politics is the merging of realistic political understanding with a sensitively tempered use of the various approaches within the disciplines (e.g. psychology, social psychology, psychiatry, and certain aspects of anthropology).[33]

---

[33] For a fuller discussion, see my essay "Political Psychology: A Pluralistic Universe," cited in n. 1, especially pp. 545–67, and the discussions of analytic standing of "role," "cultural," "social background," and "situational" explanations of behavior as they related to "personality" explanations, in the second essay cited in that note.

CHAPTER ONE

The Study of Personality
and Politics

The full title of this book provides the most convenient brief statement of its concern: problems of evidence, inference, and conceptualization in the study of personality and politics. Putting it less grandly, I shall be discussing how one can analyze the political consequences that result from personal characteristics of political actors. How should students of politics think about such matters? What kinds of evidence should they gather? How can they muster that evidence to reach fruitful conclusions? Stated dogmatically, and defended more fully in the remainder of the chapter, here is the line of reasoning that has led me to this particular investment of effort.

1. My most primitive assumption is that politics frequently is influenced in important ways by factors that are commonly summarized by the term "personality." I am regularly struck by how, as one's perspective on political activity becomes closer and more detailed, the political actors begin to loom as full-blown individuals who are influenced in politically relevant ways by the various strengths and weaknesses to which the human species is subject. Viewed in proximity, political participants present themselves as something considerably more than can be indicated by the impersonal categories students of politics ordinarily use to explain political behavior—as more than role-players, creatures of situation, members of cultures, and possessors of social characteristics, such as occupation, class, sex, and age.

2. It follows that the study of personality and politics ought to be a systematically developed subdivision of political science, occupying the skill and energy of numerous workers.

1

3. The study of personality and politics is, in fact, *not* a thriving scholarly endeavor. A principal reason is that the scholars who study politics do not feel equipped to analyze personality in ways that meet their intellectual standards. Personality tends to remain the preserve of journalists. This is unfortunate, since what the student of politics leaves to the journalist is not only of frequent political importance, but also is complexly elusive—hence especially in need of the kind of reflective examination that appropriately equipped scholars can provide.

4. The most fundamental item of scholarly equipment in this area consists simply of the capacity to think clearly about the kinds of issues that arise in the existing personality-and-politics literature.

5. But that literature is formidably gnarled—empirically, methodologically, conceptually, and even in the degree to which there is agreement that such a literature ought to exist. Indeed, the presence of a literature labeled "personality and politics"—a fascinating, but tangled array of efforts—is one of the paradoxical deterrents to the development of the field.

6. *Ergo*, if some of the tangle can be unraveled and if paths to satisfactory inquiry can be identified, it is possible that controversy will be defused and channeled into constructive inquiry.

I. MATTERS OF DEFINITION

THE MEANING OF "PERSONALITY" TO PSYCHOLOGISTS

For an initial indication of the degree and nature of the tangle we need do no more than attempt to define "personality and politics." Mainly because of the ambiguity of its first term, the phrase lacks uniform meaning. There are differences within psychology over what is meant by "personality," and, furthermore, the term tends to have different connotations to political scientists than it has to psychologists. As long as one is clear about one's usage in particular contexts, nothing is gained by striving for a canonical definition. But clarity *is* served by being aware of the range of usages, and a brief definitional discussion has the further advantage of beginning to lay out in fuller detail some of the problems that shall concern us.

The psychologists themselves have been chronically unable

to arrive at a commonly accepted definition of "personality." A standard discussion by Allport lists no less than fifty *types* of definitions.[1] This definitional pluralism results, to a considerable extent, from one of the basic problems for workers in this area: the continuing diversity of personality theories and, therefore, of the number and nature of terms used by different commentators to characterize individual psychological make-up.

The degree of theoretical anarchy within psychology can easily be exaggerated, however. Although theorists populate their definitions with different nomenclature, it is frequently the case that one theoretical vocabulary can readily be translated into another. Furthermore, there is general agreement among psychologists about the standing of the term "personality." Its referent is to an *inferred entity* rather than to a directly observable phenomenon. "Personality" refers to a construct that is introduced to account for the regularities in an individual's behavior as he responds to diverse stimuli.

Adjusting for differences of nomenclature and nuance, one also finds much consensus among psychologists on the separable components of personality. Personality theorists posit "structures" that are adapted to screening reality (cognition), to expressing feelings (affect), and to relating the self to others (identification). On the other hand, there is less consensus about the degree to which a personality theory ought to stress the aspects of inner life that have traditionally interested clinical psychologists and others who claim Freud as part of their intellectual heritage—especially the processes of ego-defense. These are the means through which individuals, often without realizing it, adapt their behavior to the need to manage their inner conflicts. And there is also less agreement about the degree to which theories should emphasize as a principal part of personality the closer-to-the-surface psychological dispositions that *are* widely studied by political scientists—namely, attitudes and all the related psychological orientations that are the regular grist of the mills of survey research.

THE MEANING OF "PERSONALITY" TO POLITICAL SCIENTISTS

Whatever may be the specific features he considers important, the psychologist's usage ordinarily is comprehensive. For

---

[1] Gordon Allport, *Personality* (New York: Holt, 1937), pp. 24–54.

him "personality" subsumes all important psychic regularities. Political scientists, however, appear to assign it a much more restricted meaning, or so one may infer contextually from numerous statements in the political-science literature about the relevance to political behavior of the typically undefined (and reified) entity to which they assign the label "personality." First of all, the political scientist's usage ordinarily excludes political attitudes. Secondly, political scientists often further contract the term to refer to the layers of the psyche in the clinician's traditional domain—inner conflict and the ego defenses and their manifestations.

In equating "personality" with ego defense and "personality and politics" with the effects of personal psychopathology on political behavior, the political scientist accurately identifies a persisting, if controversial, strand in political and social analysis. The potential relevance for political analysis of Freud's categories and hypotheses was first explored in detail for a political science audience in 1930 by Harold D. Lasswell in his *Psychopathology and Politics*.[2] By that date Lasswell was able to point to numerous efforts by psychoanalysts (including Freud himself) to view politics through their intellectual lenses. And there have been many post-1930 attempts to explain politics and other large-scale social phenomena in depth psychological terms: sweeping macro-formulations about politics and society by writers such as Erich Fromm, Herbert Marcuse and Norman O. Brown;[3] work in the culture-and-personality, national character tradition of Benedict, Gorer and Mead; attempts to use clinical

---

[2] Harold D. Lasswell, *Psychopathology and Politics* (Chicago: University of Chicago Press, 1930); reprinted in *Political Writings of Harold D. Lasswell* (Glencoe, Ill.: Free Press, 1951); and paperback edition of *Psychopathology and Politics*, with "Afterthoughts: Thirty Years Later" (New York: Viking Press, 1960). The paperback edition omits a bibliographical appendix.

[3] Erich Fromm, *Escape from Freedom* (New York: Rinehart, 1941); Herbert Marcuse, *Eros and Civilization* (rev. ed.; Boston: Beacon Press, 1966); and Norman O. Brown, *Life Against Death* (Middletown, Conn.: Wesleyan University Press, 1959). Other sweeping accounts include: Franz Alexander, *Our Age of Unreason* (rev. ed.; Philadelphia: Lippincott, 1951); Ranyard West, *Conscience and Society* (New York: Emerson, 1945); and R. E. Money-Kyrle, *Psychoanalysis and Politics* (New York: Norton, 1951). Examples of the types of writings referred to in the remainder of the paragraph are cited below in connection with my own remarks on the state of the personality-and-politics literature.

psychological notions to explain conflict among nations; plus such less global enterprises as the very many quantitative studies of the imperfectly understood psychological syndrome labeled "authoritarianism," psychological biographies of public figures, and clinical case-studies of members of the general population. It is of these diverse enterprises, rather than, for example, the literature on the psychology of voting, that political scientists tend to think when they refer to personality and politics.

THE USAGE AND FOCUS OF THIS WORK

My focus in what follows is *in part* on depth psychology and the analysis of politics. Many social scientists would dismiss this as even a partial concern. The disadvantages of considering depth psychological issues are suggested by the great volume of polemical and clarificatory literature on psychoanalysis that continues to pour out even now. Yet one can accept the many demonstrations of the chaotic logical and empirical standing of psychoanalytic concepts and propositions but nevertheless feel it vital not to lose sight of the phenomena to which these concepts and propositions are addressed.[4] For political depth psychologists may have a point when they argue that much political behavior —for example, much of the "irrationality" which often seems so luxuriant in politics—may have ego-defensive origins. And as long as this possibility exists, it is desirable to clarify the standards for accepting and rejecting hypotheses that explain political behavior in these terms.

My attention to ego-defensive processes is, however, only an aspect of a broader interest in personality, in the comprehensive psychologist's sense of the totality of more or less stable personal psychological characteristics. Like most political scientists, when I employ the word "personality," I tend not to be referring to straightforward political attitudes. And by and large, this book

---

[4] For a sample of the polemical issues, see the symposium edited by Sidney Hook, entitled *Psychoanalysis: Scientific Method and Philosophy* (New York: New York University Press, 1959). Among the more interesting constructive efforts at clarification are: A. C. MacIntyre, *The Unconscious: A Conceptual Analysis* (London: Routledge and Kegan Paul, 1958) ; Peter Madison, *Freud's Concept of Repression and Defense: Its Theoretical and Observational Language* (Minneapolis: University of Minnesota Press, 1961) ; and B. A. Farrell, "The Status of Psychoanalytic Theory," *Inquiry*, 7 (1964), 104–23.

does not discuss the principal issues in the study of attitudes, if only because this aspect of political psychology is already rather well developed, especially as it relates to electoral behavior. I tend instead to apply "personality" to the broad gamut of non-political psychological attributes which lead us to conclude that people are, for example, out-going, hostile, or phlegmatic—or that they have other, perhaps more complex, personal qualities. But part of my argument is that we need to be wary of such restrictive connotations, since, as we shall see, many of the standard difficulties in the political personality literature come from the failure to think in a sufficiently broad way about the full configuration of psychological and non-psychological determinants of political behavior. Moreover, much of what needs to be said about the effect on politics of personality in any of the more restricted senses applies broadly to the political consequences of psychological variables in general. This is so emphatically the case that henceforth I shall use such phrases as "political psychology," "political personality," and "personality and politics" interchangeably, making finer distinctions only when necessary.

II. THE NEED FOR SYSTEMATIC STUDY OF PERSONALITY AND POLITICS

We may now consider in more detail the undefended assertion that there is need for a systematically developed personality-and-politics literature. Fifty-some years ago, Walter Lippmann observed that "to talk about politics without reference to human beings . . . is just the deepest error in our political thinking."[5] This would appear both on formal and on empirical grounds to be an unassailable assertion no matter which of the two standard kinds of definitions of "politics" we use. We can treat as political all of the activities that go on in and around government. Or we can, in Lasswell's usage, define the term "functionally" to refer to some distinctive pattern of behavior that may manifest itself in any of the conventionally designated institutional settings[6]—for

---

[5] Walter Lippmann, *Preface to Politics* (New York: Mitchell Kennerley, 1913), p. 2.

[6] Lasswell seems first to have introduced the distinction between functional and conventional definitions of politics in *Psychopathology and Politics*, *op. cit.*, Chap. 4.

example, the exercise of power and influence, efforts to resolve conflict resolution, or, in David Easton's often quoted phrase, "authoritative allocations of values."[7] By either tack, politics is a matter of human behavior, and behavior, in the formulation of Kurt Lewin and many others, is a function of both the *environmental situations* in which actors find themselves and the *psychological predispositions* they bring to those situations.

There is of course nothing novel in the assertion that behavior is a consequence of the actor's environment and his psychological dispositions. Yet this assertion is so fundamental to an appreciation of why psychological evidence frequently is essential for political analysis that it deserves to be dwelled upon. Consider the following statement of the point by Lazarus in his textbook:

> The sources of man's behavior (his observable action) and his subjective experience (such as thoughts, feelings, and wishes) are twofold: the external stimuli that impinge on him and the internal dispositions that result from the interaction between inherited physiological characteristics and experience with the world. When we focus on the former, we note that a person acts in such-and-such a way because of certain qualities in a situation. For example, he attacks a friend because the friend insulted him, or he loses interest in a lecture because the teacher is dull or uninformed, or he fails in his program of study because the necessity of supporting himself through school leaves insufficient time for studying. It is evident that a man's behavior varies greatly from moment to moment, from circumstance to circumstance, changing with the changing conditions to which he is exposed.
>
> Still, even as we recognize the dependency of behavior on outside stimuli, we are also aware that it cannot be accounted for on the basis of the external situation alone, but that in fact it must arise partly from personal characteristics.[8]

---

[7] David Easton, *The Political System* (New York: Knopf, 1953), Chap. 5 and *passim*.

[8] Richard S. Lazarus, *Personality and Adjustment* (Englewood Cliffs, N.J.: Prentice-Hall, 1963), pp. 27–28. For a discussion of political psychology

One is immediately able to proliferate examples of political events that were critically dependent upon the personal characteristics of key actors, or of actors in the aggregate. Take Republican politics in 1964. An account of the main determinants of the Republican Presidential nomination that year and of the subsequent election campaign would have to include much more than descriptions of the personal characteristics of the party leaders and members. But any account would be incomplete that did not acknowledge the impact of such factors as the willingness of one of the strongest contenders for the nomination to divorce his wife and marry a divorced woman; the indecisiveness of the party's elder statesman; the emotional proclivities that produced a politically damaging outburst of temper in a news conference (two years earlier) by the man who had been the party's 1960 Presidential candidate; the self-defeating political style of the man who received the 1964 nomination (his unwillingness to placate his opponents within the party, his propensity to remind voters of the issues on which he was most vulnerable); and countless more unpuzzling, but no less psychologically important aspects of the actions of the protagonists. Not to mention psychological factors that had their effect through the aggregation of the behavior of many less visible actors: for example, the psychologies of voters in the Republican primaries of that year and of delegates to the national convention.

Attempts to explain the outcomes of adversary relationships often place in particularly clear relief the need for psychological data. For example, the overwhelming defeat in 1967 of numerically superior, better-equipped Arab armies by Israel quite obviously was a function of gross discrepancies between the levels of skill and motivation of the two sides, both among leaders and subordinates. A further example—one which lays out with a rather grim clarity the possible life-or-death policy relevance of reliable knowledge of the inner tendencies of political actors—is provided by the 1962 Cuban Missile Crisis. This event can usefully be discussed in some detail, not only in its own right, but also in terms of an academic debate of more than "academic" significance that broke out in its midst.

in which the interaction of psychological and situational determinants of behavior is especially emphasized, see James Davies, *Human Nature in Politics* (New York: Wiley, 1963).

For the few days of the Missile Crisis, the United States and the Soviet Union seemed chillingly close to nuclear war. Soviet missiles, potentially capable of neutralizing the American defense system, were being set up in Cuba. Soviet ships, some of them carrying additional missiles, were on the high seas in transit to Cuba. President Kennedy issued an ultimatum demanding the removal of the missiles already in Cuba and stating the American intention to inspect the Soviet ships and stop those which were carrying missiles. It was by no means clear whether the Soviet reaction would be to fire the first shot in what might quickly become the third and final World War, or to comply with inspection, halt the missile-carrying ships in mid-voyage, and withdraw the missiles which had already been landed.

At the immediate point of the crisis over the ships and in the subsequent days until the missiles had been withdrawn, decisions were inevitably being based upon assumptions about the psychological predispositions of the Soviet leaders—assumptions about how Khrushchev and his associates were likely to respond to the various possible American actions, including that of inaction.[9] The missile-bearing ships *did* stop and return to the Soviet Union. Somewhat later, the missiles which had already been set up in Cuba *were* withdrawn. At either of these two stages, miscalculations of the Russian leaders' psychology would have led to a drastic change in the international balance of power or, depending upon the further actions of the American leaders, to shooting and possibly a full-scale war.

In the interim between the halting of the Soviet ships and the withdrawal of the missiles already in Cuba, an exchange took place in the correspondence columns of the *New York Times* which underlined the intimate connection between assumptions about the psychology of political actors and the decisions made by policy-makers. One group of writers sought to stress the urgency of exercising restraint and, in particular, of providing the Soviet leaders with face-saving means of withdrawal.

> If the United States is to be effective in the world today, those who are pushing for an "all-out" approach must restrain their enthusiasm. Both victory and peace

---

[9] The Soviet decision-makers were, of course, equally dependent upon assumptions about the psychology of their American counterparts.

depend upon keeping the size of an international issue
under control and upon *making it as easy as possible
for other countries to accept a solution. . . .* The effectiveness of our pressure will depend not only on how
much pressure is applied but on how easy we make it
to yield. . . . The United States has demonstrated its
determination and its unwillingness to be pushed
around by the Soviet Union. Our flexibility in negotiation should not be handicapped by the insistence of
extremists that other countries lose face.[10]

Another correspondent, Bernard F. Brodie, took sharp exception to these seemingly unexceptionable "common-sense"
warnings, suggesting that the writers, by failing to take account
of the "special character" of the Soviet leaders, were proposing a
policy likely to endanger the peace. In making his point, Brodie
explicitly cited one of the leading academic writers on personality and politics, Nathan Leites.

The argument that it is the wiser part of diplomacy
for us to make sure that Khrushchev has an easy way
out of his predicament and to avoid anything smacking
of "humiliation" is an argument appropriate to pre-
1914 diplomacy. Neither his venturesome missile advance into the Caribbean nor his unabashed retreat
under strong American reaction would fit the patterns
of pre-1914 diplomacy. Both are, on the other hand,
beautifully explained in anticipation by such a "codification" of Bolshevik behavior as that published . . . by
. . . Dr. Nathan Leites. . . . This study has now received monumental confirmation in the Cuban affair.
Among the Soviet characteristics that Dr. Leites
pointed out . . . were the following: It is tantamount
to a moral imperative to the Communist leader that he
must advance against the opponent wherever opportunity affords; he must not, in other words, be lax in
carrying forward the revolution. On the other hand, it
is equally imperative that he must at no point submit
to grave risk or hazard the basic achievement already
consolidated. He must, therefore, be absolutely ready to

[10] Letter of Roger Fisher, Donald G. Brennan, and Morton H. Halperin,
New York Times, October 28, 1962 (italics added).

retreat wherever occasion requires it, without regard to
childish notions of "humiliation" and the like, provided, of course, the menace is real and not fake. . . .
     We had absolutely nothing to thank . . . [Khru-
shchev] for, but if we wanted to be humane to him, the
best way was to make our threat absolutely unambiguous—to save him and his colleagues occasion for won-
dering whether their headlong retreat was really necessary. What would be intolerable to Khrushchev personally and to his position in the Soviet Union would
be the feeling that he had yielded prematurely to a weak
threat rather than having backed away appropriately
from a serious menace. *We should* thus *expect from the*
premature softening of our tone not only no payoff but
actually the reverse. . . .[11]

I will not go further into the specifics of this particular
debate. The contending positions are certainly not exhaustive,
and on further analysis they might even prove not to be mutually
exclusive. My point is that the issues raised by the debate are
obviously of fundamental significance for the understanding and
control of political affairs. This is true both of the actual content
of the *New York Times* exchange and of the analytic problems
arising in the infinitely larger set of situations in which the
Cuban Missile Crisis can be included. This set consists of instances in which political (or other) stimuli have been administered to political actors with consequences for their behavior
which we can only correctly anticipate if we have knowledge of
the actors' psychological characteristics—of the personal elements that mediate between stimulus and political response.
     One might think therefore that substantial resources would
be devoted to clarifying and resolving questions bearing on the

---

[11] *New York Times*, November 13, 1962 (italics added). Brodie's reference
is to Nathan Leites' *The Operational Code of the Politburo* (New York:
McGraw-Hill, 1951) and to his *A Study of Bolshevism* (Glencoe, Ill.: Free
Press, 1953). For a later formulation by Leites, taking account of the missile
crisis, see his "Kremlin Thoughts: Yielding, Rebuffing, Provoking, Retreating,"
RAND Corporation Memorandum RM-31618-ISA (May, 1963). Cf. Alexander
L. George, "Presidential Control of Force: The Korean War and the Cuban
Missile Crisis," paper presented at the 1967 Annual Meeting of the American
Sociological Association. Also see Edward D. Hoedemaker's remarks on the
Missile Crisis in his "Distrust and Aggression: An Interpersonal-International
Analogy," *Journal of Conflict Resolution*, 12 (1968), 69–81.

psychology of politics. Yet in fact, the entire enterprise of exploring the personal antecedents of political and other large-scale social phenomena is widely suspect. We therefore know much less than we should about psychological aspects of politics and have failed to perfect the tools for redressing this deficiency.

III. WHY SYSTEMATIC POLITICAL PERSONALITY STUDY HAS BEEN SLOW TO DEVELOP

I have already suggested that one reason why the study of personality and politics is not a highly developed endeavor is the state of the existing literature. Before examining that literature and its vicissitudes in some detail, we may note several further causes of the laggard state of political personality studies.

For much of the brief history of empirical political science, political analysis has seemed to proceed in a quite acceptable fashion without employing explicit psychological assumptions. If one is studying "normal" actors in a familiar culture, it is often convenient simply to look at variations in the setting of politics or merely to deal with the portion of the actor's psychological characteristics that relate to his social position (socioeconomic status, age, and sex, for example).

Implicit, common-sense psychological assumptions become less satisfactory, however, when one attempts to explain (a) actors in one's own culture whose behavior deviates from expectations or (b) actors from a different culture. An example of the first is Woodrow Wilson's determined unwillingness, under certain circumstances, to follow the American politician's practice of compromising with one's adversaries, as described by George and George;[12] an example of the second is the possible applicability of Leites' theory of Bolshevik leadership to the Cuban Missile Crisis. But when the political scientist does sense the importance of making explicit his assumptions about psychological aspects of politics, he is put off by the state of psychology. Rather than finding *a* psychological science on which to draw for insight, he finds a congeries of more or less competing models and frames of

---

[12] Alexander L. George and Juliette L. George, *Woodrow Wilson and Colonel House: A Personality Study* (New York: John Day, 1956) ; and paperback edition with new Preface (New York: Dover, 1964).

reference, with imperfect agreement on the nature of man's inner dispositions, on the appropriate terms for characterizing them, and on the methodologies for observation.

If the political scientist persists in his determination to make systematic use of psychology, he is likely to experience further discouragement. Much of the research and theory he will encounter will seem singularly irrelevant to explaining the kind of complex behavior that interests him. And where psychological writers *do* address themselves to his subject matter, their political observations will often seem naive and uninformed. Psychologists' insights seem irrelevant to political scientists for the good reason that many psychologists do not conceive of their science as one which *should* attempt to explain concrete instances of social behavior. Instead, the psychologist attempts to discover general principles that underlie the specific types of social behavior. Thus a deliberate attempt is made, as one psychologist puts it, to treat psychology as "socially indifferent"—to strip away and ignore those aspects of behavior that are specific consequences of the fact that it has occurred, say, on a Congressional committee or at a political party convention.

> When colleagues in other disciplines (mainly sociology, anthropology, political science, and economics) turn to psychology for help they are disappointed, and, indeed, often aggrieved. What they begin to read with enthusiasm they put down with depression. What seemed promising turns out to be sterile, palpably trivial, or false and, in any case, a waste of time. . . . Psychologists do study and must study things and activities possessing social content. There is no other way . . . . It is only that psychology has been a science that abstracts out of all these content-characterized behaviors the concepts which form the jargons of its subdisciplines. . . .

The writer goes on to suggest why it is that when psychologists pronounce on problems of politics and society, their observations so often strike politically knowledgeable readers as dubious.

> I am impressed with how naive and conventional my colleagues [in psychology] and I are when confronted with most social phenomena. We are ignorant of the

historical dimensions of most social activity, we do not see the complex interweaving of institutions and arrangements. . . . In general, psychologists tend to be like laymen when they confront social phenomena, particularly those that involve large-scale patterns. And the reason for all of this is that the main areas of social activity are only the *place* where psychologists study interesting sorts of things, rather than being the *focus of inquiry*.[13]

However, the principal further reason for lack of progress has been the problem to which we must now turn: the controversial state of the existing literature.

IV. THE STATE OF THE PERSONALITY–AND– POLITICS LITERATURE

A CLASSIFICATION OF TYPES OF PERSONALITY-AND-POLITICS INQUIRY: INDIVIDUAL, TYPOLOGICAL, AND AGGREGATIVE ANALYSES

Much of what is done in the analysis of personality and politics can be grouped under the following three rough headings: *single-case* psychological analyses of individual political actors, *typological* (and, in effect, multi-case) analyses of the psychology of political actors, and analyses of *aggregation*—that is, analyses of the collective effects of individuals and types on the functioning of political institutions, ranging all the way from informal face-to-face groups through organizations and political patterns at the international level.

The single-case literature includes the in-depth studies of members of the general population by such investigators as Lane[14] and Smith, Bruner and White.[15] It also includes psychological biographies of public figures.[16] I am using "typological" to

[13] Richard A. Littman, "Psychology: The Socially Indifferent Science," *American Psychologist*, 16 (1961), 232–36 (italics in original).

[14] Robert E. Lane, *Political Ideology* (New York: Free Press of Glencoe, 1962).

[15] M. Brewster Smith, Jerome Bruner, and Robert White, *Opinions and Personality* (New York: Wiley, 1956).

[16] For example, George and George, *op. cit.*; Erik H. Erikson, *Young Man Luther: A Study in Psychoanalysis and History* (New York: Norton, 1958); Lewis J. Edinger, *Kurt Schumacher: A Study in Personality and Political*

refer to all classifications of political actors in psychological terms—from mere classification of the members of a population in terms of the categories of a single psychological variable, such as "political efficacy," through complex typologies identifying syndromes of interrelated attributes. The best known, best developed, and possibly most controversial of the typological literatures is that on authoritarianism.[17] Other of the politically relevant psychological typologies are designed to classify people in terms of dogmatism,[18] misanthropy,[19] Machiavellianism,[20] and tradition-inner-and-other directedness.[21] There also are various psychological classifications of actual political role incumbents, such as Lasswell's agitator-administrator-theorist trichotomy[22] and Barber's four-fold spectator-advertiser-reluctant-lawmaker division.[23]

"Aggregation," the term for the third kind of analysis, is borrowed from the literature on the connection between micro- and macro-economics.[24] Among the aggregative analyses of personality and politics, we find the many writings on national character[25] and the efforts to connect intrapersonal emotional

---

Behavior (Stanford, Calif.: Stanford University Press, 1965); Arnold Rogow, *James Forrestal: A Study of Personality, Politics, and Policy* (New York: Macmillan, 1963); E. Victor Wolfenstein, *The Revolutionary Personality: Lenin, Trotsky, Gandhi* (Princeton, N.J.: Princeton University Press, 1967); and Betty Glad, *Charles Evans Hughes and the Illusions of Innocence* (Urbana: University of Illinois Press, 1966). Also see A. F. Davies, *Private Politics* (Melbourne: Melbourne University Press, 1966).

[17] Theodor W. Adorno, Else Frenkel-Brunswik, Daniel J. Levinson, and R. Nevitt Sanford, *The Authoritarian Personality* (New York: Harper, 1950); Richard Christie and Marie Jahoda, eds., *Studies in the Scope and Method of "The Authoritarian Personality"* (Glencoe, Ill.: Free Press, 1954).

[18] Milton Rokeach, *The Open and Closed Mind* (New York: Basic Books, 1960).

[19] Morris Rosenberg, "Misanthropy and Political Ideology," *American Sociological Review*, 21 (1956), 690–95.

[20] Richard Christie and F. Geis, *Studies in Machiavellianism* (New York: Academic Press, forthcoming).

[21] David Riesman, with Nathan Glazer and Reuel Denney, *The Lonely Crowd* (New Haven, Conn.: Yale University Press, 1950).

[22] Harold D. Lasswell, *Psychopathology and Politics, op. cit.*

[23] James D. Barber, *The Lawmakers* (New Haven, Conn.: Yale University Press, 1965).

[24] Gardner Ackley, *Macroeconomic Theory* (New York: Macmillan, 1961).

[25] For example, Geoffrey Gorer, "Burmese Personality" (New York: Institute of Intercultural Studies, 1943, mimeograph); Ruth Benedict, *The Chrysanthemum and the Sword* (Boston: Houghton Mifflin, 1946); and Geoffrey Gorer, *The American People* (New York: Norton, 1948).

tension with conflict among nations,[26] as well as, on the one hand, more microscopic studies of behavior in groups and, on the other, the sorts of global psychologizing about man and society referred to earlier in the chapter.

There is an unfolding logic that makes these three divisions heuristically useful as a way of organizing the issues that arise in personality-and-politics inquiry, even though any actual contribution may in fact contain more than one of the three modes of analysis. Moderately discrete and separable methodological issues arise, depending upon whether one chooses (a) to diagnose a single actor, (b) to classify actors and explain the origin and behavior of the types in the classification, or (c) to make use of knowledge obtained from the study of individuals and types in order to explain aspects of the larger system of which they are a part. Each analytic mode has somewhat distinctive requirements and has been subject to distinctive difficulties. Furthermore, there are interesting interdependencies among the three modes, as can be easily seen schematically in the following diagram:

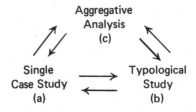

Frequently, for example, it is our inability to explain why some single political actor has behaved in a fashion that does not seem consistent with our normal expectations for behavior in comparable situations that initially turns our attention to political personality. In the course of inferring the personality structures that account for the idiosyncrasies of our subject's behavior, we then may come to suspect that in important respects *our* actor resembles certain other political actors, and, if we pursue the resemblances, we find ourselves moving inductively in the

[26] Otto Klineberg, *Tensions Affecting International Understanding* (New York: Social Science Research Council, Bulletin 62, 1950) ; Leon Bramson and George W. Goethals, *War: Studies from Psychology, Sociology, Anthropology* (New York: Basic Books, 1964).

direction of creating a typology (a → b). But it is also possible
that an existing typology with which there is associated a body of
theory and empirical evidence will lead us to move deductively
toward a set of predictions about our biographical subject and
the ways in which his behavior is patterned (b → a). Thus, for
example, Alexander and Juliette George in *Woodrow Wilson and
Colonel House* were able to make effective use of the clinical
literature on compulsive types to analyze President Wilson's
personality and behavior.[27]

Moving from individuals and types of individuals to aggregate structures, we find that there are many theories about the
relevance for systems of the distribution within them of personality types (b → c). An example of such a theory is provided by
Fromm's speculations about the significance of a high incidence
of authoritarian personality types for the collapse of Weimar
Germany.[28] And it is true in politics, perhaps more so than in
other spheres of life, that particularly well-placed single individuals can have a substantial impact on the aggregate system
(a → c). Finally, we have a long, if not completely edifying,
history of inquiry going under such headings as "culture-and-
personality," "social-structure-and-personality," and, more recently, "political socialization," to remind us that the causal arrow
also points in the opposite direction—that systems have impact
on the individuals and types of individuals that compose them
(c → a and c → b). We also have well-established traditions of
normative political analysis, going back to the ancients, in which
the merits of alternative modes of political organization are eval-
uated partly on the basis of the consequences of systems for the
psychic well-being of their members.

SOURCES OF DIFFICULTY IN THE LITERATURE

Critics of the personality-and-politics literature have pointed
to difficulties that are generally applicable to the *genre* as a whole
and to criticisms that are more specific to one or another of the
modes. The overriding theme in all of the criticisms is that

---

[27] See Alexander George's remarks in "Power as a Compensatory Value
for Political Leaders," *Journal of Social Issues*, 24:3 (1968), 29–50.

[28] Erich Fromm, *op. cit.*

personality explanations of political behavior tend to be undemonstrated—and possibly undemonstrable—half-insights. We may first consider criticisms of the specific analytic modes.

Single-case psychological analyses of political actors have frequently been taken to task for the "subjectivity" inherent in the diagnosis of individuals. Critics have decried the alleged absence of standards for making reliable and valid single-case interpretations. They have argued that such interpretations are not replicable, and they have especially pointed to the seeming arbitrariness of the interpretations based on depth psychology. In addition, the more clinical of the case histories have often been said to overemphasize elements of pathology and to be insufficiently sensitive to sources of personal strength and creative adaptation. It is especially easy to level such an accusation against many of the earlier psychoanalytic political biographies, —for example, the psychiatrist L. Pierce Clark's 1933 book on Abraham Lincoln, an analysis that fails totally to provide a satisfactory account of Lincoln's extraordinary political capacities.[29]

Typological personality-and-politics inquiries also have had distinctive tribulations. Investigators employing quantitative typological analytic procedures have encountered formidable problems in developing reliable and valid measures of personality and its political correlates. Thus, for example, much of the very extensive research on authoritarianism conducted during the 1950's was seriously compromised by problems of measurement error.[30] During an earlier research epoch, numerous studies were

[29] L. Pierce Clark, *Lincoln: A Psycho-Biography* (New York: Scribners, 1933). Erikson consciously sets out to remedy the emphasis on pathology in his *Young Man Luther, op. cit.*

[30] For representative efforts to remedy the measurement difficulties in the early authoritarian personality studies, see Martha T. Mednick and Sarnoff A. Mednick, *Research in Personality* (New York: Holt, Rinehart, and Winston, 1963). The work of Herbert McClosky is exemplary in its sophisticated attention to instrument validation. See, for example, his "Conservatism and Personality," *American Political Science Review*, 52 (1958), 27–45; Herbert McClosky and John H. Schaar, "Psychological Dimensions of Anomy," *American Sociological Review*, 30 (1965), 14–40; and Herbert McClosky, "Personality and Attitude Correlates of Foreign Policy Orientation," in James Rosenau, ed., *Domestic Sources of Foreign Policy* (New York: Free Press of Glencoe, 1967), pp. 51–109.

carried out in which psychometric measures of personality and political orientation were correlated with one another: in general the correlations proved to be weak and unstable, largely, I think, because phenomena of considerable complexity and subtlety were being studied via overly crude indices of both the independent and dependent variables.[31] Underlying all of the difficulties is a serious lack of clear conceptualization in many typological studies.

It is, however, probably the aggregative analyses of personality and politics—the psychological accounts of national character, of international tensions, and of the functioning of various institutions—that have been most widely criticized.[32] In many such analyses, there seems to be little inhibition about applying psychological notions directly and without qualification to the explanation of social processes. "Reductionism" is the standard label for the fallacy of advancing necessary and sufficient explanations of (say) Germany in terms of the personality, and perhaps early life experiences of the typical German.

"Reductionism" is a pejorative tag that applies generally to explanations of complex phenomena in terms of only a portion of their components. And reductionism in its various forms is one of the general banes of personality-and-politics inquiry, above and beyond the difficulties critics have noted with each of the three modes of inquiry. The preoccupation with psychopathology in some psychological biographies involves a kind of reductionism. So does the nearly exclusive emphasis in the early authoritarian personality work on ego-defensive determinants of ethnic prejudice and political deference. Stated in terms of what is ignored, the difficulty with reductionist personality-and-politics analyses is one that has already been alluded to: they pay insufficient attention to the full range of possible psychological and non-psychological determinants of behavior. There is a failure in such analyses to seek multivariate contextual explanations in

---

[31] For a discussion of the early "trait-correlational" political-psychology literature, see Smith, Bruner, and White, *op. cit.*, Chap. 2.

[32] See, for example, Theodore Abel, "Is a Psychiatric Interpretation of the German Enigma Necessary?" *American Sociological Review*, 10 (1945), 457–64; and Reinhard Bendix, "Compliant Behavior and Individual Personality," *American Journal of Sociology*, 58 (1952), 292–303.

which the different factors that affect political behavior are considered together and in terms of the ways they interact with one another.

Finally, among the overall criticisms of this *genre*, there is a class of objections which deny on more or less formal grounds that *in principle* much can come of personality-and-politics inquiry. These are objections based on such considerations as the allegedly greater capacity of social than of personality characteristics to explain behavior, the ostensibly greater influence of situational than of personality variables, the limited possible impact of individual personalities on events, and the unimportance of ego defenses in everyday life. On close examination, these objections, all of which need a good bit of clarification, prove *not* to be valid reasons for avoiding the study of personality and politics. But they are, nevertheless, interesting since they provide important suggestions about how personality-and-politics inquiry ought to proceed.

I shall describe and discuss in depth the formal objections to political personality study in the next chapter; but first it will be instructive to review a number of promising recent developments in the literature, including a formulation designed to make explicit the kind of contextual, multivariate thinking needed to avoid the various reductionisms.

Promising Trends in the Study of Personality and Politics

My lament about the lack of a systematic personality-and-politics literature may leave the impression that *no* interesting or useful work has been done in this field. Quite the contrary. There is much that is intriguing in the older work, not the least of which is in Lasswell's early contributions. And recently there has been scattered, but extremely promising progress on precisely the matters that led to the past criticisms of each of the three kinds of inquiries and more generally of the overall political personality endeavor.

There have been a number of impressive contributions to the single-case analysis literature, perhaps the most widely acclaimed being the treatment of Luther in Erik Erikson's *Young Man Luther* and of Wilson in *Woodrow Wilson and Colonel*

THE STUDY OF PERSONALITY AND POLITICS

House: A Personality Study by Alexander and Juliette George.[33] Light-years separate these sophisticated works from the early pathographies of political figures. Both Erikson and the Georges succeeded in applying depth psychological notions to complex and problematic protagonists without reducing them to their ego-defenses, without ignoring the impact of non-psychological considerations and without failing to consider their strengths along with their weaknesses. The George and George volume is of particular interest to political psychologists both because it deals with a major modern political figure and because it is methodologically exemplary. Although the Georges presented their account of Wilson largely as a chronological narrative, keeping detailed defense of the explanatory inferences they were making to a minimum, their narrative was illuminated by exceptional methodological and theoretical self-consciousness. The Georges have discussed the assumptions and procedures that guided their analysis of Wilson in an appendix to *Woodrow Wilson and Colonel House* and in a number of other writings.[34] In doing so, they have made a major contribution to specifying and perfecting the ordinarily tacit criteria that govern single-case psychological analyses, thus helping make the single-case psychological analysis a less subjective, more replicable enterprise. In Chapter Three, where I discuss evidence and inference in the single-case analysis, I draw extensively on the Georges' analysis of Woodrow Wilson as a source of illustrations, as well as on their methodological work on the logic of single-actor diagnosis.

Typological analysis has also progressed. James D. Barber's *The Lawmakers*[35] provides an important example. Barber interviewed and administered questionnaires to Connecticut state legislators. He found it possible to generate the following four-fold typology out of the two dichotomous variables of (*a*) the member's attitude toward his membership in the legislative group, as indicated by willingness to return to the legislature for additional

[33] See Erikson, *op. cit.*, and George and George, *op. cit.*

[34] Alexander L. George, "Power as a Compensatory Value for Political Leaders," *op. cit.*; "Some Uses of Dynamic Psychology in Political Biography" (unpublished paper, 1960); and Alexander L. George and Juliette L. George, "Woodrow Wilson: Personality and Political Behavior" (paper presented at the 1956 Annual Meeting of the American Political Science Association).

[35] Barber, *op. cit.*

terms, and (*b*) his level of activity in the group, as shown by various objective indicators of legislative behavior:

Activity in Legislature

		High	Low
Attitude toward legislative membership	positive	Lawmakers	Spectators
	negative	Advertisers	Reluctants

Barber found a remarkable degree of variation in the motives and behavior of the legislators, but was able to isolate a good bit of patterning by means of his typology. For example, the legislators Barber calls the Lawmakers—those members who are both active in the legislature and positively oriented to it—proved to have strong needs to engage in intelligent problem-solving based on rational canvassing of alternatives. Each of the remaining three types also tended to exhibit distinctive patterns of needs and distinctive political styles—needs and styles which were generally not pointed toward achieving policy goals in the legislature. The antithesis of the Lawmakers, those members who were both inactive and uncommitted to the legislature, tended to be in office to fulfill a dutiful obligation. These are Barber's Reluctants. His inactive but committed Spectators exhibited a Riesmanesque tendency to be dependent upon their political participation for signs of emotional reassurance. Finally, the active but uncommitted Advertisers tended to be "young men on the make"—exploitative types whose political activity was a way of obtaining personal attention and career advancement.

In generating a typology out of the relationships among a few central variables, Barber pursues a strategy that Lasswell enunciated in *Psychopathology and Politics*[36] and subsequently expanded upon.[37] Lasswell suggests that typological analysis can fruitfully begin by identifying "nuclear types" of the sort that result from Barber's two dichotomous variables. Then, Lasswell

---

[36] Barber, *op. cit.*, Chap. 4.

[37] Harold D. Lasswell, "A Note on 'Types' of Political Personality: Nuclear, Co-Relational, Developmental," *Journal of Social Issues*, 24:3 (1968), 81–91.

points out, it becomes strategic to identify the clusters or syndromes of interrelated further characteristics that are associated
with the nuclear defining characteristics. Thus Barber's Lawmaker type tends to be a college graduate who is from a party-
competitive urban area and who is high in self-esteem; the Spectator tends to be female, from a small town, and highly deficient
in self-esteem; and the other two types also show clusters of
distinctive characteristics. Similar findings, including possibilities for subtypes, emerge from Barber's recent work on presidential style. Lasswell calls this second stage of typological analysis
"co-relational" typing: he makes it clear that the logic of inquiry
leads one from nuclear to co-relational types.

The logic of inquiry further tends to lead from co-relational
types to, in Lasswell's phrase, developmental types:

> Many of the terms which are used to describe adult
> traits are no doubt unpredictable from the less dif-
> ferentiated traits of infancy, childhood, and youth. But
> the growth of full-blown developmental types requires
> the sifting and refinement of terms until they are ade-
> quate to the description of sequences of growth. De-
> velopmental types will describe a set of terminal, adult
> reactions, and relate them to those critical experiences
> in the antecedent life of the individual which dispose
> him to set up such a mode of dealing with the world.[38]

Barber is especially attentive to developmental aspects of
typology in his later work on types of American presidents,
which extends the kind of analysis used in *The Lawmakers*.
Consistent with the emphasis in modern personality theory on
individual development as a life-long process, rather than merely
a consequence of early childhood experiences, Barber finds that
the early adult years seem to have been critical for the presidents'
later political behavior. In particular, his canvass of biographical
records points to the later significance of the president-to-be's
first independent political successes.[39]

The Lasswell-Barber strategy of systematically constructing

---

[38] Lasswell, *Psychopathology and Politics, op. cit.*, p. 61.
[39] James D. Barber, "Classifying and Predicting Presidential Styles: Two
Weak Presidents," *Journal of Social Issues*, 24:3 (1968), 51–80, and his "Adult
Identity and Presidential Style: The Rhetorical Emphasis," *Daedalus*, 97
(1968), 938–68.

psychological typologies of political actors is one that I shall
return to in Chapter Four, where I attempt to illustrate the
problems of typological research through a logical reconstruction
of the best known, but perhaps most vexed of the political
psychology typologies, that of the authoritarian personality.

Just as very promising single-case and typological work has
begun to appear, advances also are evident in analyses of how
psychological phenomena aggregate—of their effects on the collectivities that are composed of political actors. The stances that
various theorists have taken on the connection of the micro-phe-
nomena of individual psychology and behavior with the macro-
phenomena of social and political institutional functioning cover
the gamut of possibilities. They range from Durkheimian unwillingness to explain "social facts" psychologically, through reductionist failures to realize that social and political systems have
characteristics that are not predictable by mere addition of the
psychological properties of their members.

These epistemological debates about the connection between
micro- and macro-phenomena are, as Singer has pointed out,
endemic in the natural sciences as well as the social sciences.[40] Or
at least they are endemic among theorists. Those who engage in
empirical inquiry "appear content," in the words of a reviewer
on recent developments in molecular biology, "to note the difficulties and then to get on with the work at hand."[41] Political
science examples of "getting on" with the empirical work are the
efforts of Browning and Jacob to weave togetner data on the
characteristics of political systems and data on the motivational
needs of politicians[42] and Browning's subsequent attempts via
computer simulation to determine what kinds of politicians will
be recruited in what kinds of political systems with what consequences.[43]

But if we think in terms of the broader conception of

[40] J. David Singer, "Man and World Politics: The Psychological Interface," *Journal of Social Issues*, 24:3 (1968), 127–56.

[41] John L. Howland, "The Strategy of Molecular Biology," *Choice*, 4
(1968), 1209–12.

[42] Rufus P. Browning and Herbert Jacob, "Power Motivation and the
Political Personality," *Public Opinion Quarterly*, 28 (1964), 75–90.

[43] Rufus P. Browning, "The Interaction of Personality and Political System in Decisions to Run for Office: Some Data and a Simulation Technique,"
Journal of Social Issues, 24:3 (1968), 93–110.

"personality" and consider under the aggregative heading all examples of the use of psychological data to explain institutional patterns, then it is the voting literature that shows the most dramatic progress. There have been recent instances in that literature of convincing, data-based explanations of large-scale political patterns in terms of micro-data. Investigators at the University of Michigan Survey Research Center have used survey data to analyze such persistent institutional patterns as the loss of Congressional seats in mid-term elections by the Presidential party in the United States and the rise and fall of volatile "flash" political parties, such as the Poujadists in France.[44] These explanations, which have the further interest of being contrary to received belief, will be part of my concern in the account of aggregation in Chapter Five.

In addition to the foregoing developments in individual, typological, and aggregative analysis, there also has been an easing of certain of the difficulties that have plagued all the analytic modes. In particular, there is now much less of the explanatory one-sidedness for which students of political personality have so often been chastised. There have been a number of formulations designed to sensitize workers in this area to the need for sufficiently comprehensive and multivariate explanation. Perhaps the most useful of these is M. Brewster Smith's "A Map for the Analysis of Personality and Politics,"[45] which is a further development of Smith's work with Bruner and White on *Opinions and Personality*.

V. A "MAP" FOR THINKING ABOUT PERSONALITY AND POLITICS

Smith's formulation is designed to serve as a reminder of the complex interdependency of different classes of psychological

[44] See Angus Campbell, Philip E. Converse, Warren E. Miller, and Donald Stokes, *Elections and the Political Order* (New York: Wiley, 1966), pp. 40–62, 269–91.

[45] M. Brewster Smith, "A Map for the Analysis of Personality and Politics," *Journal of Social Issues*, 24:3 (1968), 15–28. Also see Alex Inkeles and Daniel J. Levinson, "The Personal System and the Socio-Cultural System in Large-Scale Organizations," *Sociometry*, 26 (1963), 217–29.

and social determinants of political—as well as other—behavior. For a full exposition, it is necessary to turn to Smith's lucid paper; but the general formulation, which is outlined graphically in Figure One, can be summarized here. (I shall return frequently to Figure One in later chapters, using it as a touchstone for discussing a number of the questions that arise in thinking about personality and politics.)

In essence the figure is a sophisticated expansion of a point we have already noted: behavior is a function of the actor's psychological predispositions and the environmental influences that impinge upon him (stimulus → organism → response). The end product of this equation, political behavior, is shown in the panel numbered V, at the center right of Figure One. The remainder of the figure consists of an economical, but still rather extensive, set of elaborations on the environmental and predispositional antecedents of behavior. Psychological predispositions are summarized in Panel III. Panels I, II and IV are designed to differentiate social and other environmental determinants of behavior into three classes:

1. the immediate situation within which behavior occurs (Panel IV);
2. the immediate social environment, extending from birth through adult life, within which the actor's psychological development occurs (Panel II); and
3. the "distal" or remote social environment which the actor (especially if he is a member of the general population rather than a leader) does not experience directly, but which shapes the immediate environments that socialize him and provide him with situational stimuli (Panel I). The distal environment has two central components: the overarching features of the contemporary sociopolitical system and the historical antecedents of these features.

The phenomena summarized by the three environmental panels are clearly empirically continuous with each other, but analytically separable.

The solid arrows in the figure indicate the foregoing and other types of causal relationships of which students of personality and politics need to take account. The dotted arrows note certain feedback relationships: the further effects of an actor's

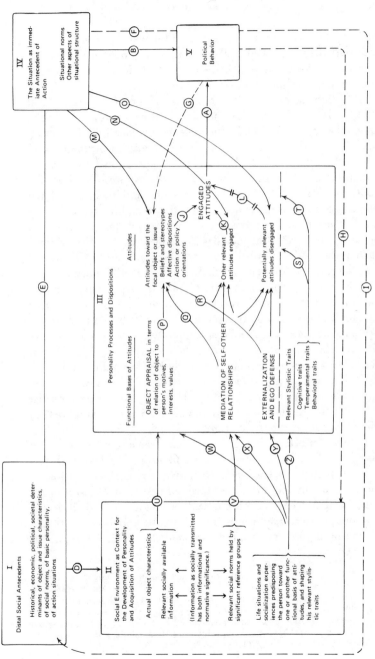

FIGURE ONE. TYPES OF VARIABLES RELEVANT TO THE STUDY OF PERSONALITY AND POLITICS

Source: M. Brewster Smith, "A Map for the Analysis of Personality and Politics," *Journal of Social Issues*, 24:3 (1968), 25; repr. in Fred I. Greenstein and Michael Lerner, eds., *A Source Book for the Study of Personality and Politics* (Chicago: Markham, 1971), 42.

political behavior on the situation within which he acts and on his own attitudes, and the effects that are of concern in aggregative inquiries—the impact of behavior, individually and in summation, on the distal social environment.

Within the central, psychological portion of his map (Panel III), Smith locates the dispositions and processes of personality. Like other psychologists, he includes in "personality" the subcategory "attitudes." He analytically distinguishes attitudes from the ordinarily more enduring and deeply-rooted personality structures in which they have their bases. As we have seen, the contents of Panel II (i.e., both attitudes and their underlying bases) are analytically constructed rather than directly observed: all that can be directly observed is environmental variables and behavior, but the latter includes not only gross physical actions such as the casting of a ballot or participation in a *coup d'état*, but also the expression of one's beliefs in a confidential interview.

Political scientists sometimes tend to equate the concept "attitude" with its most prevalent indicator—a discrete response to a question of opinion in a public opinion poll. Smith defines a person's attitudes as the "dispositions . . . he brings to any situation he encounters . . . when they represent integrations of cognitive, emotional, or conative tendencies around a psychological object such as a political figure or issue."[46] In short, the term is used to summarize the full array of subjective orientations that we bring to bear in reacting to situations. Smith's paraphrase of his definition in the upper right of Panel III, Figure One, lists not only "affective dispositions" (emotional tendencies), but also "beliefs and stereotypes" (cognitive tendencies) and "action or policy orientations" (conative tendencies). Attitudes, then, can be thought of as the "face" of personality closest to the situational antecedents of political behavior: indeed, it is the situation, *as perceived by the actor*, an attitudinal datum, that is of central importance for predicting and explaining behavior.[47] It

---

[46] Smith, *op. cit.*, p. 21.

[47] For a discussion of how the notion "attitudes" might be further specified into a series of more precise terms describing relevant psychological antecedents of political behavior (e.g., the actor's values, aims, information about his situation, and estimates of future developments), see a comment by Alexander L. George on an earlier statement by Smith of his conceptualization, "Comment on 'Opinions, Personality, and Political Behavior,'" *American Political Science Review*, 52 (1958), 18–26.

also sometimes is instructive to think of attitude and situation as being in a kind of a push-pull relationship: the stronger the attitudinal press for a course of action, the less need for a situational stimulus, and vice versa. A further point about the interface of attitudes and situations is that situational sanctions are effective only when they are addressed to subjectively relevant values.[48]

It is to the interaction of attitudes and situational stimuli that one must look first in order to explain behavior. But to understand the conditions of attitude formation, arousal, stability and change, it may then be useful to consider the deeper personality structures: what Smith, extending his work with Bruner and White, calls the "functional bases of attitudes." Smith's distinctions partially parallel the Freudian categories of ego, super-ego, and id, as well as the similar categories in many other personality theories:

1. One underlying structure which may be more or less well-developed in any individual is specialized toward dealing with reality—toward assessing and adapting to the environment. To the degree that an attitude, say an importer's belief in the desirability of low tariffs, has its basis in the need to establish such means–end relationships, it is said to serve the function of *object appraisal.*

2. A second fundamental personality structure—again, one which varies in importance from person to person—serves to cope with inner conflict. Of special concern are the deeper, anxiety-producing conflicts that have their source in the need to manage impulses to express unacceptable primitive desires that were supressed or repressed in the course of development. When an attitude is influenced by the need to accommodate to inner conflicts, when it is an outer manifestation of inner psychic tensions, it is said to serve the function of *externalization and ego defense.* The relationships between inner needs and such atti-

---

[48] On "push–pull," see Fred I. Greenstein, "Harold D. Lasswell's Concept of Democratic Character," *Journal of Politics,* 30 (1968), 696–709. Also see J. Milton Yinger, "Research Implications of a Field View of Personality," *American Journal of Sociology,* 68 (1963), 580–92. On the dependence of sanctions for their effectiveness upon the psychology of those to whom they are applied, see Melvin Spiro, "Social Systems, Personality, and Functional Analysis," in Bert Kaplan, ed., *Studying Personality Cross-Culturally* (New York: Harper & Row, 1961), pp. 93–128.

tudes may run the gamut of mechanisms of defense: projection, displacement, splitting, idealization, identification with the aggressor, and so on along the various lists of how the sometimes contradictory demands of impulse, conscience, and reality may be managed.

3. A third underlying aspect of personality that may influence political attitudes consists of the various and ubiquitous tendencies of the self to adopt positive or negative orientations to reference groups and exemplars. To the degree that attitudes and behavior result from needs to be like or unlike significant others in one's immediate or distant environment, the function of *mediation of self-other relations* (referred to less aptly in *Opinions and Personality* as "social adjustment") is being performed.[49]

Any single attitude or political action may, as the psychoan-

---

[49] At this point, it is possible to restate more clearly some of the points made earlier in the chapter. When psychologists, such as Smith, use the word "personality," they have in mind the entire contents of Panel III. Political scientists, however, sometimes tend to use the term as if it referred only to one of the three functional bases of attitudes—"externalization and ego defense"—thus ignoring a large part of the non-attitudinal, non-psychodynamic aspects of psychological functioning, although these may often be important sources of political behavior. Generally speaking, I follow the psychologists' usage, specifying my meaning further where appropriate (as in Chapter Two, where it is necessary to establish what "personality" means in a variety of objections to the study of personality and politics). But the purpose of this work is to suggest that political analysts should be more attentive to the aspects of psychic functioning represented at the left of the panel (including, but not exclusively, the ego defenses)—and to indicate how they can deal rigorously with such matters. Occasionally, as in Chapter Five, I speak of the left side of Panel III as the "underlying personality processes," in order to distinguish this aspect of psychic functioning from attitudes.

We should note that Smith identifies a further category of less-dynamic psychological characteristics that may determine attitudes. These characteristics are under the heading "relevant stylistic traits," indicated under the dotted line in Panel III. An example of such a trait might be the disposition to make use of abstraction in one's cognitive functioning. For example, in *Opinions and Personality*, Smith and his associates found that one of their case-study subjects, whom they called Charles Lanlin, tended to perceive political objects in a highly fragmented manner, not relating them to one another. This seemed mainly to be a simple extension of a mode of cognitive performance which showed little capacity for abstracting. Lanlin's political views bore the stamp of this aspect of his personal style, but nothing would be gained by saying that fragmented political attitudes were in some sense performing a function for him. In contrast, the functional terminology is not jarring when applied, say, to the aggressive attitudes and behavior of an individual who, by exhibiting aggressiveness, is able to conceal from himself emotionally threatening impulses to be passive.

alysts put it, be "over-determined," having its basis in more than one of the underlying structures. But frequently it may be possible to establish that a particular attitude serves one or another predominant function for an individual. For another individual, the same attitude may have a different functional basis. Therefore, these two individuals may well respond quite differently to any single effort to arouse, reinforce, or change the attitude. An attitude change procedure that succeeds with attitudes based on object-appraisal needs may backfire if applied to attitudes that serve to shore up an individual's ego-defenses.[50] Thus Smith's formulation serves as a reminder to assess the place of attitudes in a political actor's psychic economy, as well as ascertaining the content of his attitudes, the situational antecedents of his behavior, his social environmental background, and his broader, distal sociopolitical setting.

VI. THE PLAN OF THE BOOK

We must, of course, be more specific about the requirements of personality-and-politics analysis than the grand and sweeping assertion that ended the previous paragraph; therein lies the task of the remainder of this book. To recapitulate the remarks I have already made about the agenda of the next five chapters:

Chapter Two considers, at some length, several formal objections to personality and politics research, arguing that rather than being obstacles to inquiry, they have a variety of positive implications about how the political psychologist may usefully go about his business.

Chapters Three through Five follow from the triadic classification of modes of personality-and-politics analysis. The third

---

[50] The classical analyses of how the same attitude may serve different functions for different individuals have arisen in writings on the causes and possible cures of intergroup prejudices. Provision of new information may eliminate prejudices that have their origin in object appraisal; but the very same doses of information may actually stiffen the prejudices of individuals whose intergroup views are expressions of inner conflict. For the latter, some more or less psychotherapeutic attitude change technique may be nessasary. But neither psychotherapy nor new information will reach the individual whose prejudice mainly performs the function of relating him to others in his environment.

chapter deals with evidence and inference in single-case analysis, drawing for examples from the Georges' analysis of Wilson; the fourth chapter deals with the tasks of typological analysis, concentrating on a reconstruction of the theoretical premises of the controversial literature on authoritarianism; the fifth chapter, which treats aggregation, also draws for examples on the authoritarianism literature and additionally makes a number of rather schematic methodological observations.

In Chapter Six, I draw together a number of strands from the previous chapters by way of summary and go on to suggest certain additional contributions that can be made by the analyst of personality and politics. As will be evident throughout, what I have to say is provisional and preparatory: at no point is it my purpose to present a set of crystalized mechanical procedures that would substitute for what continues to be the central scholarly desideratum—intellectual energy and imagination.

CHAPTER TWO

Objections to the Study of
Personality and Politics

A bewildering variety of criticisms have been leveled at the heterogeneous literature on personality and politics. The criticism has been so profuse that there is considerable accuracy to the sardonic observation of David Riesman and Nathan Glazer that the field of culture-and-personality research, within which many of the past accounts of personality and politics fall, has "more critics . . . than practitioners."[1] As we have seen, some of the criticisms are directed toward methodological difficulties of the existing research; but others are more fundamental, formal objections that would seem to apply even to methodologically sound inquiry. These objections typically seem to take the form of answers in the negative to the (often implicit) question: "Is personality important as a determinant of political behavior?"

The more intellectually challenging of the various formal objections—i.e., the assertions that *in principle* personality-and-politics research is not promising, even if one avoids the specific

---

[1] David Riesman and Nathan Glazer, "*The Lonely Crowd:* A Reconsideration in 1960," in Seymour M. Lipset and Leo Lowenthal, eds., *Culture and Social Character* (New York: Free Press of Glencoe, 1961), p. 437. For examples of discussions that are in varying degrees critical of personality and politics writings, see Edward A. Shils, "Authoritarianism: 'Right' and 'Left,'" in Richard Christie and Marie Jahoda, eds., *Studies in the Scope and Method of "The Authoritarian Personality"* (Glencoe, Ill.: Free Press, 1954), pp. 24–49; Sidney Verba, "Assumptions of Rationality and Non-Rationality in Models of the International System," *World Politics,* 14 (1961), 93–117; Reinhard Bendix, "Compliant Behavior and Individual Personality," *American Journal of Sociology,* 58 (1952), 292–303; and David Spitz, "Power and Personality: The Appeal to the 'Right Man' in Democratic States," *American Political Science Review,* 52 (1958), 84–97.

methodological pitfalls of case-study, typological, and aggregative inquiry—seem to fall under five headings. In each case, the
objection is one that can be generalized to the study of how
personality relates to any social phenomenon. And in each case,
the objection proves on analysis to have certain positive implications for the study of the relationship between politics and "personality," in several senses of the latter term. Listed elliptically,
the five objections are that:

1. Personality characteristics tend to be randomly distributed in institutional roles. Personality, therefore, "cancels out"
and can be ignored by analysts of political and other social
phenomena.

2. People's personality characteristics are less important
than their social characteristics in influencing behavior. This
makes it unpromising to concentrate research energies on studying the impact of personality.

3. Personality is not of interest to political and other social
analysts because individual actors (personalities) are severely
limited in the impact they can have on events.

4. Personality is not an important determinant of behavior
because individuals with varying personal characteristics will
tend to behave similarly when placed in common situations. And
if the ways that people vary do not affect their behavior, it is not
useful to study personal variation.

5. Finally, there is a class of objections deprecating the
relevance of personality to political analysis in which "personality" is equated with particular aspects of individual psychological functioning. We shall be concerned with one of the objections
falling under this heading—*viz.*, the assertion that deep psychological needs of the sort summarized by the term "ego-defensive"
do not have an important impact on behavior and that, therefore,
"personality" in this sense of the term need not be studied by the
student of politics.

The first two of these objections seem to be based on fundamental misconceptions. Nevertheless, they do point to interesting
problems for the student of political psychology. The final three
objections are partially well-taken, but need to be rephrased in
conditional form as "Under what circumstances?" questions. The
remainder of this Chapter consists of expanded accounts of each

of the five objections and of the peremptory judgments I have just rendered on them.

I. TWO ERRONEOUS OBJECTIONS

THE THESIS THAT PERSONALITY "CANCELS OUT"

The assumption underlying the first objection seems to be, as Alex Inkeles points out, that "in 'real' groups and situations, the accidents of life history and factors other than personality which are responsible for recruitment [into institutional roles] will 'randomize' personality distribution in the major social statuses sufficiently so that taking systematic account of the influence of personality composition is unnecessary." As Inkeles easily shows, this assumption is false on two grounds.

First, "even if the personality composition of any group is randomly determined, random assortment would not in fact guarantee the *same* personality composition in the membership of all institutions of a given type. On the contrary, the very fact of randomness implies that the outcome would approximate a normal distribution. Consequently, some of the groups would by chance have a personality composition profoundly different from others, with possibly marked effects on the functioning of the institutions involved." Secondly,

> there is no convincing evidence that randomness *does* consistently describe the assignment of personality types to major social statuses. On the contrary, there is a great deal of evidence to indicate that particular statuses often attract, or recruit preponderantly for, one or another personality characteristic and that fact has a substantial effect on individual adjustment to roles and the general quality of institutional functioning.[2]

The objection turns out, therefore, to be based on unwarranted empirical assumptions. It proves not to be an obstacle to re-

---

[2] Alex Inkeles, "Sociology and Psychology," in Sigmund Koch, ed., *Psychology: A Study of a Science*, 6 (New York: McGraw-Hill, 1963), 354.

search, but rather—once it is examined—an opening gambit for identifying a crucial topic of investigation for the political psychologist: How are personality types distributed in social roles and with what consequences?

THE THESIS THAT SOCIAL CHARACTERISTICS ARE MORE IMPORTANT THAN PERSONALITY CHARACTERISTICS

The second objection—asserting that individuals' social characteristics are "more important" than their personality characteristics—seems to result from a conceptual rather than empirical error. It appears to be an objection posing a pseudo-problem that needs to be dissolved analytically rather than resolved empirically.

Referring back to the "map" in Chapter One, let us consider the referents of "social characteristic" and "personality characteristic." By the latter we refer to some inner predisposition of the individual (Panel III of the figure on p. 27). The term "characteristic" applies to a state of the organism. Using the "environment → predispositions → response" paradigm, we assume that the environmental stimuli (Panel IV) which elicit behavior (Panel V) are mediated through the individual's psychological predispositions.

But we also assume that the psychological predispositions (or "characteristics") are themselves to a considerable extent environmentally determined, largely by prior social experiences (Panel II). It is to these prior environmental states, which may occur at any stage of the life cycle and which may or may not persist into the present, that we commonly refer when we use the expression "social characteristics." In this case, the term "characteristic" refers *not* to a state of the organism (Panel III), but rather to the environment within which the organism has developed (Panel II). This is made particularly clear by the common usage of "*objective* social characteristics."

It follows that social and psychological characteristics are in no way mutually exclusive. They do not compete as candidates for explanation of social behavior, but rather are complementary. Social characteristics can *cause* psychological characteristics; they are not substitutes for psychological characteristics. The erroneous assumption that social characteristics could even in principle be more important than psychological characteristics probably arises in part from the misleading impression of identity fostered by using the same noun in the two expressions.[3]

This confusion also very probably is contributed to by the standard procedures social scientists use to eliminate spurious correlations, namely, controlling for "third factors" and calculating partial correlations. When used indiscriminately and without reference to the theoretical standing of the variables that are being analyzed, control procedures can lead to the failure to recognize what Herbert Hyman once described as "the distinction between developmental sequences or configurations and problems of spuriousness."[4] An example of how the failure to recognize this distinction arises is provided by Urie Bronfenbrenner's interesting research report entitled "Personality and Participation: The Case of the Vanishing Variables."[5] Bronfenbrenner reports a study in which it was found that measures of personality were associated with participation in community affairs. However, as he notes, "it is a well-established fact that extent of participation varies as a function of social class position, with lower classes participating least." Bronfenbrenner therefore proceeds to measure the relationship between personality and participation, while controlling for social class (and certain other factors). The result: "Most of the earlier . . . significant relationships between personality measures and participation now

---

[3] My criticism of the second objection would, of course, not stand in any instance where some acquired inner characteristic (such as a sense of class consciousness) was being defined as a social characteristic, and in which it was being argued that this "social" characteristic was "more important" than a "personality" characteristic. In terms of my usage, this would imply an empirical assertion about the relative influence of two types of psychological, or "personality," variables. By now, it should be clear that my remarks on the meaning of terms are simply short-handed approaches to clarify the underlying issue; at no point do I want to engage in the quixotic enterprise of attempting to establish "correct" usage.

[4] Herbert Hyman, *Survey Design and Analysis* (Glencoe, Ill.: Free Press, 1955), pp. 254–74. The phrase in quotation marks is the heading of a section in which Hyman discusses this matter and is at p. 254.

[5] Urie Bronfenbrenner, "Personality and Participation: The Case of the Vanishing Variables," *Journal of Social Issues*, 16 (1960), 54–63. For an alternative, and I think more useful, approach to analyzing the effects of personality on participation, see David Horton Smith, "A Psychological Model of Individual Participation in Voluntary Organizations: Applications to Some Chilean Data," *American Journal of Sociology*, 72 (1966), 249–66.

disappear, leaving only two significant correlations, both of them quite low." One common interpretation of such a finding would be that Bronfenbrenner had shown the irrelevance of personality to participation; but his finding should not be so interpreted. Hyman's remarks, since they place the problem of relating social-background data to psychological data in its more general context, are worth quoting at some length.

> . . . the concept of spuriousness cannot *logically* be intended to apply to antecedent conditions which are associated with that particular independent variable as part of a developmental sequence. Implicitly, the notion of an uncontrolled factor which was operating so as to produce a spurious finding involves the image of something *extrinsic* to the . . . apparent cause. Developmental sequences, by contrast, involve the image of a series of entities which are *intrinsically* united or substitutes for one another. All of them constitute a unity and merely involve different ways of stating the same variable as it changes over time. . . . Consequently, to institute procedures of control is to remove so-to-speak some of the very cause that one wishes to study. . . . How shall the analyst know what antecedent conditions are intrinsic parts of a developmental sequence? . . . One guide, for example, can be noted: instances where the "control" factor and the apparent explanation involve *levels of description from two different systems* are likely to be developmental sequences. For instance, an explanatory factor that was a personality trait and a control factor that was biological such as physique or glandular functions can be conceived as levels of description from different systems. Similarly, an explanatory factor that is *psychological* and a control factor that is sociological can be conceived as two different levels of description, i.e., one might regard an attitude as derivative of objective position or status or an objective position in society as leading to psychological processes such as attitudes. Thus, the concept of spuriousness would not be appropriate.[6]

---

[6] Herbert Hyman, *op. cit.*, pp. 254–57 (italics in the original). Also see Hubert Blalock, "Controlling for Background Factors: Spuriousness Versus Developmental Sequences," *Sociological Inquiry*, 34 (1964), 28–39, for a discussion of the rather complex implications of this distinction for data analysis.

In the Bronfenbrenner example, then, an individual's "objective" socioeconomic background—as opposed to such subjective concomitants as his sense of class consciousness—needs to be analyzed as a possible social determinant of the psychological correlates of participation. This enables the analyst to take account of the fact that, as Allport[7] puts it, "background factors never directly cause behavior; they cause attitudes [and other mental sets]" and the latter "in turn determine behavior." Allport's statement does not gainsay the use of controls. "I am not, of course, arguing against the use of breakdowns or matched groups," he adds. "They should, however, be used to show where attitudes come from and not to imply that social causation acts automatically apart from attitudes."

By suggesting the developmental source of a psychological state, a control often helps to explain the dynamics and functions of that state in the adult personality. A good example can be found in the well-known Hyman and Sheatsley critique of *The Authoritarian Personality*. At one point, Hyman and Sheatsley examine certain patterns of attitudes and certain typical ways of viewing the world which the authors of *The Authoritarian Personality* tended to explain in terms of complex processes of personal psychopathology. Hyman and Sheatsley suggest that such attitudes (for example, highly punitive notions about how society should deal with sexual deviance) may be learned *cognitions* rather than manifestations of ego-defensiveness. They were able to suggest this by using controls to show that these attitudes are typical beliefs among lower socioeconomic-status strata and, therefore, may simply be conventionally learned orientations of individuals from such backgrounds. But what Hyman and Sheatsley do *not*—and on purely formal grounds *cannot*—show is that such attitudes are in some sense "social" or "cultural" *rather* than psychological.[8]

---

[7] Gordon Allport, "Review of *The American Soldier*," *Journal of Abnormal and Social Psychology*, 45 (1950), 172.

[8] Herbert Hyman and Paul B. Sheatsley, " 'The Authoritarian Personality' —a Methodological Critique," in Richard Christie and Marie Jahoda, eds., *op. cit.*, pp. 50–122. As M. Brewster Smith has pointed out to me, the tendency of some sociologists to "control away" psychological variables inappropriately is paralleled by "a naïve application of the analysis of variance model" on the part of some psychologists who "fail to realize that prior conceptual decisions are required before it can be interpreted causally." Smith comments that "for

The more general lesson that emerges from our examination of the second objection is that students of personality and politics will often find it necessary to lay out developmental schemes of explanation placing social and psychological factors in the sequence in which they seem to have impinged upon each other.

II. THREE PARTIALLY CORRECT OBJECTIONS

The three remaining objections bear on (a) how much impact individual actors can have on political outcomes; (b) whether the situations in which political actors find themselves impose uniform behavior on individuals of varying personal characteristics, thus making it unprofitable for the political analyst to study variations in the actors' personal characteristics; and (c) the numerous questions that can be raised about the impact on behavior of particular classes of personal characteristics, including the so-called ego-defensive personality dispositions that I shall be discussing. Once these objections are rephrased in conditional form, it becomes possible to state propositions indicating the circumstances under which each objection is or is not likely to be valid. But it must be emphasized that the propositions I shall be advancing in what follows are not hypotheses stated with sufficient precision to be testable. Given the appropriate theoretical interests, these propositions *can* be further specified so as to be testable—and falsifiable. But their present function is as sensitizers—that is, as general indications of the circumstances under which political analysts are and are not likely to find it desirable to study "personality" in the senses of the term implicit in the objections.

When Do Individual Actions Affect Events ("Action Dispensability")?

The objection to studies of personality and politics which emphasizes the limited capacity of single actors to shape events is similar in its essentials to the nineteenth- and early twentieth-cen-

---

practical prediction in a *stable* political system, one can often ignore the psychological mediation. In an unstable one it is risky to do so. In any case, theoretical understanding requires spelling out the mediation." Cf. the discussion by Angus Campbell and his associates of "the funnel of causality," in *The American Voter* (New York: Wiley, 1960), Chap. 2.

tury debates over social determinism—that is, over the role of individual actors (Great Men or otherwise) in history. In statements of this objection, emphasis is placed on the need for the times to be ripe in order for the historical actor to make his contribution. "What impact could Napoleon have had on history if he had been born in the Middle Ages?" is the type of question that is asked. Possibly because of the parlor-game aura of the issues it raises the problem of the impact of individuals on events has not had as much disciplined attention in recent decades as have the two remaining issues I shall be treating. Nevertheless, at one time or another it has received the attention of Tolstoy, Carlyle, William James, Plekhanov, and Trotsky (in his *History of the Russian Revolution*). The main attempt at a balanced general discussion seems to be Sidney Hook's vigorous, though unsystematic, 1943 essay *The Hero in History*.[9]

Since the degree to which actions are likely to have significant impacts is clearly variable, we can begin clarification by asking: *What are the circumstances under which the actions of single individuals are likely to have a greater or lesser effect on the course of events?* For shorthand purposes, this might be called the question of *action dispensability*. This is possibly not the only question that has arisen in hero-and-history debates, but it has the merit of presenting a discrete analytic problem. We can conceive of the actions performed in the political arena as being on a continuum, ranging from those that are indispensable for outcomes that concern us through those that are utterly dispensable. And we can make certain very general observations about the circumstances which are likely to surround dispensable and indispensable actions.

This notion of action dispensability is, as we shall see, separable from the related notion of act*or* dispensability—that of whether we need to explain the action in terms of the actor's personal characteristics. The first is, as it were, the question of under what circumstances nations are likely to be saved (or lost) by the juxtaposition of the little Dutch boy's finger and the dike; the second is addressed to whether we must take account of the psychology of the little boy. In each case, there would be some advantage in speaking of "substitutability" rather than "dispensability," since the former term has the merit of suggesting a

---

[9] Sidney Hook, *The Hero in History* (New York: John Day, 1943).

handy means of rough and ready reasoning about the *degree* of importance of an actor or of his personal characteristics: one may engage in the mental exercise of substituting other possible acts (including inaction) and of hypothesizing the likely behavior of other historically available actors. But the antonym, "nonsubstitutability," is less successful than "indispensability" as a way of indicating the circumstances under which a particular act was a necessary link in some chain of events or under which the actor's personality qualities were a necessary antecedent of his act.

In rephrasing the actors-are-limited objection to the study of personality and politics in terms of action dispensability, we clarify the nature of the objection. What is at stake is more a social issue (concerning the influence of participants in decision-making processes) than a psychological issue. In terms of Figure One on page 27, our reference is to the feedback arrow at the bottom of the chart that indicates the possible effect of individual political behavior (Panel V) on the distal social environment (Panel I). Psychological data are only a part of what is needed for analyzing such effects, and analyses of them do not invariably raise important psychological issues.

The following three propositions suggest circumstances under which the actions of an individual are likely to be links in a chain of further events. The propositions are necessarily quite abstract because of the very great generality of the question "when do actions affect events?" But further specification can readily be introduced depending upon the context of investigation (e.g., the kinds of action being studied) and upon the concerns of investigators (e.g., the kinds of effects that are of interest). The likelihood of personal impact varies with (1) the degree to which the actions take place in an environment which admits of restructuring, (2) the location of the actor in the environment, and (3) the actor's peculiar strengths or weaknesses.

1. *The likelihood of personal impact increases to the degree that the environment admits of restructuring.* Technically speaking, we might describe situations or sequences of events in which modest interventions can produce disproportionately large results as "unstable." They are in a precarious equilibrium. The physical analogies are: massive rock formations at the side of a

mountain which can be dislodged by the motion of a keystone, tinder-dry forest land, highly explosive compounds with properties like that of nitro-glycerine, and the weakened dikes of our little-Dutch-boy example.

Instability in this sense is by no means synonymous with what is loosely known as "political instability," a phrase commonly used to refer to a variety of unsettled phenomena, including political systems in which governments rise and fall with some frequency and systems in which violence is common. Many of the situations commonly referred to as unstable do not at all admit of restructuring. In the politics of many of the "unstable" Latin American nations, for example, most conceivable substitutions of actors and actions would lead to little change —at least in such "larger" political arrangements as the likelihood that officials will be changed by *coup* rather than by election. Thus, to return to physical analogy, an avalanche in motion down a mountainside is for the moment in stable equilibrium, since it cannot be influenced by modest interventions, just as the stationary rock formation that begot the avalanche was in unstable equilibrium.

The situation which does not admit readily of restructuring appears typically to be one in which a variety of factors press toward the same outcome so that the outcome can be expected to occur even if some of the contributing factors are eliminated.[10] The outcome that can be expected to occur "no matter what happens" can in fact be a *non*-outcome, as in the numerous instances of pattern maintenance involving the persistence of timeworn institutional arrangements. Or it may be the sort of highly likely occurence to which such vague notions as "historical inevitability" are applied: a chain of events that is decisively under way and almost certain to arrive at a particular outcome. In situations that do not readily admit of restructuring, a key variable is likely to be the self-fulfilling prophesies generated by the actors' own perceptions of the degrees and ways in which the situation is manipulable, and by whom.

Hook, in *The Hero in History*, offers the outbreak of World

---

[10] I take this point from Wassily Leontief's interesting essay "When Should History be Written Backwards?," *The Economic History Review*, 16 (1963), 1–8.

War I and of the February Revolution as instances of historical sequences which, if not "inevitable," probably could not have been averted by the actions of any single individual. In the first case, the vast admixture of multiple conflicting interests and intertwined alliances and, in the second case, the powerful groundswell of discontent were such as to leave the impression that no action by any single individual—excluding the far-fetched hypothetical instances that invariably can be imagined —would have averted the outcome. On the other hand, Hook attempts to show in detail that without the specific actions of Lenin the October Revolution might well not have occurred. By implication, he suggests that Lenin was operating in an especially unstable environment. A similar argument might be advanced about the degree to which key leaders (notably Hitler) could exercise leverage over the political environment of Europe just prior to the outbreak of World War II, on the basis of the various accounts at our disposal of the state of affairs that preceded the invasion of Poland in 1939. In defending such an argument, however, it would be vital to avoid taking the circular route of simply showing that the environment *had* been manipulated by a single actor.[11]

2. *The likelihood of personal impact varies with the actor's location in the environment.* To shape events, an action must be performed not only in an unstable environment, but also by an actor who is strategically placed in that environment. It is, for example, a commonplace that actors in the middle and lower ranks of many bureaucracies are unable to accomplish much singly, since they are restrained or inhibited by others. Robert C. Tucker points out what may almost be a limiting case on the other end of the continuum in an essay on the lack of restraint on Russian policy-makers, both under the Czars and since the Revo-

---

[11] But such an argument, based on an account of the properties of the environment, ought to be possible. In order to find indicators of "manipulability," (compare the indicators of other dispositional concepts, such as "fragility"), it is not necessary to bring about the end-state to which the concept points. It *would*, however, be appropriate (and non-tautological) to collect trend-data on the circumstances under which environments had changed in response to individual actors. For an account of the outbreak of World War II which parallels Hook's analysis of Lenin and the October Revolution, see Alan Bullock, *Hitler: A Study in Tyranny* (rev. ed.; New York: Harper, 1960).

lution. He quotes with approval Nikolai Turgenev's mid-nine-teenth-century statement that, "in all countries ruled by an un-limited power there has always been and is some class, estate, some traditional institutions which in certain instances compel the sovereign to act in a certain way and set limits to his caprice; nothing of the sort exists in Russia."[12] Tucker also has pointed to the tendency in totalitarian states for the political machinery to become "a conduit of the dictatorial psychology"[13]—that is for there to be a relatively unimpeded conversion of whims of the dictator into governmental actions as a consequence of his au-thoritarian control of the bureaucratic apparatus.

3. *The likelihood of personal impact varies with the per-sonal strengths or weaknesses of the actor.* My two previous observations can be recapitulated with an analogy from the pool-roöm. In the game of pocket billiards, the aim of the player is to clear as many balls as possible from the table. The initial distri-bution of balls parallels my first observation about the manipula-bility of the environment. With some arrays a good many shots are possible; perhaps the table can even be cleared. With other arrays no successful shots are likely. The analogy to point two— the strategic location of the actor—is, of course, the location of the cue ball. As a final point, we may note the political actor's peculiar strengths or weaknesses. In the poolroom, these are paralleled by the player's skill or lack of skill. Skill is of the utmost importance, since the greater the actor's skill, the less his initial need for a favorable position or a manipulable environ-ment, and the greater the likelihood that *he himself* will contribute to making his subsequent position favorable and his environment manipulable. By the same token, a singularly inept politician may reduce the manipulability of his environment.[14]

---

[12] Robert C. Tucker, *The Soviet Political Mind* (New York: Praeger, 1963), pp. 145–65; quotation from Turgenev at p. 147.

[13] Robert C. Tucker, "The Dictator and Totalitarianism," *World Politics*, 17 (1965), 583.

[14] Putting it a bit more formally, the skill (or ineptness) of the actor at t_1 may be a key determinant of the manipulability of his environment at t_2. To the degree that we take environmental conditions as given (i.e., considering them statically at a single point in time), we underestimate the impact of individuals on politics. For examples of political actors shaping their own roles and environments, see Hans H. Gerth and C. Wright Mills, *Character and Social Structure* (New York: Harcourt, Brace, 1953), Chap. 14.

The variable of skill is emphasized in Hook's detailed examination of Lenin's contribution to the events leading up to the October Revolution. Hook concludes that Lenin's vigorous, persistent, imaginative participation in that sequence was a necessary (though certainly not sufficient) condition for the outcome. Hook's interest, of course, is in lending precision to the notion of the Great Man. Therefore, he is concerned with the individual who, because of especially great talents, is able to alter the course of events. For our purposes, the Great Failure is equally significant: an actor's capabilities may be relevant to an outcome in a negative as well as a positive sense. In each case, what presumably concerns us is a personal input—including again the failure to take available courses of action—that diverts the course of events from what would have been expected if the actor's personal capacities had been more typical.[15]

WHEN DOES PERSONAL VARIABILITY AFFECT BEHAVIOR ("ACTOR DISPENSABILITY")?

Even when it is acknowledged that some action taken by an individual has been a crucial node in a decision-making process, it may sometimes be argued that the action is one that would have been performed by any actor in the same situation or role. There are, as Shils notes, many circumstances under which "per-

---

[15] Without getting into the bog of technical philosophical debate about testing counter-factuals (propositions taking the form: "if x had not occurred, then . . ."), this observation suggests a means of empirical leverage on action dispensability—and it is also relevant to the discussion which follows of actor dispensability. When we say that in some single instance an action or actor was indispensable, we are evidently stating a covert, multi-instance proposition about likely outcomes, under a series of circumstances in which the only variation consists of acts or actors like the ones to which we are imputing indispensability. For a highly imaginative study of political leadership which brings this point home, see Donald B. Rosenthal and Robert L. Crain, "Executive Leadership and Community Innovation: The Fluoridation Experience," *Urban Affairs Quarterly*, 1 (1966), 39–57. Rosenthal and Crain show that the position taken by mayors on water fluoridation is an extraordinarily good predictor of the outcome of community fluoridation decisions. The point that analyses of the single instance often involves thinking in multiple-case terms emerges again in my remarks in Chapter Three on single-case analysis.

For a classical discussion of how to reason about the "what-would-have-happened-if?" questions raised by analyses of action dispensability, see Max Weber, *The Methodology of the Social Sciences* (Glencoe, Ill.: Free Press, 1949), pp. 172ff.

sons of quite different dispositions" can be found to "behave in a more or less uniform manner."[16] Easton, making the same point, gives the example of political party leaders who differ in their personality characteristics and who are "confronted with the existence of powerful social groups making claims on their parties." Their "decisions and actions," he suggests, will tend "to converge."[17]

Raised to the level of an objection to the study of personality and politics, the argument here is that political behavior (Panel V of the figure on page 27) is frequently dependent upon situational stimuli (Panel IV) to the exclusion of variations in the actors' personal characteristics (Panel III). If individuals vary in personality but perform identically when exposed to common stimuli, we clearly can dispense with the study of their personality differences: a variable cannot explain a uniformity.

Proponents of the view that situational and other pressures eliminate or sharply reduce the effects of personality often note that there are circumstances under which this tends not to be the case. Similarly, the advocates of personality-and-politics analysis identify much the same sorts of circumstances in qualifying the assertion that personality factors have an important impact on politics. Typically, the qualifications in such discussions are more interesting than the overall direction of the argument. Statements on this matter by such writers as Lane, Shils, Gold-hamer, Levinson, and Verba[18] provide us with a bewilderingly extensive array of propositions addressed to the following re-phrasing of the objection: *Under what circumstances do different actors (placed in common situations) vary in their behavior and under what circumstances is their behavior uniform?*

Although "*actor dispensability*" appears to be the most convenient way to label this question, what is at issue is not the actor but his personal characteristics and the degree to which they are dispensable from an explanation of his political behav-

---

[16] Edward A Shils, in Christie and Jahoda, eds., *op. cit.*, p. 43.

[17] David Easton, *The Political System* (New York: Knopf, 1953), p. 196.

[18] Robert E. Lane, *Political Life* (Glencoe, Ill.: Free Press, 1959), pp. 99–100; Shils, in Christie and Jahoda, eds., *op. cit.*, pp. 24–49; Herbert Gold-hamer, "Public Opinion and Personality," *American Journal of Sociology*, 55 (1950), 346–54; Daniel J. Levinson, "The Relevance of Personality for Political Participation," *Public Opinion Quarterly*, 22 (1958), 3–10; and Sidney Verba, *op. cit.*, pp. 93–117.

ior. The question of actor dispensability is logically distinct from our previous question about the circumstances under which, not an actor's characteristics, but his actions are dispensable from an account of some political outcome (act*ion* dispensability). Nevertheless, the greater our interest in the latter, the more likely it is that we will be interested in the former. For example, even if considerations of situational and role pressures lead us to believe that there is very little variation in the ways American presidents can be expected to respond to the warning system that signals a missile attack, the consequences of any presidential action under these circumstances are so great that even small variations acquire profound interest.

A personality-oriented political analyst might object to the basic formulation of actor dispensability—to the very notion that under some circumstances different actors behave uniformly—on the grounds that in fact behavior is *never* uniform. The objection is not well taken, but raises an important consideration. Every different act is of course different in the trivial, definitional sense. It is also empirically true that if we inspect actions with sufficient care, we can always detect differences among them—even such substantially "situation-determined" actions as "the way in which a man, when crossing a street, dodges the cars which move on it"[19] vary from individual to individual. Nevertheless, the objection lacks force in that it denies the principle (necessary for analytic purposes) that we can classify actions, treating them as uniform for some purposes. It is this ability that enables Shils, in a passage following the assertion quoted earlier, to make an important sociological observation about the ways that organizations inhibit the expression of personal variation: "To a large extent," he comments, "large enough indeed to enable great organizations to operate in a quite predictable manner . . . [different individuals] will conform [i.e., behave uniformly] despite the possibly conflicting urges of their personalities."[20]

Yet the objection serves as a reminder that what we treat as

---

[19] This is a quotation from a well-known passage in Karl Popper's *The Open Society and Its Enemies*, 2 (New York: Harper Torchbook Edition, 1963), 97, arguing that sociology is an "autonomous" discipline because psychological evidence is so often of limited relevance—compared with situational evidence—to explanations of behavior. For a critique of Popper's analysis, see Richard Lichtman, "Karl Popper's Defense of the Autonomy of Sociology," *Social Research*, 32 (1965), 1–25.

[20] Shils, in Christie and Jahoda, eds., *op. cit.*, p. 44.

uniform behavior depends upon our principle of classification, which in turn depends upon our theoretical interests. For one analytic purpose, we might classify as uniform the very same acts that in the light of other purposes we would analyze in terms of their variation. This is equally true of situational stimuli and psychological characteristics: for some purposes certain kinds of variations are of interest; for others they are not. In fact, one source of the untidiness in the list of propositions on actor dispensability that follows is that the propositions are addressed to something as general as personal variability (which is all that "personality" appears to mean in the present objection), rather than to specific kinds of variability.

In contrast to the schematic triad of very abstract propositions I advanced on the unfashionable question of action dispensability, it is possible to find dozens of assertions of circumstances under which personal variability does or does not have behavioral consequences. Since the notion of personal variability is too broad to permit very great rigor, it seems most useful simply to summarize and organize a number of the more suggestive assertions without detailed criticism, reiterating that as presently formulated the assertions are sensitizers and sources of hypotheses, rather than testable, falsifiable formulations. Some order can be introduced if the many assertions are organized, as all but one of them can be, in terms of the elements in the environment → predispositions → response equation to which they are addressed. Not only are some environmental stimuli more likely than others to allow the expression of personal differences. It is also possible to identify kinds of personal predispositions which, if present in an individual, reduce the likelihood that other of his predispositions will come into play. Finally, it is possible to identify types of responses that commonly need to be explained in terms of inner variation.

The first six propositions consist of three sets of paired assertions about complementary environmental and predispositional conditions of personal variation; of the remaining five propositions, three refer to types of action, one to a predispositional variable, and one is not classifiable in these terms. Although this basis of organization lends some order to the diversity of assertions, the propositions plainly are not mutually exclusive or exhaustive, and there are several points of what appears to be contradiction.

1. *Ambiguous situations leave room for personal variability to manifest itself.* As Sherif puts it, "the contribution of internal factors increases as the external-stimulus situation becomes more unstructured."[21] (A classically unstructured environmental stimulus, leaving almost infinite room for personal variation in response, is the Rorschach ink blot.)

Budner distinguishes three types of ambiguous situations.[22] Each of his distinctions meshes with one more of the various concrete examples that have been given of circumstances under which environments foster actor dispensability or indispensability. Budner's first type is:

(a) *The "completely new situation in which there are no familiar cues."*

Shils comments that in new situations "no framework of action [has been] set for the newcomer by the expectations of those already on the scene. A new political party, a newly formed religious sect will thus be more amenable to the expressive behavior of the personalities of those who make them up than an ongoing government or private business office or university department with its traditions of scientific work."[23]

Goldhamer argues that the public opinion process moves from unstructured conditions admitting of great personal variability to more structured conditions that restrain individual differences. Immediate reactions to public events, he argues, reflect personal idiosyncrasies; but gradually the individual is constrained by his awareness that the event has become a matter of public discussion. "There is reason to believe that, as the individual becomes aware of the range and intensity of group preoccupation with the object, his orientation to it becomes less individualized, less intimately bound to an individual perception and judgment of the

---

[21] Muzafer Sherif, "The Concept of Reference Groups in Human Relations," in Muzafer Sherif and M. O. Wilson, eds., *Group Relations at the Crossroads* (New York: Harper, 1953), p. 211.

[22] Stanley Budner, "Intolerance of Ambiguity as a Personality Variable," *Journal of Personality*, 30 (1962), 29–50. Quotations at p. 30.

[23] Shils, in Christie and Jahoda, eds., *op. cit.*, pp. 44–45.

object. . . . [H]e is drawn imperceptibly to view this object anew, no longer now as an individual percipient, but as one who selects (unconsciously, perhaps) an 'appropriate' position in an imagined range of public reactions . . . a limitation is thus placed on the degree to which the full uniqueness of the individual may be expected to influence his perceptions and opinions."[24]

The second type of ambiguity referred to by Budner is (b) *"a complex situation in which there are a great number of cues to be taken into account."*

Levinson suggests that the availability of "a wide range of . . . socially provided . . . alternatives" increases "the importance of intrapersonal determinants" of political participation. "The greater the number of options for participation, the more the person can choose on the basis of personal congeniality. Or, in more general terms, the greater the richness and complexity of the stimulus field, the more will internal organizing forces determine individual adaptation. This condition obtains in a relatively unstructured social field, and, as well, in a pluralistic society that provided numerous structured alternatives."[25]

Finally, Budner refers to (c) *"a contradictory situation in which different elements suggest different structures."*

Several of Lane's examples fall under this heading: "Situations where reference groups have politically conflicting points of view. . . . Situations at the focus of conflicting propaganda. . . . Current situations which for any individual are in conflict with previous experience."[26]

2. *The opportunities for personal variation are increased to the degree that political actors lack socially standardized mental sets which might lead them to structure their perceptions and resolve ambiguities.* Socially standardized mental sets may be

---

[24] Goldhamer, *op. cit.*, pp. 346–47.
[25] Levinson, *op. cit.*, p. 9.
[26] Lane, *op. cit.*, p. 99.

largely cognitive, as in the shared bodies of knowledge that characterize members of a profession. (One assumes that physicians will be less variable in their reactions to an accident victim than will laymen.) The shared mental sets may also be largely affective, taking the form of stereotyped attitudes.

Verba, in an essay on "Assumption of Rationality and Non-Rationality in Models of the International System," comments that "the more information an individual has about international affairs, the less likely it is that his behavior will be based upon non-logical influences. In the absence of information about an event, decisions have to be made on the basis of other criteria. A rich informational content, on the other hand, focuses attention on the international event itself. . . ."[27]

Wildavsky, in an account of adversary groups in the Dixon-Yates controversy, points to ways in which the preconceptions of members of factions lead them to respond in predictable fashions that are likely to be quite independent of their personal differences. "The public versus private power issue . . . has been fought out hundreds of times at the city, state, county, and national levels of our politics in the past sixty years. A fifty year old private or public power executive, or a political figure who has become identified with one or another position, may well be able to look back to twenty-five years of personal involvement in this controversy. . . . The participants on each side have long since developed a fairly complete set of attitudes on this issue which have crystallized through years of dispute. . . . They have in reserve a number of prepared responses ready to be activated in the direction indicated by their set of attitudes whenever the occasion demands. . . ."[28]

3. *The impact of personal differences on behavior is increased to the degree that sanctions are not attached to certain of the alternative possible courses of behavior.*

---

[27] Verba, *op. cit.*, p. 100. By "non-logical," Verba means influences resulting from ego-defensive personality needs, but his point applies generally to personal variability.

[28] Aaron Wildavsky, "The Analysis of Issue-Contexts in the Study of Decision-Making," *Journal of Politics*, 24 (1962), 717–32.

"The option of refusing to sign a loyalty oath," Levinson comments, "is in a sense 'available' to any member of an institution that requires such an oath, but the sanctions operating are usually so strong that non-signing is an almost 'unavailable' option to many who would otherwise choose it."[29]

4. If, as the third proposition asserts, the degree to which certain of the alternative courses of action are sanctioned reduces the likelihood that personal characteristics will produce variation in behavior, then: *intense dispositions in a contrary direction to the prevailing sanctions increase the likelihood that personal characteristics will affect behavior.*

"Personality structure will . . . be more determinant of political activities when the impulses and the defenses of the actors are extremely intense"—for example, "when the compulsive elements are powerful and rigid or when the aggressiveness is very strong."[30]

5. As numerous studies of conformity to "group pressures" indicate, *to the degree that individuals are placed in a group context in which their "decision or attitude is visible to others,"*[31] *personal variation is reduced.*

6. By the same token, *intense needs to take one's cues from others will tend to reduce the effects of variation.*

Personality may dispose some individuals to adopt uncritically the political views of their environment, but as a result, Goldhamer comments, the view adopted will "have a somewhat fortuitous character in relation to the personality and be dependent largely on attendant situational factors."[32] Dispositions toward conformity are, of course, a key concern of political psychologists. The point here is merely that these dispositions reduce the impact of the individual's other psychological characteristics on his behavior.

[29] Levinson, *op. cit.*, p. 10.
[30] Shils, in Christie and Jahoda, eds., *op. cit.*, p. 45.
[31] Verba, *op. cit.*, p. 103.
[32] Goldhamer, *op. cit.*, p. 353.

7. *The greater a political actor's affective involvement in politics, the greater the likelihood that his psychological characteristics* (apart from his sense of political involvement) *will be exhibited in his behavior.*

Goldhamer comments that "the bearing of personality on political opinion is conditioned and limited by the fact that for large masses of persons the objects of political life are insulated from the deeper concerns of the personality." He, however, adds in a footnote: "This should not be interpreted to mean that personality characteristics are irrelevant to an understanding of the opinions and acts of political personages. . . . [Among such activists] political roles are so central to the entire life organization that a close connection between personality structure and political action is to be expected."[33]

Levinson argues that "the more politics 'matters,' the more likely it is that political behavior will express enduring inner values and dispositions. Conversely, the less salient the issues involved, the more likely is one to respond on the basis of immediate external pressures. When a personally congenial mode of participation is not readily available, and the person cannot create one for himself, he may nominally accept an uncongenial role but without strong commitment or involvement. . . . In this case, however, the person is likely . . . to have a strong potential for change toward a new and psychologically more functional role."[34]

In the following propositions, we move from environment and predisposition to response, i.e., to political actions themselves.

8. *The more demanding the political act—the more it is one that calls for an active investment of effort—the greater the likelihood that it will be influenced by personal characteristics of the actor.*

Lane suggests that there is little personal variation in "the more conventional items, such as voting, expressing

---

[33] Goldhamer, *op. cit.*, p. 349.
[34] Levinson, *op. cit.*, p. 10.

patriotic opinions and accepting election results as final."
On the other hand, his list of actions which "reveal . . .
personality" includes "selecting types of political behavior
over and above voting."[35] Examples of these types of more
demanding activity are: writing public officials, volunteer-
ing to work for a political party and seeking nomination for
public office. A particularly demanding class of action is—
to return to propositions three and four—*contra-sanction*
behavior. Such behavior is therefore likely to reveal personal characteristics in ways that sanction-congruent behavior does not.

9. *Variations in personal characteristics are likely to be
exhibited in certain kinds of spontaneous behavior—notably actions that proceed from personal impulse, without effort or pre-
meditation.*

Goldhamer refers to "a person's . . . casual rumina-
tions while walking along the street, sudden but perhaps
transient convictions inspired by some immediate experience, speculations while reading the newspaper or listening
to a broadcast, remarks struck off in the course of an
argument. . . . If we have any theoretical reason for sup-
posing that a person's opinions are influenced by his personality structure, it is surely in these forms of spontaneous
behavior that we should expect to find the evidence of this
relationship."[36]

10. *Even when there is little room for personal variability
in the instrumental aspects of actions, there is likely to be variability in their expressive aspects.* Examples of expressive aspects
of actions include evidences of the personal *style* of an actor (for
example, his mannerisms), the *zealousness* of his performance,
and the *imagery* that accompanies his behavior at the preparatory and consummatory phases of action (for example, fantasies
about alternative courses of action). "Instrumental" refers to the
gross aspects of goal attainment—for example, the very fact that
an individual votes or writes a letter to a Congressman.

---

[35] Lane, *op. cit.*, p. 100.
[36] Goldhamer, *op. cit.*, p. 349.

Lane suggests that "the idiosyncratic features of personality" are likely to be revealed in the "images" political actors hold "of other participants." There also is "scope for the expression of personal differences," Lane points out, in "the grounds" one selects "for rationalizing a political act," and in one's style "of personal interaction in political groups."[37]

Shils, after arguing that "persons of quite different dispositions" often "will behave in a more or less uniform manner," then adds: "naturally not all of them will be equally zealous or enthusiastic. . . ."[38]

Riesman and Glazer point out that, although "different kinds of character" can "be used for the same kind of work within an institution," a "price" is paid by "the character types that [fit] badly, as against the release of energy provided by the congruence of character and task."[39]

The final proposition, going over some of the same ground as several of its predecessors (such as propositions one, seven, and eight), refers to political roles and does not fit neatly into any of the three elements of the environment → predispositions → response equation.

11. *Personality variations will be more evident to the degree that the individual occupies a position free "from elaborate expectations of fixed content."*[40] Typically these are leadership positions. We have already seen that such positions figure in the conditions of action indispensability; their importance for the student of personality and politics is evident *a fortiori* when we

---

[37] Lane, *op. cit.*, p. 100.

[38] Shils, in Christie and Jahoda, eds., *op. cit.*, p. 43.

[39] Riesman and Glazer, in Lipset and Lowenthal, eds., *op. cit.*, p. 438.

[40] Shils, in Christie and Jahoda, eds., *op. cit.*, p. 45. The term "role" is commonly used so as to have both an environmental referent (the prevailing expectation about his duties in a role incumbent's environment) and a predispositional referent (the incumbent's own expectations). For most analytic purposes, clarity would be served if these two dimensions were distinguished from each other. For a valuable discussion, see Daniel Levinson, "Role, Personality and Social Structure in the Organizational Setting," *Journal of Abnormal and Social Psychology*, 58 (1959), 170–80.

note that the leader's characteristics also are likely to be reflected in his behavior, thus meeting the requirement of actor indispensability.

The military leader, it has been said, may have an especially great impact. "Even those who view history as fashioned by vast impersonal forces must recognize that in war personality plays a particularly crucial part. Substitute Gates for Washington, and what would have happened to the American cause? Substitute Marlborough or Wellington for Howe or Clinton, and what would have happened? These are perhaps idle questions, but they illustrate the fact that the course of a war can depend as much upon the strengths and failings of a commander-in-chief as upon the interaction of geography and economics and social system."[41]

UNDER WHAT CIRCUMSTANCES ARE EGO-DEFENSIVE NEEDS LIKELY TO MANIFEST THEMSELVES IN POLITICAL BEHAVIOR?

The final objection to the study of personality and politics that we shall consider is one in which "personality" denotes neither the impact of individuals on the political process (action dispensability), nor the mere fact of individual variability (actor dispensability), but rather denotes specific ways that "personalities" vary. Once we have found it necessary to explain political behavior by referring to personal variations, objections can be made to whatever specific personality variables we choose to employ. In this case, the counter-ploy of rephrasing the objection in the form of contingent propositions is especially constructive: propositions about the circumstances under which *specific kinds of psychological variations* ("ego strength," intelligence, and the

---

[41] William Willcox, *Portrait of a General* (New York: Knopf, 1964), pp. ix–x. Willcox does not indicate in this passage whether the personality variables that have military consequences are simply skill-levels, or whether he also is thinking, for example, of aspects of personality that relate to emotional functioning; however, in the full context of his book it is clear that he has in mind not only skill but also other personality variables. This is an instructive ambiguity, since it serves as a reminder of the weakness of propositions about personal variability in general: it is possible that Willcox's assertion correctly applies to variations in military skill, but not, for example, to variation in emotional functioning. (Compare the statement by Verba quoted under the second proposition on actor dispensability.)

like) have political consequences are closer to the requirements of empirical research than are propositions about variability in general.

As we have seen (Chapter One, pp. 4–5), political scientists often equate the study of personality and politics with the applications of depth psychology in such works as Lasswell's *Psychopathology and Politics*, Fromm's *Escape from Freedom*, and *The Authoritarian Personality*.[42] Consequently, many commentators who argue that personality does not have an important impact on politics have in mind the political consequences of the defensive processes through which individuals deal with their inner conflicts. They may argue, for example, that such processes do not have much bearing on politics because the psychic forces evident in the pathological behavior of the disturbed do not come into play in the daily behavior of normal people.

Rephrasing this objection conditionally, we arrive at the following question: *Under what circumstances are ego-defensive needs likely to manifest themselves in behavior?* It should be emphasized that the selection of this particular question about actors' characteristics carries no implication that personality ought to be equated solely with the unconscious, the irrational, and the emotional. Indeed, one of the great needs of contemporary political analysis is for convenient means of personal characterization that go beyond political attitudes, but do not merely focus on deeper motivational processes and structures.

Much of what I have said about actor dispensability also applies to the circumstances under which ego-defensive needs are likely to manifest themselves. Wherever the circumstances of political behavior permit personal variation to affect political outcomes, it is possible that this variation will take the form of ego-defensive reaction to inner psychic conflict. These circumstances include: "unstructured" political situations; settings in which sanctions are weak or conflicting so that individuals of diverse inclinations are not coerced into acting uniformly; and the various other considerations discussed under the previous

---

[42] Harold D. Lasswell, *Psychopathology and Politics* (Chicago: University of Chicago Press, 1930), reprinted in *Political Writings of Harold D. Lasswell* (Glencoe, Ill.: Free Press, 1951); Erich Fromm, *Escape from Freedom* (New York: Rinehart, 1941); and T. W. Adorno, *et al.*, *The Authoritarian Personality* (New York: Harper, 1950).

heading. These circumstances make it *easier* for ego-defensive personality needs to come to the fore. They do not, of course, make it necessary—or even very likely—that behavior will have a significant basis in ego defense.

Given the foregoing circumstances that make ego-defensive behavior easier, what, then, makes it likely (or at least adds to the likelihood) that deeper psychodynamic processes will be at work? We may briefly note the following three classes of factors, locating them conveniently in terms of environment, predispositions, and response.

1. *Certain types of environmental stimuli undoubtedly have a greater "resonance" with the deeper layers of the personality than do others.* These are the stimuli which evoke disproportionately emotional responses; people seem to be overly sensitive to them. They include certain kinds of issues politicians learn to be wary of; examples are capital punishment, cruelty to animals, and, in recent years, fluoridation of drinking water. In addition, politicians themselves certainly vary in terms of the degree to which they appeal to various kinds of needs with which the ego defenses are typically associated. Often the stimulus value of an emotionally sensitive issue is to only a small segment of the electorate; nevertheless, the capacity of such issues to arouse fervid response may be such that a Congressman would rather confront his constituents on a knotty economic matter like revision of the tariff affecting the district's principal industry than on, in the phrase of the authors of *Voting*, a "style issue"[43] like humane slaughtering.

> One element in these sensitive issues, Lane and Sears suggest, may be that they touch upon "topics dealing with material commonly repressed by individuals. . . . Obvious examples are war or criminal punishment (both dealing with aggression) and birth control or obscenity legislation (both dealing with sexuality). Socially 'dangerous' topics, such as communism and religion, also draw a host of irrational defensive maneuvers. The social 'dangers' that they

---

[43] Bernard Berelson, *et al.*, *Voting* (Chicago: University of Chicago Press, 1954), p. 184.

represent frequently parallel unconscious intra-psychic 'dangers.' For example, an individual with a strong unconscious hatred for all authority may see in Soviet communism a system which threatens intrusion of authoritarian demands into every area of his life. His anti-communism may thus stem more from a residual hatred for his father than from any rational assessment of its likely effects on his life." Lane and Sears do not, however, imply that the sensitivity of an issue is a necessary indicator that it has activated deeper personality needs, although it *is* a rule of thumb of clinical practice to search for signs of ego-defensiveness when an individual's emotional response to a stimulus appears "out of all proportion."

Lane and Sears also suggest that "opinions dealing with people (such as political candidates) or social groups (such as 'bureaucrats,' 'blue bloods,' or the various ethnic groups) are more likely to invite irrational thought than opinions dealing with most domestic economic issues. Few people can give as clear an account of why they like a man as why they like an economic policy; the 'warm-cold' dimension seems crucial in many 'person perception' studies, but the grounds for 'warm' or 'cold' feelings are usually obscure. Studies of ethnic prejudice and social distance reveal the inaccessibility of many such opinions to new evidence; they are often compartmentalized, and usually rationalized; that is, covered by a plausible explanation which an impartial student of the opinion is inclined to discount."[44]

2. *The likelihood that ego-defensive needs will affect political behavior also is related to the degree to which actors "have"*

---

[44] The quotations are from Robert E. Lane and David O. Sears, *Public Opinion* (Englewood Cliffs, N.J.: Prentice-Hall, 1964), p. 76. Compare Heinz Hartmann, "The Application of Psychoanalytic Concepts to Social Science," in his *Essays on Ego Psychology* (New York: International Universities Press, 1964), pp. 90ff. Lane and Sears also suggest that "irrational" opinion formation is fostered where the "referents of an opinion" are "vague," where the issue is "remote" and it is "difficult to assess its action consequences," and where the "terms of debate" are "abstract." These are points which, in terms of the present discussion, apply generally to the possibility that personal variability will affect behavior (actor dispensability), as well as more specifically to the possibility that ego defense will come to the fore.

ego-defensive needs. This assertion is not quite the truism it appears to be. We still have very little satisfactory evidence of various patterns of psychopathology in society[45] and even less about the degree to which emotional disturbance tends to become channelled into political action.

Although it is not a truism, the proposition—in spite of being less general than the propositions on all types of psychological variation—needs to be elaborated into a series of more specific hypotheses about the different *kinds* of ego-defensive adaptations as they relate to political behavior. For example, one of the more interesting findings of the prejudice studies of a decade ago was an observation made, not in the well-known *Authoritarian Personality*, but rather in the somewhat neglected *Anti-Semitism and Emotional Disorder* by Ackerman and Jahoda.[46] Personality disorders which manifested themselves in depressive behavior, it was noted, were not accompanied by anti-Semitism. But anti-Semitism was likely if the individual's typical means of protecting himself from intra-psychic conflict was extra-punitive—that is, if he was disposed to reduce internal tension by such mechanisms as projection. There is no reason to believe that this observation will prove to apply only to the restricted sphere of anti-Semitism.

3. *Finally, certain types of response undoubtedly provide greater occasion for deep personality needs to find outlet than do others*—for example, such responses as affirmations of loyalty in connection with the rallying activities of mass movements, and the various other types of responses deliberately designed to channel affect into politics. Both in politics and in other spheres of life, it should be possible to rank typical classes of actions in terms of the degree to which the appropriateness of expressing affect is taken as a norm. And it is reasonable to expect, although this needs to be empirically demonstrated, that action in these spheres will be especially likely to express ego-defensive needs.

---

[45] But see Leo Srole, *et al.*, *Mental Health in the Metropolis* (New York: McGraw-Hill, 1962). Also see Jerome G. Manis, *et al.*, "Estimating the Prevalence of Mental Illness," *American Sociological Review*, 29 (1964), 84–89, and the sources there cited.

[46] Nathan W. Ackerman and Marie Jahoda, *Anti-Semitism and Emotional Disorder* (New York: Harper, 1950).

III. SUMMARY AND CONCLUSIONS

Five of the more intellectually challenging assertions about the lack of relevance of personality to the endeavors of the student of politics have been considered. Two of these seem to be based on misconceptions, albeit interesting ones. The three additional objections can be rephrased so that they no longer are objections, but rather provide the occasion for advancing propositions about how and under what circumstances personality affects political behavior. In rephrasing these objections, we see three of the many ways in which the term "personality" has been used in statements about politics: to refer to the impact of individual political actions, to designate the fact that individual actors vary in their personal characteristics, and to indicate the specific content of individual variation. When "personality" is equated with specific aspects of individual variation, the term often proves to refer to the deeper ego-defensive, psychological processes.

This diversity of meaning makes it clear that general questions—such as, "Should personality be taken into account in analyses of politics?"—are not susceptible to general answers. Rather, the global questions must be broken down into the variety of sub-questions implied in them, and these, when pursued, lead not to simple answers, but to an extensive examination of the terrain of politics in terms of the diverse ways in which "the human element" comes into play. Having considered the issues that are raised by the standard global objections for personality-and-politics analysis, we may now turn to more specific problems of evidence, inference, and conceptualization as they arise in single-case, typological, and aggregate inquiry.

CHAPTER THREE

Psychological Analysis
of Single Political Actors

I. COMMON ASPECTS OF SINGLE–ACTOR AND TYPOLOGICAL ANALYSES

"Personality": A Circularly Used Construct

The discussion in this and the next two chapters can be framed in terms of the following stripped-down and slightly relabeled version of M. Brewster Smith's five-part map of types of variables that are relevant to the study of personality and politics:

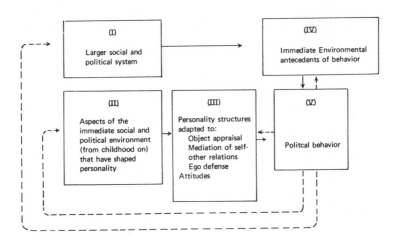

The political behavior of concern in this chapter is that of single political actors. Using the map, we can sketch in simplified form the kinds of intellectual operations that underlie the complex enterprise of analyzing a single actor psychologically. Our prime sources of observables in that enterprise are indicated in Panel IV on the immediate environmental antecedents of behavior and in Panel V on the behavior itself. We observe our subject's behavior in order to establish its *pattern*. We attend, of course, not only to his gross actions, but also and especially to his verbal actions. We interpret the behavioral pattern in terms of the environmental stimuli that appear to evoke it. (The fortunate analyst of a contemporary actor may himself be able to administer some of the behavior-evoking stimuli, in the form of interviews and psychological tests.)

From our observations of the regularities of behavior in varying settings we arrive at an analytic construct—an intellectually generated account of our subject's psychological characteristics (Panel III), including his attitudes and the personality processes in which they are based. These processes include his style of cognitive functioning (object appraisal), his ways of orienting himself socially (mediation of self-other relations), and his ways of managing inner conflict (ego defense). If we are fortunate, we may have a further source of observations on which to base our personality construct—namely, information about the past environmental influences that shaped our subject's present mode of psychic functioning (Panel II). And once we have formulated a construct that summarizes the more or less stable dispositions of our subject, we use that construct—along with data on environmental stimuli—to explain specific political actions of the individual under analysis.

The very same items on our map and the same processes of observation, construct-building, and inference are involved in the task that will concern us in Chapter Four: the development of psychological typologies. There our purpose is to classify multiple cases rather than to diagnose single cases. Otherwise, as in single-case analysis, we observe the patterning of behavior in its situational context in order to generate a personality construct. If possible, we also analyze the background experiences that shaped the personality. And we use the personality construct we have formulated, plus situational data, to explain behavior.

The seeming circularity of generating a personality construct *from behavior* and using the construct *to explain behavior* does not in fact involve a tautology as long as we do not use the same item of behavior to infer a disposition and then use the inferred disposition to explain the item of behavior. Nor do any problems arise from the use of a concept which describes phenomena that cannot be directly observed. There are ample precedents for using such concepts, an example from the natural sciences being the construct "electron."[1]

PHENOMENOLOGY, DYNAMICS, AND GENESIS: THREE COMPLEMENTARY APPROACHES TO CHARACTERIZING PERSONALITY

The processes of single-actor and typological ·personality diagnosis that I have just described can usefully be conceived of as involving three overlapping but analytically separable operations: the characterization of the *phenomenology*, the *dynamics*, and the *genesis* of personality.

1. *Phenomenology.* Here I refer to the observed behavioral phenomena upon which all further analysis depends—the regular patterns of behavior that the individual or type exhibits under varying environmental conditions. Phenomenological accounts are more or less static, more or less unexplained descriptions of the presenting symptoms. In terms of the figure that begins the chapter, the analyst of phenomenology focuses on the behavior panel (V). We may also, however, think of phenomenological analyses as dipping superficially into the personality panel (III), since descriptions are possible only in terms of interpretive criteria indicating which of the observable data are of interest, and these criteria are summarized in the personality construct.

2. *Dynamics.* To the degree that accounts of personality go beyond faithful characterizations of "symptomology" into diag-

---

[1] Some behavioral scientists, notably the psychologist B. F. Skinner, have attempted to dispense with psychological constructs—i.e., with the inferred entities that populate Panel III of the figure. For a cogent discussion of why the use of such formulations is probably inevitable, see Noam Chomsky, "Review of *Verbal Behavior* by B. F. Skinner," *Language*, 35 (1959), 26–58. For a systematic discussion of the general role of hypothetical entities in science, see Carl G. Hempel, "The Theoretician's Dilemma: A Study in the Logic of Theory Construction," in his *Aspects of Scientific Explanation* (New York: Free Press of Glencoe, 1965), pp. 173–226.

nosis, the concern shifts from phenomenological description to dynamic interpretation. The analyst begins to ask why the individual or type that concerns him exhibits a particular syndrome: this question leads the analyst to advance a theory of the intrapsychic processes which "must" be responsible for holding together the disparate elements of the syndrome. Analyses of dynamics can be thought of as a step back from the behavior panel of our figure: these analyses are concerned with the explicit personality construct indicated in Panel III. Dynamic analyses vary in the degree to which they rely on complex theoretical assumptions. Such analyses range from relatively atheoretical descriptions of the contingencies under which different aspects of phenomenology are manifested, through explanations in terms of inner events that can only be characterized in terms of the concepts of the various schools of personality theory. Hence the term "dynamics" can be seen to cover a host of rather disparate explanatory operations; in using it, I do not mean to imply that psychic functioning is "dynamic" in any of the several uses of the word.

3. *Genesis.* Accounts of personality dynamics tend to lead the analyst still further to the left side of the map. Having observed and explained an individual or type in terms of contemporary functioning, the analyst frequently is led to search for the aspects of inborn structure, maturation, and experience that culminated in the observed presenting features and the inferred underlying dynamics.

Like my classification of personality-and-politics research into individual, typological, and aggregative studies, the foregoing distinctions describe a *reconstructed* logic of inquiry. Actual research—what Abraham Kaplan calls "logic-in-use"[2]—does not follow neat *post hoc* schematizations. An investigation will, and in fact *must*, move in highly irregular ways from phenomenological through dynamic and genetic considerations. Descriptions of symptomology are constantly illuminated by dynamic assumptions and vice versa; a bit of information on genesis may lead to a changed emphasis in interpreting dynamics, or even in describing phenomenology. There is a ceaseless interplay among the three operations.

----

[2] Abraham Kaplan, *The Conduct of Inquiry* (San Francisco: Chandler, 1964), pp. 3–11.

This reconstruction of personality diagnosis into the complementary tasks of characterizing phenomenology, dynamics, and genesis, although not a faithful account of research procedures, has several uses. First, it organizes the tasks of personality diagnosis roughly in the order of the degree to which an investigator's findings are likely to be readily accepted by other investigators. Analysts of quite different intellectual orientations are reasonably likely to be able to agree on phenomenological analyses, since procedures are well developed for reaching consensus on whether an individual or type exhibits some observable trait or pattern. Agreement is harder to come by on dynamic interpretations, especially those that are dependent upon the concepts and assumptions of some one of the competing personality theories. And explanations of genesis are perhaps most likely to be controversial. In principle one might expect more agreement on the observables of developmental experience than on the concept-ridden variables of dynamic interpretations. But in practice the paucity of satisfactorily detailed and verified observations of developmental experience reduces the chances of widely accepted genetic explanations. Furthermore, genetic explanations are weakened because there is still imperfect knowledge of general principles of human development, and because many of the more interesting genetic hypotheses posit relationships that are in principle likely to be weak, or at any rate complex and difficult to document—relationships between phenomena remote from one another in time and connected by many mediating links.

A second use of the phenomenology-dynamics-genesis distinction is to order diagnostic operations in terms of their priority for the analyst of any specific pattern of political activity. It is the aspect of psychological interpretation that most readily can be agreed upon which proves to be most urgent. Phenomenological analyses can be thought of as actuarial accounts of how an individual or type is likely to respond to varying stimuli, and such information is bound to be helpful in efforts to explain or predict any particular action. Dynamic and genetic explanations also are of interest to the student of behavior, but being "further back" in the chain of social-psychological antecedents, their explication has a lower priority.

The third and most fundamental use for this set of distinctions is theoretical clarification. In the remainder of this chapter, after touching upon some of the general issues that arise in single-case analysis, I shall use the three distinctions as headings under which to explicate the explanatory structure of a single-case analysis. In the following chapter, the same headings will serve as the basis for discussing the rationale of a well-known typology. These efforts at clarification serve to identify key methodological and empirical problems that might otherwise not become evident.

II. PROBLEMS SPECIFIC TO SINGLE-ACTOR PSYCHOLOGICAL ANALYSIS

There are two general clusters of single-actor analyses in the personality-and-politics literature—the case studies of members of the general population by investigators such as Lane[3] and Smith, Bruner, and White,[4] and psychological biographies. In the former, data on single individuals are usually presented to illustrate theoretical or methodological arguments. Having an illustrative purpose, the authors do not concentrate their main efforts on establishing the superiority of their diagnoses of such pseudonymous individuals as "Ferrara," "Lanlin," or "Sullivan," over other possible diagnoses. For the author of the psychological biography, on the other hand, accuracy of diagnosis is a compelling matter. The biographer frequently seeks to establish whether some action of his protagonist was a necessary condition of a historical outcome (action dispensability), and, if so, whether the action is one that needs to be explained in terms of the protagonist's personal characteristics (actor dispensability). His diagnosis of his subject's personality becomes the linchpin, the crucial connecting link, in a larger account of a historical outcome.

We cannot expect such diagnoses to achieve the standardization and precision possible in multi-case, typological studies. Nevertheless, there is no reason why single-actor diagnosis should remain a wholly literary endeavor, dependent upon the whims of the analyst. It should be possible to stipulate and

---

[3] Robert E. Lane, *Political Ideology* (New York: Free Press of Glencoe, 1962).

[4] M. Brewster Smith, Jerome Bruner, and Robert White, *Opinions and Personality* (New York: Wiley, 1956).

perfect the criteria for conducting such analyses—for selecting evidence for discussion from the array of available biographical data and for making explanatory inferences, including those especially controversial inferences that sometimes need to be made about the deeper (ego-defensive) levels of personality functioning.[5]

In attempting to identify such criteria, I have found it helpful to consider the procedures used by Alexander and Juliette George in *Woodrow Wilson and Colonel House*.[6] The Georges' work is instructive for a variety of reasons, some of which were briefly suggested in Chapter One. To begin with, Wilson himself was a historical figure to whom the notions of action and actor dispensability can easily be applied. There was no question either to his contemporaries or to subsequent commentators that his actions (and inactions) had a major impact on historical outcomes and that they were highly *personal* actions. Wilson behaved in ways we would not expect other comparably placed political actors to behave. Moreover, his behavior cries out for an analysis that goes beyond common-sense, non-technical psychology. Neither his contemporaries nor his many biographers have felt able to account for his oscillation between skill and catastrophic ineptness in dealing with other political figures, and for other enigmatic aspects of his conduct.

The Georges' analysis of Wilson warrants extended analysis because of the authors' exceptional craftsmanship. Many social scientists have echoed Bernard Brodie's judgment that this is one of the more satisfactory of the psychological biographies and that it is the first interpretation of the character of Wilson "which impresses one as having depth, coherence, and consistency."[7]

---

[5] The development of standards for psychological case studies has been a longstanding, if intermittent, interest in the social sciences. Important early efforts include: John Dollard's classic *Criteria for the Life History* (New Haven, Conn.: Yale University Press, 1935); and Gordon W. Allport, *The Use of Personal Documents in Psychological Science* (New York: Social Science Research Council Bulletin 49, 1942). For more recent discussions see Note 11 below.

[6] Alexander L. George and Juliette L. George, *Woodrow Wilson and Colonel House: A Personality Study* (New York: John Day, 1956); paperback edition with new Preface (New York: Dover, 1964). My interest here is in the Georges' analysis of Wilson, not their less fully developed account of Colonel House.

[7] Bernard Brodie, "A Psychoanalytic Interpretation of Woodrow Wilson," *World Politics*, 9 (1957). 413–22.

The Georges' success in dealing with Wilson is partly a result of such aspects of the logic of discovery as their long-standing immersion in the details of his life, the depth and subtlety of their familiarity with psychoanalytic theory, their empathetic capacities, and the many years they allowed themselves for developing, testing, and reframing their hypotheses about Wilson. But it is their attention to the logic of demonstration that concerns us here.

The Georges invested extraordinary effort in making explicit to themselves their criteria for analyzing Wilson. This involved them in the general activity of clarifying the requirements of explanation in psychological case studies. Although they put on paper a number of important discussions of single-actor psychological explanation,[8] in the body of *Woodrow Wilson and Colonel House* they chose to subordinate their methodological interests to the demands of narrative exposition. Consequently the explicit diagnostic statements about Wilson in that work tend to be brief and sketched only in outline. These statements and the narrative itself are, however, powerfully buttressed by the authors' background analyses. This no doubt explains the striking ring of truth to which Brodie[9] refers.

The quality of the Georges' work and the authors' methodological self-awareness enables us to assume that difficulties in their analysis of Wilson are not merely minor faults in craftsmanship. Instead, the difficulties are likely to be problems intrinsic to conducting and communicating the findings of psychological case studies. As an illustration especially of the communication problems that arise in the absence of generally-recognized standards for psychological biography, consider the following jibes at the Georges' analysis by the historian, Page Smith:

[8] Alexander L. George and Juliette L. George, "Woodrow Wilson: Personality and Political Behavior" (paper presented at the 1956 Annual Meeting of the American Political Science Association); and the following papers by Alexander George: "Some Uses of Dynamic Psychology in Political Biography" (unpublished paper, 1960); "Power as a Compensatory Value for Political Leaders," *Journal of Social Issues*, 24:3 (1968), 29–50. Also see the methodological appendix to *Woodrow Wilson and Colonel House*.

[9] Brodie, *op. cit.* I do not mean to recommend abandonment of narrative exposition or even of elliptical and partially implicit interpretation. The mode of exposition one uses depends upon one's purpose. But as single-actor case studies come to be more concerned with demonstration, there will be a need for experimentation with expository approaches that complement straightforward narrative—for example, extensive use of methodological appendices.

They found that [Wilson] had the usual father problem—a strong and authoritarian parent who repressed young Woodrow.

That young Wilson's "resentment and rage" . . . at his father's treatment of him were "almost entirely repressed" (in the world of Freud, the love of a son for a strict and demanding father is not really love, of course, but repressed rage and hostility) is indicated by "the esteem and apparent affection in which he held his father throughout his life."

The Georges observe what has been observed by many others—that Wilson in his adult life showed a strong impulse toward political domination (as indeed have most successful politicians), which represented "for him a compensatory value, a means of restoring the self-esteem damage [by his father] in childhood."

After a good many more such observations, the Georges reach the conclusion that Wilson's personality flaws—rigidity, self-righteousness, the desire to have his own way, and the refusal to compromise—doomed the League of Nations to rejection by the Senate. All very well, but hardly a revelation. Any scholar familiar with Wilson's character is aware of the traits enumerated by the Georges. And what, after all, have they told us that is purely and simply the result of their use of Freudian tools? Only some shaky speculations about Wilson's relations with his father which do not in the end add to our understanding of his triumphs and his ultimate tragedy. The virtues of the book derive from the fact that the Georges are conscientious historians and skillfully explicated Wilson's political career.[10]

As we shall see, Smith fails to follow much of the George and George analysis. Nevertheless, his remarks are of interest because they include critical points that regularly appear in skeptical reviews of psychological biographies. These points are

---

[10] Page Smith, *The Historian and History* (New York: Knopf, 1964), pp. 125–26. The first three of the quoted statements appear in the original as a continuous passage; the fourth statement appears a paragraph later in Smith's text.

not only evident in comments on such conspicuously unsatisfactory efforts as Zeligs' study of the Hiss-Chambers affair and the Freud-Bullitt volume on Wilson,[11] but are also seen in reviews of such well-executed works as Erikson's brilliant, if highly "intuitive," treatment of Luther.[12]

---

[11] Meyer A. Zeligs, *Friendship and Fratricide: An Analysis of Whittaker Chambers and Alger Hiss* (New York: Viking Press, 1967). The Zeligs book was widely viewed as not only displaying the vices of the older psychological biographies (reductionism, exclusive preoccupation with pathology in the author's treatment of Chambers), but also as a partisan defense of Hiss. This work appeared at the same time as the equally controversial posthumous work by Sigmund Freud and William C. Bullitt, *Thomas Woodrow Wilson, Twenty-Eighth President of the United States: A Psychological Study* (Boston: Houghton Mifflin, 1967), which had been written in the 1930's with the stipulation that it not be published until after the death of Wilson's widow. Neither work advanced the cause of psychological biography, but both are useful illustrations of the difficulties in single-actor psychological analyses. The second work has been the source of authorship disputes, with members of the psychoanalytic fraternity arguing from internal evidence that whatever contribution Freud had made was severely distorted by Bullitt. The Georges knew of this manuscript, but did not have access to it. A number of the reviews of both of these works raise interesting, if inconclusive points about the potentialities of psychological biography. Examples of such reviews are: Meyer Shapiro, "Dangerous Acquaintances," *New York Review of Books*, February 23, 1967, pp. 5–9; "Brotherly Hatred," *The Times Literary Supplement* (London), November 9, 1967, p. 1057; Ernest van den Haag, "Psychoanalysis and Fantasy," *National Review*, March 21, 1967, pp. 295ff.; Erik Erikson and Richard Hofstadter, "The Strange Case of Freud, Bullitt and Wilson," *New York Review of Books*, February 9, 1967, pp. 3–8.

There are several recent general discussions of the problems of psychological biography. A particularly interesting, if fugitive, item is the long introduction by B. A. Farrell to the English paperback edition of Sigmund Freud's *Leonardo* (Harmondsworth, Middlesex: Penguin, 1963). Also, see the long, thoughtful two-part article by Lewis J. Edinger, entitled "Political Science and Political Biography," *Journal of Politics*, 26 (1964), 423–39, 648–76; various of the articles reprinted in Bruce Mazlish, *Psychoanalysis and History* (Englewood Cliffs, N.J.: Prentice-Hall, 1963); John A. Garraty, *The Nature of Biography* (New York: Knopf, 1957); A. F. Davies, "Criteria for the Political Life History," *Historical Studies of Australia and New Zealand*, 13:49 (1967), 76–85; Richard L. Bushman, "On the Uses of Psychology: Conflict and Conciliation in Benjamin Franklin," *History and Theory*, 5 (1966), 225–40; Fred I. Greenstein, "Art and Science in the Political Life History: A Review of A. F. Davies' *Private Politics*," *Politics: The Journal of the Australasian Political Science Association*, 2 (1967), 176–80; Erik H. Erikson, "On the Nature of Psycho-Historical Evidence: In Search of Gandhi," *Daedalus*, 97 (1968), 695–730; and Betty Glad, "The Role of Psychoanalytic Biography in Political Science" (paper delivered at the 1968 Annual Meeting of the American Political Science Association).

[12] Erik H. Erikson, *Young Man Luther: A Study in Psychoanalysis and History* (New York: Norton, 1958).

III. THE GEORGES' ANALYSIS OF WILSON[13]

The 300 or so vividly written pages of the Georges' volume serve at once to provide a summary account of Wilson's life and works and to isolate in detail certain episodes and periods of his development that are critical to their analysis. In their treatment of Wilson's early years, they especially note his relationship with his father and his adolescent and young-adult efforts to find a vocation and a sense of purpose. Their treatment of the adult Wilson examines in depth how he handled his three major executive roles: the Presidency of Princeton, the Governorship of New Jersey, and the Presidency of the United States. Wilson's career in each of these roles was marked by a remarkably regular sequence of stages: (1) dramatic accomplishments shortly after taking office, (2) followed by a period of contention and controversy, and (3) finally, defeat under circumstances that offered ample possibilities for success. In particular, his failure to obtain Senate ratification of the Versailles Treaty under conditions that are generally conceded to have been highly favorable to his cause was closely analogous to the bitter, self-defeating behavior that ended what had begun as a brilliant Presidency of Princeton.

What follows is a quite selective inventory of some of the Georges' principal themes, designed to illustrate how biographical data can be clarified in terms of a reconstructed logic. These statements on the phenomenology, dynamics, and genesis of Wilson's personality will be clearest in the context of reading *Woodrow Wilson and Colonel House*, although they should make sense in their general outlines to the reader who is unfamiliar with that work.

PHENOMENOLOGY: WILSON'S PRESENTING CHARACTERISTICS

"Any scholar familiar with Wilson's character is aware of the traits enumerated by the Georges," Page Smith comments. His assertion is consistent with a point made in the opening

---

[13] The following expository remarks are based on the Georges' book and on their various papers. The quotations are from *Woodrow Wilson and Colonel House* unless otherwise indicated and can readily be found in that work's excellent index, which also serves as a handy summary of the authors' principle statements about Wilson and his contemporaries.

sections of this chapter: it is relatively simple to achieve agreement among analysts on matters of phenomenology. Smith refers to Wilson's "rigidity, self-righteousness, . . . desire to have his own way," and "refusal to compromise." These aspects of Wilson's political style, he acknowledges, "doomed the League of Nations to rejection by the Senate."

Yet Wilson had another side that Smith overlooks. Wilson could on some occasions be enormously ingratiating to other political actors whose support he needed; and at certain points in his career, "rigidity" was the least appropriate term one could employ in characterizing him. This was notably the case during his rise to political prominence when he rapidly underwent a conversion from conservatism to progressivism. During this period, he assiduously curried the favor of William Jennings Bryan, a politician for whom he had earlier expressed the greatest contempt. The Georges recount numerous other instances of Wilson's seemingly quite striking flexibility, even on matters of principle. Thus, it is too simple merely to characterize Wilson by the set of "well-known" traits that Smith lists.

Similarly, Smith misses a crucial aspect of the Georges' analysis of Wilson when he suggests that Wilson's "strong impulse toward domination" manifested itself in an orientation toward power of the sort one might expect to find in "most successful politicians." For Wilson's approach to power was anything but normal. Quite unlike the typical American public figure, he used some of his power resources to the hilt with no regard to declining marginal utility; and he used other power resources not at all. At such times as the period when the New Freedoms legislation was passed and that of the catastrophic deadlock with the Senate over confirmation of the Versailles Treaty, his predilection was to *impose* his own will. His adversaries were not even permitted symbolic, face-saving concessions. Yet on other occasions he showed utter indifference to opportunities to exploit the resources at his disposal. For example, he evidently took no interest whatsoever in supervising or even reviewing the activities of a number of members of his administration, such as the Secretary of Agriculture. At various times in his role as chief United States negotiator in Paris—a role which the Georges characterize with extraordinary subtlety—he was unbending in pursuit of certain of his goals; but he ignored some of the opportunities at his disposal to obtain precisely these goals, notably possibilities to re-open consideration of issues on which he had reluctantly yielded at early stages in the peace conference. Once forced to bend on an issue, he could not bring himself to return to it.

Single elements in Wilson's phenomenology are not puzzling. Even some aspects of the curiously contradictory *pattern* of his behavior might seem to lend themselves to relatively simple explanations. We might, for example, argue that it is fully consistent with the "role requirements" of political success to be more flexible when seeking power than when exercising power. However, the full phenomenological pattern—the whole ensemble of traits that Wilson exhibits—is exceptionally puzzling when analyzed only in terms of the psychologically-shallow notion of role requirements. For very few American politicians, placed in the situations Wilson was in, would have shown the same mixture of extreme expediency and extreme rigidity, the same alternation between maximization and minimization of power resources, and the other inconsistencies that marked Wilson's political style. As Arthur Link, the historian who has been most comprehensive in his treatment of Wilson, put it: "Being neither mind-reader nor psychiatrist, the biographer can only agree with Colonel House that Wilson was 'one of the contradictory characters in history' and hope that the man will reveal himself in the pages that follow."[14] One accomplishment that the Georges share with other of Wilson's biographers is their capacity to allow the man to "reveal himself" through an acute delineation of his phenomenology; but their distinctive contribution is in the presentation and partial documentation of a theory of dynamics appropriate for explaining his "contradictory" political behavior.

THE GEORGES' ACCOUNT OF WILSON'S PERSONALITY DYNAMICS

At the simplest and least controversial level of dynamic analysis, the Georges are able to specify what can be called the dynamic aspects of Wilson's personality phenomenology; i.e., the contingencies under which he behaved in different ways. Thus, as

---

[14] Arthur S. Link, *Wilson: The New Freedom* (Princeton, N.J.: Princeton University Press, 1956), p. 70.

we have seen, they specify that the occasions when he showed flexibility to the point of seeming opportunism were when he was *seeking* power; and his rigidities were evident when he was *exercising* power. Further, they point out that once in power, Wilson's need to dominate and to avoid being dominated, his need to be fully in control of political outcomes, manifested itself only with respect to issues that he conceived himself—often in distinctly messianic terms—to be uniquely competent to pronounce upon and to shape. Issues he defined as being outside this exalted category interested him not at all. There seems to have been virtually no middle ground.

On the issues that he defined as central to his leadership aspirations—to his mission to do "noble works"—the Georges note that Wilson was both unbending and totally unable to see virtue in the positions of those who disagreed with him. Through what seems frequently to have been genuine rationalization, Wilson perceived his opponents to be wholly mean in motive. Hence they had to be *totally* overwhelmed; to compromise with such unacceptable forces, even to provide them with face-saving means of retreat, was to be tarnished. Thus the moral acceptability of his own refusal to share power: with such adversaries it was, he seems to have reasoned, both legitimate and necessary to seek complete domination.

Under such circumstances, when Wilson did not have the strength to dominate, he was himself crushed—or an impasse resulted. The Georges observe that in the more bitter of these conflicts, disagreements over principle were heavily colored with clashes of personality. This was true both in the Princeton graduate-school controversy, which was marked by Wilson's burning antagonism to Dean Andrew West, and in the Versailles Treaty crisis, which revolved around his equally acrimonious relations with Henry Cabot Lodge. The single male adversary was especially likely to force Wilson into a self-defeating stance of implacable unwillingness to compromise, even when compromise was plainly in his interest, since only minor concessions were necessary to triumph. Wilson was especially susceptible to the adversary who, like Lodge, was gifted at deriding him by way of supercilious deprecation of his abilities. (Lodge once said of the League Covenant, the document on which Wilson had taken such pains: "As an English production, it does not rank high. It might get by at Princeton but certainly not at Harvard.")

At a deeper, necessarily more speculative and, hence, more controversial level of dynamic interpretation, George and George tentatively identify in Wilson's behavior a number of standard ego defense mechanisms, such as reaction formation and denial. In addition, they find a partial fit between his life style and the adaptive patterns present in the clinical characterology of compulsiveness. They also draw upon Lasswell's theorizing in *Power and Personality*[15] about the power-centered type and conclude that Wilson's compulsive need to dominate under the circumstances described above served the defensive function of protecting him from his deep-seated "low self-estimates."

In seeking to document such provisional interpretations, the Georges do not rely upon any single observation, but rather muster a variety of kinds of evidence in a cumulative argument. We can indicate their mode of analysis best by reconstructing through an abbreviated sketch the way that they attempt to establish whether ego-defensive needs contributed to Wilson's extreme unwillingness to compromise under certain circumstances and, if so, what kind of ego-defensive needs were influential.

For each of the circumstances in which Wilson was unwilling to compromise, and consequently was defeated, the possibility of a non-ego-defensive explanation cannot be rejected.[16] The

---

[15] Harold D. Lasswell, *Power and Personality* (New York: Norton, 1948). The Georges relied heavily on this discussion of Lasswell's as a source of preliminary hypotheses about Wilson. Alexander George has subsequently suggested ("Power as a Compensatory Value for Political Leaders," *op. cit.*, p. 38n.) the additional merits of various of Erikson's notions for the single-case political analyst. George especially commends the analyses of adolescent identity-formation in James D. Barber's work on American Presidents. See Barber's "Classifying and Predicting Presidential Styles: Two Weak Presidents," *Journal of Social Issues*, 24:3 (1968), 51–80; and his "Adult Identity and Presidential Style: The Rhetorical Emphasis," *Daedalus*, 97 (1968), 938–68.

[16] The Georges were aware of a variety of alternative explanations that make no reference to processes of ego defense in the extensive literature on Wilson: for example, interpretations of his life and career largely in terms of his Calvinist heritage and interpretations of his behavior during the League Crisis largely in medical terms. They chose not to address themselves explicitly to alternative hypotheses, just as they chose more generally to keep methodological discussion to a minimum in the book. Some of the variables referred to in

failure of an actor to take the steps most appropriate to attain his goals is not necessarily (perhaps not even often) a consequence of the confounding of his reality-coping efforts with unconscious intrapersonal needs to ward off conflicts. Irrationality may, for example, result simply from imperfect information that leads to faulty calculations; and the actor may not be "irrational" at all in the sense of being unable to connect means with ends, but rather may have consciously chosen not to pay the price (in other values) for a particular end-in-view. For example, the utility for him of obtaining passage of a certain bill might be less than the "disutility" of bribing a key committee chairman—or even, depending upon his scale of values, the disutility of giving up a Saturday game of golf. A non-ego-defensive interpretation of Wilson's repeated failures to attain certain coveted ends would be furthered if it could be shown that his action in situations in which his inflexibility led to defeat, including those of his actions that actually molded the situations, could *normally* be expected of political actors in comparable circumstances with similar opportunities, restraints, and provocations. Statistical normality does not preclude ego-defensiveness, nor does deviance from norms insure that a defensive interpretation is appropriate; but deviance is a potential indicator of ego-defensiveness, given at least one other concomitant—*behavior that is substantially at odds with the actor's own conscious views of his goals and of the means appropriate to attain them.*

Were the situations in which Wilson found himself ones that precluded alternative courses of action—that would have led other comparably placed actors to behave similarly? The Georges, like many of Wilson's contemporaries and many other historians, reach a strong negative conclusion. At Princeton, and

---

ostensible "alternative" explanations need not be viewed as competitive with the ego-defensive explanation offered by the Georges. For example, the Georges themselves emphasize that the Calvinist ethos was an important influence in Wilson's thought and behavior; but they clearly also felt that Wilson was not merely a typical representative of "the spirit of Calvinism" and that a theory of his psychodynamics was needed, for example, to explain why Calvinism was an obstacle to compromise under some circumstances and not others. Similarly, the psychological biographer needs to be sensitive to medical considerations; but it is naïve to explain behavior in "purely" medical terms as if the effects of illness (such as the one or more strokes Wilson suffered) were not—like the cultural heritage—mediated through personal character.

even more so in the conflict with Lodge and his allies in the Senate, Wilson had excellent opportunities to attain his ostensible ends. Especially during the struggle over confirmation of the Paris Treaty, he had only to admit other actors into the decision-making process and to make relatively slight accommodations and compromises. His actions were not those that one would expect from most actors in a political system notable for its pragmatic bargaining traditions.

Nor did his actions seem to be a function of Wilson's own conscious views of his goals and the appropriate means for attaining them. George and George are able to present examples of explicit statements made by Wilson earlier in his career extolling precisely the kinds of compromises he adamantly resisted during the graduate-school and League-of-Nations controversies, apart from also being able to show the actual instances of flexibility and adaptability noted above. For example, a decade before taking office, Wilson had commented on how the President should deal with Senate opposition, laying down a prescription that was almost the perfect reciprocal of his later behavior during the League crisis: "He may himself be less stiff and offish, may himself act in the true spirit of the Constitution and establish intimate relations with the Senate on his own initiative, not carrying his plans to completion and then laying them before the Senate to be accepted or rejected." As Wilson put it on another occasion, Presidents "must not be impossible," insisting "upon getting at once what they know they cannot get!"

The foregoing line of reasoning, which I have made somewhat more explicit than do the Georges, is only part of their procedures of interpreting Wilson's personality dynamics. Continually, and in ways that cannot be fully summarized here, they focus microscopically upon details of behavior and utterance. They comment, for example, on the peculiarly intense fervor with which Wilson felt called upon to deny that he himself had any personal stake in precisely those points of contention about which he was most unyieldingly insistent—the matters on which the dotting of the *i*'s and the crossing of the *t*'s had to be wholly his own. In addition, they point to the *recurrence* of his most self-defeating actions. If an actor repeatedly thrusts himself into quite similar encounters, it becomes increasingly evident that his own more or less deep-seated personality dispositions, rather than straightforward reactions to environmental stimuli, need to be called upon to account for the regularities in his behavior.

Finally, the Georges consulted various technical literatures in search of general insights into individuals with Wilson's characteristics. One of the more instructive sources of insight was the clinical literature on compulsiveness, which helped the Georges to identify and account for the juxtaposition of a variety of traits and behavior patterns in Wilson—for example, his stubbornness, his punctiliousness, his extreme orderliness, his pedantry, and his disposition to moralize. Individually, these were all traits that had been recognized by other biographers; but none of the previous biographers had seen the traits as part of a syndrome that could be related to the psychodynamics described in the clinical account of the compulsive personality type. Drawing further on technical literature and with far more self-consciousness than is common in single-case analyses, the Georges specified operational indicators of such key terms as "low self-estimates," "unwillingness to share power," and "compensation"—terms which appear in the hypothesis that Wilson's pursuit of power served compensatory functions.

Thus, the Georges came to have at their disposal an extensively elaborated, precisely formulated set of propositions about Wilson. They therefore were able to predict circumstances under which, if their basic diagnosis of Wilson's personality dynamics is correct, one would expect Wilson to have experienced a variety of quite distinctive kinds of feelings in connection with his pursuit and exercise of power—feelings such as euphoria, depression, and the driven need to push onward in the immediate wake of a success. And they were fortunate enough to have a sufficiently detailed body of historical data to test and find support for many of their predictions, since Wilson was a prolific letter writer and his official biographer, Ray Stannard Baker, was a resourceful collector of memoirs on Wilson by his contemporaries.

 GENETIC HYPOTHESES: THE GEORGES' ANALYSIS OF WILSON'S DEVELOPMENT

Brodie comments succinctly on the standing of the George's developmental analysis and at the same time summarizes its principal themes:

The authors are inevitably on weaker ground when they try to explain the genesis of the Wilsonian neurosis than when they describe the manner in which it expressed itself full-blown. Not that their explanation is implausible. On the contrary, it is arresting and persuasive, and the evidence to support it is weighty, though necessarily presumptive and incomplete. It is one thing to observe compulsive behavior and identify it for what it is; it is quite another to find the original causes. . . . [T]he authors find as the origin of the adult Wilson's inner deformity the experience of the child and youth with a demanding and yet mocking father. Dr. Joseph Ruggles Wilson, a Presbyterian minister who was noted for his caustic wit, took an extraordinarily active role in his son's education. He used ridicule freely as a sanction to force his son to meet his own perfectionist standards, particularly with respect to the use of language. The son's resentment and rage were almost entirely repressed, as indicated by, among other things, the esteem and apparent affection in which he held his father throughout his life. However, the rage expressed itself early in an atrociously poor performance in his first years at school. This failure, which the authors interpret as an unconscious *refusal* to learn, of course called for more of the father's characteristic intervention. All of his life Wilson felt inferior to his father— significantly enough, in looks as well as in morals and accomplishment. All his life he struggled against an inner feeling of inadequacy and worthlessness *which must ever be disproved.*[17]

It is Brodie's overly terse summary of one of the Georges' indicators of Wilson's hostility toward his father that Page Smith quotes in the passage on page 71 ("the esteem and apparent affection in which he held his father throughout his life"). The Georges, however, are not employing the caricatured psychoanalytic principle that Smith enunciates ("in the world of Freud, the love of a son for a strict and demanding father is not really love, of course, but repressed rage and hostility"). Rather, what the Georges identify is a much more complicated pattern of childhood and subsequent experience and behavior.

---

[17] Brodie, *op. cit.*, pp. 415–16.

Although other biographers had at their disposal the rich materials on Wilson's family background collected by Ray Stannard Baker, again it was the Georges who, because of their analytic perspectives, were first able to see the significance of seemingly disparate items of information about Wilson's relationship with his father and about certain other aspects of his early development. Indeed, so careful a scholar as Arthur S. Link, after studying all the sources both published and unpublished, concluded that "Wilson's boyhood was notable, if for nothing else, because of his normal development."[18]

Years before, Baker had mentioned Wilson's inability to read with any facility until he was eleven. Neither Link (who does not mention it in his chapter on Wilson's "Formative Years") nor any of Wilson's other biographers attached any significance to this remarkable fact; and Baker attributed it to Wilson's delight in listening while others read aloud.[19] Nor did other biographers find it significant that in a family of scholars, Wilson was such a conspicuously poor student or that, although the son of a minister, he had difficulty learning the catechism. The elder Wilson took personal charge of young Thomas Woodrow's early education and did not enroll him in school until he was ten. The Georges doubt that Dr. Wilson, who took such pains with his son's education and revered masterly use of the English language above all other intellectual skills, neglected to try to teach young Wilson his letters. They suggest that the young Wilson's capacity to learn may have been reduced by his father's perfectionist demands and, further, that the boy may have re-

---

[18] Arthur S. Link. *Wilson: The Road to the White House* (Princeton, N.J.: Princeton University Press, 1947), p. 2. The controversial "Freud-Bullitt" volume on Wilson (see Note 11 above) also rejects the "normal-development" thesis about Wilson's childhood and touches on some of the themes that the Georges treat. As I have noted, this work was written before the Georges began their research, but was not available to them until long after they had written their book and the various papers referred to in this chapter. The material Baker collected on Wilson's childhood is summarized in Ray Stannard Baker, *Woodrow Wilson: Life and Letters*, 1 (Garden City, N.Y.: Doubleday, 1927). In addition, the Georges consulted the original collection of papers Baker assembled, which is in the Library of Congress.

[19] For an unconvincing attempt to explain away the reading retardation in the context of a more general deprecation of psychological interpretations of Wilson, see the anonymous "Woodrow Wilson: The President as Professor," *Times Literary Supplement* (London), September 5, 1968, pp. 933–44. Baker's remarks are in his *Woodrow Wilson, Life and Letters*, 1, op. cit., 26.

fused to learn to read as an indirect way of expressing resentment of his father.

This line of interpretation is bolstered by materials which the Georges quote from the Baker papers, some of which Baker appears not to have exploited in his account of Wilson's development. Consider the following pair of quotations from the Baker papers on the relationship between the senior and junior Wilson:

> Relatives . . . had graphic recollections of Dr. Wilson's [Woodrow's father] severity. Helen Bones, Wilson's cousin, reported: ". . . Uncle Joseph was a cruel tease, with a caustic wit and a sharp tongue, and I remember hearing my own family tell indignantly of how Cousin Woodrow suffered under his teasing. He was proud of WW, especially after his son began to show how unusual he was, but only a man as sweet as Cousin Woodrow could have forgot the severity of the criticism to the value of which he so often paid tribute, in after life.

> Another cousin . . . recalled a typical instance of Dr. Wilson's "teasing." The family was assembled at a wedding breakfast. Tommy [Wilson later dropped the initial Thomas from his name] arrived at the table late. His father apologized on behalf of his son and explained that Tommy had been so greatly excited at the discovery of another hair in his mustache that morning that it had taken him longer to wash and dress. "I remember very distinctly the painful flush that came over the boy's face. . . ."

It is in the context of this paternal manner that the Georges are led to the conclusion that Wilson's reading retardation may have been the child's only means of resisting the relentless pressures from his father. ("Stubbornness" is sometimes interpreted in the clinical literature as an indirect means of expressing aggression; and stubbornness is one of the central elements in Wilson's later political behavior during such impasses as the League crisis.) Later, when Woodrow was able to read and write, much of his education consisted of writing compositions for his father, who repeatedly rejected the child's efforts and insisted that the compositions be written and rewritten until every trace of ambiguity was eliminated. This in the childhood of a political figure for whom it was crucial that the written word—his *own* written word—be unaltered in such documents as the Fourteen Points and who could be so readily antagonized by aspersions to his literary style.

This pattern of observations about the two Wilsons provides the setting for the Georges' interpretation that Wilson's idealization of his father involved reaction-formation. They point out that this idealization was *never* tempered by disagreement or criticism, even long after his father's death; that Woodrow repeatedly dwelled on his own inferiority to his father, whereas he often displayed what many of his contemporaries felt to be an arrogant sense of superiority to the political figures with whom he was associated; that Wilson repeatedly felt called upon to protest to his father, in the strongest possible language, the whole-heartedness of his reverence for the old man.

The following statements by Wilson from a letter to "my precious father," written at the age of 32, are not unique:

> As you know, one of the chief things about which I feel most warranted in rejoicing is that I am your son. I realize the benefit of being your son more and more as my talents and experience grow; I recognize the strength growing in me as of the nature of your strength; I become more and more conscious of the hereditary wealth I possess, that capital of principle, of literary force and skill, of capacity for firsthand thought; and I feel daily more and more bent toward creating in my own children that combined respect and tender devotion for their father that you gave your children for you.

"Dr. Wilson's death in 1903 did not diminish his hold on his son," the Georges point out.

> Joseph Tumulty, President Wilson's private secretary, has told how one day during World War I, the President interrupted a Cabinet meeting to receive an old friend of his father. While the old man praised him, the President stood like a bashful schoolboy. Then the visitor said, "Well, well, Woodrow, what shall I say to

you . . . I shall say to you what your dear old father would have said were he here: "Be a good boy, my son, and may God bless you and take care of you!" The President wept.

Even the Georges' consideration of the genesis of Wilson's personality—an analysis which I only partially recapitulate—then is based upon systematically mustered evidence and conscious principles of inference. But this portion of the analysis is understandably more tentative and inconclusive than the phenomenological and dynamic analyses. For example, the Georges are unable, or at any rate not disposed in the book, to deal with Wilson's relationships with his younger brother and there is more than a little reason to believe from clinical experience that this relationship also would be consequential for personality development. In addition, while the Georges do point out that Wilson's father also contributed positively and importantly to shaping the boy's personality into a suitable instrument for what was to be a remarkable career, they do not elaborate and document this ego-psychological assertion.

Given the difficulties attending to satisfactory genetic analysis, one might wonder whether in fact it is useful for a biographer to invest much effort on his subject's early development. After all, it is the less equivocal analyses of phenomenology and dynamics that are most relevant to explaining the subject's actual adult behavior in specific situational contexts. There are at least two reasons for concluding that developmental analysis *is* desirable. First, developmental data complement the other two sources of evidence. As Alexander George points out in one of his methodological papers which is specifically addressed to the question of dealing in case-study material with Lasswell's hypotheses about the relationship between damaged self-esteem and power needs:

> Cross-sectional observations [i.e., observations of behavior at single points of time, in this case, during the adult years] and measurements of the self-esteem status of an adult political leader may, if of a superficial character, fail to turn up indicators of the earlier low self-estimates problem experienced by the personality;

hence [in the absence of a developmental study of the individual] that individual may be incorrectly placed outside of Lasswell's hypothesis.[20]

Putting this point more generally, genetic and dynamic interpretations can interlock, serving to buttress each other. To return to the example of Wilson and his father, it is not that Wilson praised his father, but rather the fulsome quality of the praise—under circumstances that might have produced antagonism and rebellion—that leads to the provisional interpretation of the praise in terms of reaction-formation. The evidence produced by the genetic analysis—that Wilson showed none of the resentment normally evoked by a father who relies so heavily on ridicule—adds to the credibility of the dynamic analysis.

A second reason for engaging in developmental analysis is suggested by Erikson's observation that knowledge of how political leaders come to develop their distinctive personal strengths and weaknesses is a necessary prerequisite to identifying and fostering or eliminating these proclivities. Erikson stresses the need to understand and manage "negative" tendencies: "[W]e must . . . learn to recognize the afflictions of our favorite heroes, as well as the madness in those great men whom we could do without. For, short as our lives are, the influence of the men we elect, support, or tolerate as great can indeed be a curse felt far beyond the third and fourth generation."[21] But his point applies equally to the "positive" attributes of leaders. These too need to be identified with a view to their care and nurture.

IV. APPROACHES TO ENHANCING THE PROBATIVE VALUE OF SINGLE-ACTOR PSYCHOLOGICAL ANALYSES

The following points suggest a number of intellectual operations that would contribute to developing single-case psychological analyses of high probative value. Some of my assertions are based on the various George and George discussions and others

[20] Alexander George, "Power as a Conpensatory Value for Political Leaders," op. cit., pp. 47–48.
[21] Erikson, Young Man Luther, op. cit., p. 149. Also see Erikson's remarks (Young Man Luther, op. cit., p. 267) on "mastering the life cycle."

on the slowly growing literature on the problems of "objectifying" clinical diagnoses. They apply to the collection and examination of single-case data—not to the task of exposition. Self-conscious attention to demonstration in psychological case studies seems to involve such considerations as the following:

1. After his preliminary exploratory immersion in the biographical record, the investigator should be as explicit as possible in *formulating hypotheses* about the biographical subject. These may be hypotheses about the patterns and configurations in the subject's adult behavior (his phenomenology); about the psychological dynamics which need to be inferred in order to explain why the subject, under specified conditions, exhibits that pattern of behavior; and about the background experiences that seem to account for the genesis of the subject's personality. The statement of hypotheses, especially if alternative, competing hypotheses can also be specified, serves to focus the investigator directly on problems of demonstration and falsification. By and large, however, the case study does not proceed as a simple test of *a priori* hypotheses, but rather as an iterative process, beginning with the statement of preliminary hypotheses that are modified and reformulated as the data are more closely examined. The self-conscious statement of hypotheses serves further to provide criteria for what to include in the biographical account. The identification of a focus is necessary. As Hempel puts its, "any particular event may be regarded as having infinitely many different aspects or characteristics, which cannot all be accounted for by a finite set, however large, of explanatory statements."[22] This is especially evident in the case of the complex sequences of events that constitute a life history.

2. So far as possible the *hypotheses and interpretations* (the latter being hypotheses that have been provisionally accepted) *should be kept distinct from the observational data* upon which the hypotheses and interpretations are based. A common fault of single-case clinical psychological reports is that the processes of observation and interpretation are not sufficiently differentiated from each other. The reader cannot himself examine the materials upon which the interpretations are based. He cannot recon-

---

[22] C. G. Hempel, "Explanation in Science and History," in William H. Dray, ed., *Philosophical Analysis and History* (New York: Harper & Row, 1966), p. 107.

struct and, therefore, cannot assess the steps by which the analyst has arrived at an interpretation, and he does not have the raw materials with which to advance alternative interpretations of his own.

3. We have seen that the Georges were especially imaginative about devising *specific operational criteria* for distinguishing observations they were willing to accept as evidence supporting their hypotheses or that might lead them to reject or modify hypotheses. Operational criteria serve to sharpen the theoretical language in which the preliminary and subsequent hypotheses are stated, maximizing the fit between the propositions the analyst is seeking to accept or reject and the observational data he is prepared to employ for this purpose.

Once the need to specify operational indicators in single-actor analysis is identified, a further need for clarification and codification of the criteria for psychological diagnosis becomes evident. This is especially true for those criteria used in order to distinguish symptoms of ego defense. We have seen that the Georges, in diagnosing Wilson, refer to the defense mechanisms of "reaction-formation" and "denial." But what are the general standards for identifying these and other ego defenses? How, for example, can we distinguish the run-of-the-mill enthusiasm that a loving son might express for his father from the pseudo-enthusiasm of a son whose tributes serve the purpose of shielding both son and father from the son's covert sentiments in the opposite direction as seen, if we take the Georges' interpretation, in Wilson's letter to "my precious father?" Reaction-formation and denial are often said to be revealed when an individual's emotional responses are out of proportion to a stimulus; but the precise observational criteria leading to such a diagnosis have yet to be formulated. To a considerable extent, the need is merely for an explication of diagnostic procedures that *are* presently used, for it should be clear to the careful reader of clinical literature that consistent reference is made to the observables that lead clinicians to make diagnoses. There simply is too little attention given to the codification and validation of the indicators.[23]

---

[23] This point is expanded upon in my "Private Disorder and The Public Order: A Proposal for Collaboration between Psychoanalysts and Political Scientists," *Psychoanalytic Quarterly*, 37 (1968), 261–81. For a plea from a

4. Certain of the methodological standards that help place quantitative typological studies based on multi-case analysis on a firm footing are relevant, *mutatis mutandis*, to moving the single-actor study out of its story-telling stage. In particular we can move toward developing standards for perfecting *reliability* and ascertaining *validity* in psychological case studies of individuals.

By "reliability" the psychometrician refers to the consistency with which his instrument is able to measure whatever it is that the instrument may be measuring. Is the instrument capable of producing stable results, for example, when it is used by different investigators? Are the criteria of interpretation sufficiently clear and objective so that different coders will produce the same scores? Whether case-study data are extracted from an historical record or whether they are elicited directly from the subject of the investigation, there are a variety of rather easily imagined ways of augmenting the reliability of observations. These involve using the kinds of explicit operational criteria mentioned above in order to develop standardized procedures of compiling and interpreting observations. Indeed, for some purposes, strict quantitative inter-coder reliability measures could be used in order to check the precision with which different investigators were able to observe patterns in case material. French and Fromm[24] have attempted to move in this direction even with data and analytic problems as subtle and complex as psychoanalytic dream interpretation. As Christiansen shows in a review of the scattered efforts within psychoanalysis to move toward greater reliability in collecting and handling data, "clinical evidence has its inherent limitations," but at present it is less useful to dwell on the inevitable limitations of such data than on the numerous possibilities for raising "the validity of clinical evidence above its present level."[25]

5. A familiar assertion about observational techniques is that they may be reliable without being valid, although they

clinician for research designed to perfect standards of clinical inquiry, see Jules D. Holzberg, "The Clinical and Scientific Methods: Synthesis or Antithesis?" *Journal of Projective Techniques*, 21 (1957), 227–42.

[24] Thomas M. French and Erika Fromm, *Dream Interpretation* (New York: Basic Books, 1964).

[25] Bjorn Christiansen, "The Scientific Status of Psychoanalytic Clinical Evidence," *Inquiry*, 7 (1964), 47–79. Also see the articles by Michael Martin and Sydney G. Margolin in the same volume of *Inquiry*.

cannot be valid without being reliable. "Validity" refers to the degree to which a technique measures what it is intended to measure. I will stretch this notion somewhat here to apply it more generally to the problems of discriminating among alternative interpretations.

On the principle of beginning with the more accessible tasks, considerable progress would be made even if it were only possible to improve procedures for enhancing the reliability of single-case psychological analysis. Perfected techniques for making reliable observations would provide much of what is needed for one of the three main tasks of single-case analysis—that of accurately characterizing the phenomenology of the actor. And, as we have seen, data on phenomenological regularities are especially useful for analyzing political behavior. Nevertheless, confining oneself to considerations of reliability is intellectually sterile: more is needed than agnostic operationalism.

Validity, like reliability, is not an either-or matter. Just as our estimates of reliability indicate the *degree* to which we have confidence in the way we made our observations, estimates of validity also are a matter of degree, the referent being to our level of confidence in an explanation we are putting forth. An approach to validation—to enhancing confidence in single-case explanations—follows directly from the four intellectual operations I have already discussed: (1) explicitly stating hypotheses, (2) distinguishing interpretations from observations, (3) specifying operational indicators, and (4) perfecting the reliability of observations. There is a further need for the single-case analyst to state the conditions under which he will accept or reject alternative hypotheses. In order to arrive at these acceptance or rejection criteria, the analyst must make explicit his theoretical assumptions about his subject and about the general principles that govern relevant aspects of his subject's behavior. This can be done by specifying phenomenological observables and connecting them with explanatory hypotheses about dynamics and genesis.

I have described the (partly implicit) validational practices employed by the Georges, for example, in deciding whether to accept or reject the hypothesis that Wilson's failure to compromise during the League crisis had its roots in the need to manage unconscious inner conflicts. To a remarkable degree these practices parallel the procedures of external and internal comparison we would employ in quantitative multi-case analyses. For example, under the circumstances that lead to external comparisons of types of actors in a multi-case analysis—say, comparisons of the ways authoritarians and non-authoritarians perform some task— the single-case analyst often uses *implicit external comparison.* He establishes whether a particular action of Wilson's is simply a function of "rational" reaction to environmental stimuli by comparing Wilson's actions with the normal expectation for reaction by other actors to the same stimuli. In both single and multiple-case analyses there also are what can be called internal comparisons: assessments of the patterning of an individual or type's reactions to different classes of stimuli—including the personality-test stimuli that are employed by clinical psychologists. When they make internal comparisons, the single-case and multi-case analyst are on an identical methodological footing: they have at their disposal the enormous population of actions that any individual generates. The multi-case analyst must necessarily handle this volume of data quantitatively, but the single-case analyst also has this option, if it seems profitable.

Finally, in estimating validity, both multi-case and single-case analysts can derive great analytic leverage by drawing on already established principles. Multi-case analyses may not only be enhanced by reference to established general propositions. They also may serve as the basis for testing such propositions. A single-case analysis, on the other hand, cannot serve to prove or falsify a general proposition (apart from propositions that have been inappropriately stated as universals and that therefore can be falsified by a single exception). But an established general proposition—what in the philosophy-of-history literature is sometimes called a "covering law"—*can* be fruitfully drawn on to assess the validity of a single-case interpretation. Take, for example, the relationship alluded to above (in discussing Wilson's reading retardation) between stubbornness and covert aggression. It would be in the interest of any biographer of a notoriously stubborn individual to be well informed about the empirical standing of propositions connecting stubbornness with other characteristics. The biographer would quite clearly reach different diagnostic conclusions, depending upon whether the putative relationships between stubbornness and other characteristics proved to be ones that had been shown to occur with great frequency, whether they were rather rare, or whether they were in fact simply imperfectly documented hypotheses.

The use of general principles to interpret single cases does not involve what Hempel[26] calls deductive-nomological explanation; i.e., the kind of explanation that occurs when an event—like "the appearance that a spoon handle is bent at the point where it emerges from a glass of water"—is deductively subsumed under a universal law. Rather, this use of general principles involves explanation of the probabilistic sort, as in the explanation of "the subsiding of a violent attack of hay fever in a given case . . . by reference to . . . the administration of 8 milligrams of chlortrimeton." *Subjective* rather than statistical probabilities are involved. These increase with "the strength of inductive support, or the degree of rational credibility" that a covering law—for example, a psychological proposition about the likelihood that individuals who have undergone certain childhood experiences will develop certain personality characteristics —is capable of according to whatever specific interpretation is being made.

V. SUMMARY AND CONCLUSIONS

In brief recapitulation, the common elements in *single-case* and *typological* analyses are that, in each mode of inquiry, we proceed from an account of phenomenology—of the pattern of behavior in varying situations—to an account of the underlying psychological dynamics that must be inferred in order to account for the behavioral regularities under varying circumstances. A

---

[26] Hempel, "Explanation in Science and History," in Dray, ed., *op. cit.* There has been a running debate among philosophers of history about Hempel's various statements on the role of "general laws" or "covering laws" in historical explanations. See, for example, Alan Donagan, "The Popper-Hempel Theory Reconsidered," in Dray, ed., *op. cit.*, pp. 127–59. Also see Morton White, *Foundations of Historical Knowledge* (New York: Harper, 1965), esp. pp. 47–55. It seems to me difficult to deny that the single-actor analyst would at a minimum find it *heuristically* instructive to set his diagnosis against the general state of knowledge about the processes he hypothesizes to be operating in the individual he is attempting to diagnose, even though the general state of knowledge is bound to consist of statistical propositions that do not necessarily apply to the specific individual under consideration.

third task of both kinds of inquiry is that of explaining *genesis*. This can be attempted insofar as developmental data are available on how the individual or type has evolved during and since childhood in response to environmental influences on the raw materials furnished by heredity.

These three analytic operations have been identified through a logical reconstruction of the process of inquiry. Although these labels fail to describe the inelegance of what actually goes on from day to day in psychological research, such a logical reconstruction has a number of uses. It enables us to summarize data and to organize the tasks of inquiry roughly in terms of their immediate bearing on the explanation of specific items of political behavior—that is, from phenomenology through dynamics to genesis. Furthermore, the reconstruction helps us to array data and research tasks in a way that is generally consistent with the degree to which consensual, evidentially-sound explanations are available. Most fundamentally, it fosters theoretical clarity and helps to identify criteria for choice among alternative explanations.

The problems arising from the absence of well-established acceptance and rejection criteria in single-actor diagnoses are exacerbated in the case of explanations in terms of ego defense. These have an especially murky rationale. I have attempted to suggest possibilities for moving progressively toward sounder procedures by explicating what is generally agreed to be one of the more successful psychological analyses of a political actor, the Georges' study of Woodrow Wilson. Drawing on the procedures in that study and on other notions in recent discussions of clinical psychological diagnosis, it is possible to suggest a program of cumulative clarification that might make single-actor analysis less of an art and more of a systematic mode of inquiry.

There is a continuing likelihood that appropriately placed actors will behave in ways that are indispensable to political outcomes, often with momentous consequences. Hence the urgency of efforts to improve procedures for single-actor analysis, an urgency not diminished by the intrinsic difficulties.

CHAPTER FOUR

Psychological Analysis
of Types of Political Actors

The process of abstracting common features from diverse individual phenomena and classifying the *types* of regularities that one confronts is possibly as fundamental as any aspect of cognitive functioning. Using the heading "folk taxonomies," anthropologists have increasingly turned to examining the ways in which people classify the elements of their society and its environment; many of these anthropologists have concluded that this level of psychological functioning is more accessible and perhaps more revealing than the deeper emotional trends that preoccupied the earlier culture-and-personality investigators.[1] At one time, discussions of the uses of typology in everyday life especially emphasized the ways that inflexible assumptions about types (i.e., "stereotypes") impeded accurate perception. But more recently there has been a complementary emphasis on the capacity to abstract, classify, and employ categories as the *sine qua non* of dealing with reality: it would be impossible to act, it is commonly pointed out, if each environmental stimulus had to be confronted anew.

Paralleling the omnipresent typologies of everyday life are the more formal analytic typologies—only a relatively small proportion of them being psychological—which have been set forth since antiquity. In recent years, methodologists and philosophers of science have actually come to generate typologies of

---

[1] See, for example, Anthony F. C. Wallace, "The New Culture and Personality," *Anthropology and Human Behavior* (Washington, D.C.: The Anthropological Society of Washington, 1962), pp. 1–12.

typology and to begin to codify some of the principles of typology. There are a number of convenient general discussions of the requirements of constructing typologies ranging from simple classifications that call principally for use of a set of exhaustive and mutually exclusive categories, through complex syndrome typologies and the model-builder's ideal-types. There is no need here to expand upon the general assertions about the nature of typology by Lazarsfeld and Barton,[2] Hempel,[3] McKinney,[4] and Tiryakian.[5]

As I noted in Chapter One, the term "typological" provides a convenient, if necessarily loose, rubric for summarizing a wide range of multi-case studies of personality and politics. At the least complex level are the simple classifications in terms of the categories of a variable; these abound in survey research. The more one moves toward a complex typology involving the juxtaposition of a number of variables in specified relationships to one another, the more it is the case that a typology is in part a covert causal theory: a summary collection of propositions about relationships that need to be tested.

There have been, as I also noted in the introductory chapter,[6] numerous political-psychological typologies of varying clarity and complexity. We saw that a particularly clear typological construct—the typology used by Barber in *The Lawmakers*—was readily analyzable according to criteria that Lasswell has used for elucidating the explanatory structure of psychological typing. Lasswell's "nuclear," "co-relational," and "developmental" types are the basis of the slightly different formula of "phenomenology," "dynamics," and "genesis" that I used in the previous chapter to state the kinds of operations that need to engage the single-case analyst. I shall now put these same distinctions to

---

[2] Paul F. Lazarsfeld and Allen Barton, "Qualitative Measurement in the Social Sciences: Classification, Typologies, and Indices," in Daniel Lerner and Harold D. Lasswell, eds., *The Policy Sciences* (Stanford, Calif.: Stanford University Press, 1951), pp. 155–92.

[3] Carl Hempel, "Typological Methods in the Natural and Social Sciences," in his *Aspects of Scientific Explanation* (New York: Free Press of Glencoe, 1965), pp. 156–71.

[4] John C. McKinney, *Constructive Typology and Social Theory* (New York: Appleton-Century-Crofts, 1966).

[5] Edward A. Tiryakian, "Typologies," *International Encyclopedia of the Social Sciences*, 16 (New York: Macmillan, 1968).

[6] See pages 14–15 and 21–24.

work in restating a typological theory. Just as the previous chapter confined its illustrations to a single individual as analyzed by a pair of investigators, the present chapter also takes a single source of illustration: the literature on "authoritarianism."

Here, of course, we are concerned with the product of numerous investigators, and this may help to account for a paradoxical contrast between the work discussed in the two chapters. *Woodrow Wilson and Colonel House* displays exemplary methodological rigor in an investigative mode that, even when standards for inquiry are further perfected, is likely to admit of a rather low degree of exactness. The authoritarianism inquiries—the massive original "Berkeley study" as well as its countless successors—are executed in a research tradition that is methodologically highly developed. In fact, the traditions for psychometric procedure are so well established that I shall have little to say in this chapter about procedures for establishing reliability and validity. But in spite of the availability of standard methodological canons, formidable debates over evidence and inference have enveloped this body of literature.

An intellectual history of authoritarianism research provides a useful preface to reconstructing the phenomenology, dynamics, and genesis of the syndrome and certain of its variants. This, then, will lead us to a discussion of what the reconstruction implies about future research needs.

I. THE STUDY OF AUTHORITARIANISM

Stated simply, the questions that arise in the literature on the authoritarian type are: "Can we distinguish types of individuals whose personal make-up, apart from their specifically political beliefs, disposes them to act in an authoritarian manner?" "What theory or construct of personality dynamics can be used to explain this type of individual?" "What developmental experiences produce such individuals?" (Then, in discussing aggregation in Chapter Five, I shall go on to consider the methodological aspects of such further questions as: "What can be said about the circumstances under which the specifically political beliefs and the behavior of such individuals will be authoritarian?" "What can be said about the aggregate effects that individuals with democratic or authoritarian dispositions may have on the functioning of political institutions?")

One of the wonders of recent social science scholarship has been the profusion of authoritarianism research in the past two decades. An admittedly selective review of writings on the topic through 1956 contained 260 bibliographical references.[7] More recently, a short monograph was devoted entirely to reviewing selected research on authoritarianism.[8] Even as interest in this topic begins to fall off, it is rare to find an issue of a journal dealing with personality and attitude research which contains no reference to authoritarianism and no use of the various techniques designed to measure it.

The main immediate stimulus for this explosion of research was the publication in 1950 of a 990-page volume by Adorno, Frenkel-Brunswik, Levinson, and Sanford, entitled *The Authoritarian Personality*.[9] This book reported the fruits of several years of investigation into the psychology of anti-Semitism. On the basis of a rich but bewilderingly varied and uneven assortment of research procedures, the authors of this work reached a striking conclusion about the psychology of hostility toward Jews and other minority groups. Such prejudiced attitudes, they argued, were not simply beliefs which people happened to have acquired. Rather, one could identify what might be called a "bigot personality,"[10] a type of individual with deep-seated psychological needs that manifest themselves in a variety of ways over and beyond ethnic prejudice. *The Authoritarian Personality* is a book dealing more with prejudice than with the problem suggested by its title—psychological dispositions toward authority. "The title," as one of the authors points out, "was not thought of until

[7] Richard Christie and Peggy Cook, "A Guide to Published Literature Relating to the Authoritarian Personality through 1956," *The Journal of Psychology*, 45 (April, 1958), 171–99.

[8] John P. Kirscht and Ronald C. Dillehay, *Dimensions of Authoritarianism* (Lexington: University of Kentucky Press, 1967).

[9] Theodor W. Adorno, Else Frenkel-Brunswik, Daniel J. Levinson, and R. Nevitt Sanford, *The Authoritarian Personality* (New York: Harper, 1950), hereafter cited as *AP*.

[10] A phrase used in a prepublication report of the study to the general public: Jerome Himelhock, "Is There a Bigot Personality?" *Commentary*, 3 (1947), 277–84.

the writing was virtually finished."[11] But it was the title phrase that came to provide the heading under which subsequent investigation proceeded; and, in general, ethnic prejudice has become a secondary issue in research on authoritarianism.

The term "authoritarian" has at least two shortcomings as an analytic tool. First, it is applicable not only to individual psychological dispositions (our concern here), but also to the content of political beliefs and to the structure of political systems. Because of this, we may easily gloss over the possibility that authoritarianism at any one of these levels is not necessarily accompanied by authoritarianism at the other levels. For example, democratic beliefs may be imposed in an authoritarian manner; and, within an authoritarian movement, the leadership may include individuals of nonauthoritarian dispositions and may even conduct its own deliberations in a democratic fashion.

Secondly, the term seems almost inevitably to be pejorative. In a liberal democracy, "authoritarian" equals "bad." The evaluative connotations of the term interfere with efforts to use it as a neutral instrument for denoting an empirical phenomenon. A historical note on the work of the Nazi psychologist, E. R. Jaensch, may help to remind us that the term can have meaning independent of its negative connotations. In 1938, Jaensch described a psychological type with remarkable similarities to the typology presented in *The Authoritarian Personality*. But his evaluation of the type was not at all negative. Rather, he saw it as exemplifying the best virtues of National Socialist manhood.[12]

There is, of course, nothing new in the awareness that some people are more deferential toward authority than are others and

---

[11] Nevitt Sanford. "The Approach of the Authoritarian Personality," in J. L. McCary, ed., *Psychology of Personality* (New York: Grove Press, 1959), p. 256.

[12] E. R. Jaensch, "Der Gegentypus," *Beiheft zur Zeistchrift für angewandte Psychologie und Charakterkunde*, Beiheft 75 (1938). Just as the *AP* was mainly concerned with the type of individual whose dispositions are antithetical to democracy, Jaensch was most concerned with the "antitype," whose dispositions were incongruent with National Socialism. The *AP* authors were aware of Jaensch's theories, but his work was in a totally different intellectual (not to say political) tradition and was in no sense an influence on them. When the same descriptive features arise out of two such divergent lines of inquiry, it enhances one's confidence that, at least at the phenomenological level, an actual configuration is being tapped by the authoritarianism construct.

that the same people often are harsh toward their subordinates. The fawning underling is a stock character in fiction, as is the tyrannical superior. It is a safe assumption that the readers of Fielding's *Tom Jones* (1747) had no difficulty recognizing the character of Deborah Wilkins, who "seldom opened her lips either to her master or his sister till she had first sounded their inclinations, with which her sentiments were always strictly consonant," and of whom Fielding says:

> It is the nature of such persons . . . to insult and tyrannize over little people. This being indeed the means which they use to recompense to themselves their extreme servility and condescension to their superiors; for nothing can be more reasonable than that slaves and flatterers should exact the same taxes on all below them which they themselves pay to all above them.[13]

What *is* new in the twentieth-century literature on authoritarianism is the specification of a constellation of psychological correlates of this tendency to combine tyranny with servility, the elaboration of a theory of the psychological dynamics accounting for the constellation, and the further elaboration of genetic hypotheses about the typical background experiences of such individuals. This latter day formulation about a familiar phenomenon has been woven from a number of strands of contemporary social psychological thought. Some of the formulations in *The Authoritarian Personality* were presaged by research in the 1930's and 1940's into "fascist attitudes."[14] Others can be found in the World War II and Cold War national-character literature, particularly in the efforts to diagnose German, Japanese, and Russian character.[15] The discussion of authoritarian character in

---

[13] Henry Fielding, *Tom Jones*, Book I, Chaps. 6 and 8.

[14] For example, Ross Stagner, "Fascist Attitudes: Their Determining Conditions," *The Journal of Social Psychology*, 7 (1936), 438–54; and Allen L. Edwards, "Unlabeled Fascist Attitudes," *Journal of Abnormal and Social Psychology*, 36 (1941), 575–82.

[15] For example, Ruth F. Benedict, *The Chrysanthemum and the Sword* (Boston: Houghton Mifflin, 1946); Henry V. Dicks, "Personality Traits and National Socialist Ideology," *Human Relations*, 3 (1950), 111–54; and Henry V. Dicks, "Observations on Contemporary Russian Behaviour," *Human Relations*, 5 (1952), 111–75.

Erich Fromm's widely discussed *Escape from Freedom*[16] seems to have been particularly influential, as were the various efforts in the 1930's by Fromm and others connected with the Institut für Sozialforschung to blend Freud and Marx in an analysis of the role of the family "in maintaining authority in modern society."[17] Underlying all of these discussions was what is still probably the most revolutionary facet of twentieth-century social science—psychoanalysis—and, particularly, several overlapping elements in Freud's thought: his notion of the anal character, his analyses of obsessional neuroses and of paranoia, and his delineation of the mechanism of projection.

The Authoritarian Personality, therefore, served to focus attention on hypotheses which had been in the air for some time, rather than to suggest completely new hypotheses. But it did something more, and this seems to have been especially important in spurring the subsequent research. The section of the book devoted to "measurement of ideological trends" provided a number of "ready-made tests that had already been taken through many of the technical procedures of validation which every [psychological] test must pass,"[18] the most notable and widely used of these being the F- (for fascism) scale. The ready-made tests were very conveniently available to subsequent investigators, whereas the fascinating body of theory which guided the research was "in no single place in the volume"[19] conveniently stated.

In the long run, however, this emphasis on certain restricted measurement techniques proved to be most unfortunate because the authoritarian literature became progressively bogged in what was, in many respects, a comedy of methodological errors and because a number of the original insights in *The Authoritarian Personality* never received careful attention. Thus, for example, a

---

[16] Erich Fromm, *Escape from Freedom* (New York: Holt, Rinehart, and Winston, 1941). The authors of *AP* also acknowledged their indebtedness to A. H. Maslow's essay "The Authoritarian Character Structure," *Journal of Social Psychology*, 18 (1943), 401–11.

[17] Max Horkheimer, ed., *Studien über Autorität und Familie* (Paris: Alcan, 1936), p. 902.

[18] Nathan Glazer, "New Light on 'The Authoritarian Personality,'" *Commentary*, 17 (1954), 290.

[19] M. Brewster Smith, "Review of *The Authoritarian Personality*," *Journal of Abnormal and Social Psychology*, 45 (1950), 775–79.

variety of telling methodological criticisms of *The Authoritarian Personality* by Christie and Hyman and Sheatsley were published only four years after the appearance of the original work in a volume devoted to *Studies in the Scope and Method of "The Authoritarian Personality."*[20] Subsequent investigators may have been discouraged from attending to certain of the original insights because especially severe methodological strictures were raised in connection with the sections of the book based on quasi-clinical psychological techniques; and these are precisely the sections that are richest in hypotheses. A vigorous essay by Edward A. Shils in *Studies in the Scope and Method of "The Authoritarian Personality"* arguing that the authors had erroneously equated authoritarianism with "right-wing authoritarianism" and that they had fallen victim to naïve sociological assumptions may also have discouraged attention to certain of the broader themes raised by the volume.

In a later controversy, an extensive series of papers on "response set" in authoritarian research were published, thereby increasing the methodologically snarled quality of the literature. Some of these papers were devoted to showing that, at least in part, many of the findings in the authoritarian literature were attributable to a mechanical shortcoming of the F-scale, the psychological test typically used to measure authoritarianism. The test was worded so that a positive response was scored as "authoritarian"; but some subjects (especially people of low education) tended to respond "yes" to *any* question, independent of their authoritarian tendencies. Other of the papers were devoted to developing new measures that are free of response set.[21]

---

[20] Richard Christie and Marie Jahoda, eds., *Studies in the Scope and Method of "The Authoritarian Personality"* (Glencoe, Ill.: Free Press, 1954), hereafter cited as *SSMAP*.

[21] Some of the more interesting of these papers are conveniently reprinted in Chapter Six of Martha T. Mednick and Sarnoff A. Mednick, *Research in Personality* (New York: Holt, Rinehart, and Winston, 1963). For examples of studies in which non-verbal measures—i.e., actual observations of behavior—were used in studying various aspects of the authoritarianism syndrome, see Joan Eager and M. Brewster Smith, "A Note on the Validity of Sanford's Authoritarian-Equalitarian Scale," *Journal of Abnormal and Social Psychology*, 47 (1952), 265–67; and Jack Block and Jeanne Block. "An Investigation of the Relationship between Intolerance of Ambiguity and Ethnocentrism," *Journal of Personality*, 19 (1951), 303–11. Such measures of behavior, as well as perfected questionnaires, are a way out of the response set dilemma.

Yet the inconclusiveness of authoritarianism research persists partially, I think, because these critical studies have consistently failed to return in sufficient detail to basic theoretical premises. Response-set-free measures are desirable; theory-free research is not. As I shall attempt to show through a reconstruction of the theory that is implicit in the original and much of the subsequent work on authoritarianism, this typology raises a wealth of promising research questions that are both amenable to progressive empirical clarification and not readily evident when the theory is left unexplicated.

II. A RECONSTRUCTION OF THE AUTHORITARIANISM TYPOLOGY

In piecing together the phenomenology, dynamics, and genetics of the authoritarian personality syndrome I have drawn especially on the seventh chapter of *The Authoritarian Personality*, which presents the rationale for the various questionnaire items that compose the F-scale. This is the closest approximation in that work to a general theoretical exposition. I have also ranged freely through the rest of the volume and have drawn on shorter writings on the topic by Adorno and his associates. Wherever these writings seemed to evince ambiguities and inconsistencies, I have endeavored so far as possible to supply an argument that is plausible, internally consistent, and faithful to the authors' basic stance.

What emerges is a reconstruction of what we can call the "basic" authoritarianism typology. In a fascinating chapter late in the volume,[22] Adorno delineates an entire gallery of subtypical variants on the general typology, as well as a pantheon of "low-scoring" non-authoritarians. Adorno's discussion of subtypes is, however, not integrated with the discussion in the remainder of the book. In addition, the subtypes are painted with broad strokes: one cannot specify on a variable-by-variable basis how each subtype differs from the basic phenomenon that, late in their research, the authors came to call *the* authoritarian personality. Nevertheless, it is of the utmost importance to note that the

------

[22] *AP*, Chap. 19.

authors did think in terms of subtypes, since this points to the need for further reconstructions in which some of the variables I shall discuss would not be present and in which there might be additional variables. Typologies are analytic simplifications, and the "basic" typology I shall now describe is a simplification of a simplification in the sense that it will contain more features that do not happen to apply to any particular actor than would the subtypes if they were fully developed. (That is to say, Rover is more accurately described by the sub-type "Scotch terrier" or "Labrador retriever" than by the type "dog.") In no instance, of course, will a classification be a "complete" description of any individual being classified, since classifications are procedures for abstracting selective common aspects of unique individual cases.

The Phenomenology of Authoritarianism

What phenomena would meet our eye if we were to encounter a full-blown authoritarian of the sort that the authors of *The Authoritarian Personality* seem to have in mind in most of their comments about this type? Let us begin with the dozen or so traits appearing in the various observations about the authoritarian type which assume a form that more or less directly parallels activities commonly performed in the political arena. Then it will be useful to consider traits which at first glance would seem to be remote from the interests of the student of politics, but which, nevertheless, are conceived of as being part of the same basic syndrome.

For the purposes of the political analyst, *the* most central traits would appear to be the pair that the authors label as "authoritarian aggression" and "authoritarian submission"—the dominance-submissiveness tendencies of the authoritarian. Like Fielding's Deborah Wilkins, such an individual abases himself before those who stand above him hierarchically or whom he perceives to be powerful, and lords it over whoever seems to be weak, subordinate, or inferior. "German folklore," Adorno relates, "has a drastic symbol for this"—bicyclist's personality (*Radfahrernaturen*). "Above they bow, below they kick."[23]

---

[23] Theodor W. Adorno, "Freudian Theory and the Pattern of Fascist Propaganda," in Geza Roheim, ed., *Psychoanalysis and the Social Sciences*,

Also politically relevant is the tendency of such individuals to *think* in power terms, to be acutely sensitive to questions of who dominates whom. Only slightly further removed from politics is the pervasive rigidity in the authoritarian's manner of confronting the world. He is, in Else Frenkel-Brunswik's phrase, "intolerant of ambiguity."[24] He likes order and is made uncomfortable by disorder; where the phenomena he is exposed to are complex and subtle, he imposes his own tight categories upon them and ignores their nuances. His thinking, therefore, makes more than the usual use of stereotypes. Another of the traits composing this character type is "conventionalism." The authoritarian, much like Riesman's "radar-controlled" other-directed personality,[25] is described as being particularly sensitive to "external agencies" and, especially, to the prevailing standards of his own social group.

These authoritarian traits, all of which can be seen to have some rather immediate potential bearing on behavior in the political arena, hang together in a fashion which puts little strain on our common sense: dominance of subordinates; deference toward superiors; sensitivity to power relationships; need to perceive the world in a highly structured fashion; excessive use of stereotypes; and adherence to whatever values are conventional in one's setting. We can easily visualize an individual with these complementary attributes. But what is perhaps most intriguing about the authoritarian syndrome is that several additional, less obvious traits are found as a part of the presenting symptoms.

---

7 (New York: International Universities Press, 1951), p. 291n. My discussion of authoritarian traits is based on *AP*, Chap. 7 and *passim* and the Sanford discussion referred to in note 11. The latter is perhaps the single most concise and comprehensive exposition by an *AP* contributor. In identifying authoritarian aggression and authoritarian submission as the central traits in the syndrome (from the standpoint of the political analyst), I am generating what Lasswell calls a "nuclear" typology—a notion that would roughly translate, in the language of this chapter, into "the aspect of the phenomonology that provides the initial basis of classification." Lasswell's "co-relational type" includes the remaining aspects of phenomenolgy and overlaps my "dynamic typology" category. His reference to developmental types and mine to genesis appear to go over identical ground.

24 Else Frenkel-Brunswik, "Intolerance of Ambiguity as an Emotional and Perceptual Personality Variable," *Journal of Personality*, 18 (1949), 108–43.

25 David Riesman, with Nathan Glazer and Reuel Denney, *The Lonely Crowd* (New Haven, Conn.: Yale University Press, 1950).

These rather exotic, further concomitants lead us beyond phenomenology to the psychoanalytically based theory of dynamics. Indeed, to anticipate my later remarks, future research may well show that "authoritarians" who do not show certain of these concomitants fall into a subtype with quite different motivational dynamics from the "basic" type I have been describing. For example, the authoritarian is described as being superstitious, a trait which has no immediate or obvious connection with the other traits I have described. (One of the items on the F-scale is: "Although many people may scoff, it may yet be shown that astrology can explain a lot of things.") He is preoccupied with virility, tending toward "exaggerated assertion of strength and toughness." While this trait might seem at first merely to be a variant of the authoritarian's interest in power, there is the added element here of being hard-boiled and rugged. The equivalent trait in the less well-developed typology of female authoritarianism is "pseudo-femininity," a preoccupation with being "feminine and soft." The authoritarian's assumptions about human nature are generally pessimistic, and he tends to be cynical about the motives of others. He is disposed to believe that "wild and dangerous things go on in the world"—that "the world is a jungle." He shows a puritanical preoccupation with sex, a "concern with sexual 'goings on'" and "a strong inclination to punish violators of sex mores." Finally, he shows a trait of which much is made in the theoretical explanation of this pattern—"anti-intraception." This is "an attitude of impatience with and opposition to the subjective and the tender-minded." One of its more conspicuous forms is an inability to introspect, to acknowledge one's own feelings and fantasies.

The authoritarian typology, like Freud's famous juxtaposition of orderliness, parsimoniousness, and obstinacy in the anal personality type, may well have the merit of being less obvious to common sense than most of the formulations with which social scientists work. But what is its basis in reality? Are enough individuals to be found who exhibit these characteristics, or a sufficient proportion of them, to make the notion of "authoritarian personality" more than an intriguing exercise in reasoning? The answer, I believe, is yes; but it would lead into far too long and circuitous a detour if we even began to refer to the elements in the tangled body of authoritarian research on which such a conclusion might be based. The crucial point for the present purposes is to emphasize that such questions about phenomenology—like questions about the phenomenology of single actors— are *potentially* answerable. We can devise relatively uncontroversial standards for ascertaining the fit of the basic authoritarian type—and the various possible sub-types—with observational data. Questions concerning the accuracy of assertions about the dynamics and genesis of types (as about individuals) are much more problematic.[26]

THE DYNAMICS OF AUTHORITARIANISM

Although the typology of dynamics that has been proposed to account for the preceding pattern of traits can be described in the same detail as the foregoing remarks about phenomenology, we may content ourselves here with merely summarizing its main themes. In summarizing them, it is necessary to refer again to the various presenting characteristics, but to do so in the context of an account of the personality functioning of such an individual and of why, given his personality dynamics, he exhibits those phenomenological regularities.

The central ingredient in the typology of dynamics can be noted in a single sentence: The authoritarian has orientations toward figures of authority that are at once intense and *highly ambivalent.* His ambivalence is, or so the theory argues, the crux of the matter. This individual, who seems outwardly to be so servile toward those whom he perceives as his superiors, in fact also harbors exceedingly strong negative feelings toward them. Futhermore, he is unaware, or only intermittently and imper-

---

[26] On the question of whether the phenomonological typology is empirically sound, note the following statement made by Christie at the conclusion of an extensive, rigorous review of authoritarianism research. "Both the strength and weakness of *The Authoritarian Personality* lie in its basic assumptions which are rooted in psychoanalytic theory. Such an orientation has led to the uncovering of a host of data which in all likelihood would not have been discovered by investigators with differing theoretical viewpoints. Despite some methodological weaknesses in the original research, subsequent findings have been predominantly confirmatory," *SSMAP*, 195–96. Also see M. Brewster Smith, "An Analysis of Two Measures of 'Authoritarianism' among Peace Corps Teachers," *Journal of Personality*, 33 (1965), 513–35, which reports very convincing evidence about the existence of a syndrome of the sort that was described in the *AP*.

fectly aware, of the hate side of this love-hate amalgam, for the authoritarian conceals from himself his rage toward those in authority through the massive and primitive ego defense of reaction-formation. He bends over backwards in energetically excessive praise of authorities and represses—i.e., drives out of his conscious awareness—all his critical impulses toward them.[27] From this explanation of the trait of authoritarian submission, the remainder of the syndrome readily follows, given the logic of psychoanalytic personality theory.

Repression has its costs and side-effects, and repressed impulses seek alternative outlets, especially when the repression is of strong impulses such as the authoritarian's negative dispositions toward authorities. The authoritarian's repressed hostility toward those who are strong and superior is rechanneled toward those he perceives to be weak, unauthoritative, and inferior. But the repressed hostility toward authority has further, more obscure outlets and a variety of diffuse side effects. This need to express unconscious hostility contributes to the authoritarian's generally negative views of man and his works, as well as to his need to scan his environment for signs of authority relations, his tendency (via projection) to see the world as full of dangerous things and people, and his desire to punish others—for example, sex offenders—who have surrendered to their impulses. Feelings of personal weakness are covered by a façade of toughness. Still another side effect of channeling enormous energy into repression and reaction-formation is that the authoritarian's emotional capacities and even certain of his cognitive capacities are stunted. He is unable to face the prospect of canvassing his own psyche for fear of what such introspection might yield and, therefore, becomes highly dependent upon external sources of guidance.

----

[27] The authoritarian type is described as having repressed sexual, as well as hostile, impulses; but the significance of repressed sexuality in authoritarianism does not seem to have been fully explicated. At points in the *AP*, the implication seems to be simply that the authoritarian has acceded to parental taboos concerning sexuality. At other points (for example, p. 798), the implication is that the repressed sexual impulses are toward the parents and particularly the father. The latter, more classically psychoanalytic, construction is developed in some detail by Fromm in his chapter in Horkheimer, *op. cit.*, pp. 77–135; English abstract, pp. 908–11. See especially his remarks on sadomasochism.

Finally, to touch on the remaining traits in the phenomenology of authoritarianism, dependence upon external guidance provides the common element in several further surface manifestations of the syndrome which might otherwise not seem related to one another. These are: conventionality, i.e., accepting the prevailing values in one's environment; stereotypy, i.e., accepting the prevailing descriptive categories; superstition, i.e., belief that man is controlled from without by mysterious agencies; and intolerance of ambiguity and use of rigid categories—consequences of the authoritarian's discomfort when the environment provides few guideposts for thought and action.

The "basic" authoritarian type whose phenomenology and dynamics I have just described is what might be called an *ego-defensive type*. In terms of M. Brewster Smith's map of variables relevant to personality-and-politics analysis, this typology identifies a pattern of attitudes and behavior assumed to be based in "externalization and ego defense." After the fashion of classical psychoanalysis, the typology places great emphasis on irrationality—on how the self (i.e., ego) invests major energies in the task of maintaining inner equilibrium. The task of equilibrium maintenance or ego defense involves defending the self against the imperious and frequently conflicting demands of impulses and conscience.

The efforts turned to this intrapsychic purpose detract from the external requirements of mastering reality: the highly ego-defensive person is likely (in ways that vary with the specific nature of his defenses) to be flawed in his perception of and response to the environment. He may, as in the case of the ego-defensive authoritarian, see power relations where they do not exist; he may be insensitive to nuances and subtleties in interpersonal relations; he may engage in untoward acts of self-abasement or aggressiveness; and so forth. All of this is because his seeming reactions to the external world are in fact extensions of an internal set of demands. (Indeed one possible index of degree of ego defensiveness is the degree to which an individual is capable of responding to external stimuli, controlling for such additionally relevant variables as levels of intelligence and information.)

Since the empirical standing of the various concepts and theories that have their antecedents in psychoanalytic thought is controversial,[28] it is not surprising that the account of authoritarian dynamics I have just presented also is controversial. Nor is it surprising that a competing (or, as I would suggest, additional) account exists. I am referring to the observations made by various critics of *The Authoritarian Personality* and of related writings who advance what we might call a typology of *cognitive authoritarianism*.[29]

Descriptions of the cognitive (or, to use the language of Smith's map, "object appraisal") authoritarian accept at least a good part of the phenomenological portrait I have just presented. (One of the key research questions raised by a reconstruction of the sort we are engaged in is that of specifying the critical differences in presenting characteristics of the two syndromes.) In cognitive authoritarianism, the presenting characteristics are hypothesized to be based simply upon the learned (i.e., cognitive) conceptions of reality which are prevalent in certain cultures or subcultures, rather than on the labyrinthine process of reaction-formation described in the ego-defensive typology. And this patterning of the cognitive authoritarian's behavior may in fact be a more or less accurate reflection of the actual conditions of his adult life: it *is* rational to be power-oriented and deferential to authorities in some social settings; the world may really *be*

---

[28] For discussions designed to reduce polemic and seek empirical clarification of the issues underlying the controversial status of psychoanalysis, see B. A. Farrell, "The Status of Psychoanalytic Theory," *Inquiry*, 7 (1964), 104–23; Peter Madison, *Freud's Concept of Repression and Defense: Its Theoretical and Observational Language* (Minneapolis: University of Minnesota Press, 1961); and A. C. MacIntyre, *The Unconscious: A Conceptual Study* (London: Routledge and Kegan Paul, 1958). A number of interesting investigations based on the ego-defensive theory of authoritarian dynamics have been reported. For example, see Herbert C. Schulberg, "Insight, Authoritarianism and Tendency to Agree," *Journal of Nervous and Mental Disease*, 135 (1962), 481–88.

[29] For examples of the line of reasoning I am now discussing, see the essay by Hyman and Sheatsley in *SSMAP*, esp. pp. 91ff.; Herbert H. Hyman, *Political Socialization* (Glencoe, Ill.: Free Press, 1959), p. 47; and S. M. Miller and Frank Riessman, " 'Working-Class Authoritarianism': A Critique of Lipset," *British Journal of Sociology*, 12 (1961), 263–76.

I of course take the ego-defensive versus cognitive distinction from the literature on the functions served by opinions for the personality: M. Brewster Smith, *et al.*, *Opinions and Personality* (New York: Wiley, 1956), Chap. 3; the essay by Smith I have made so much use of, "A Map for the Analysis of Personality and Politics," *Journal of Social Issues*, 24:3 (1968), 15–28; and Daniel Katz, "The Functional Approach to the Study of Attitudes," *Public Opinion Quarterly*, 24 (1960), 163–204.

a jungle, as one of the F-scale items asserts. Recent research in fact suggests that the tendencies described by both the ego-defensive and the cognitive authoritarian types exist in the real world. To deal summarily with what in actuality is a matter of considerable confusion and complexity, it can be said that much of what has been called "working-class authoritarianism" does seem to have its roots in simple cognitive learning, whereas, at the higher socioeconomic levels, authoritarian orientations seem more often to have a basis in less accessible motivational sources.[30]

The Genesis of Authoritarianism

Adorno and his associates, in fact, anticipated the thesis of cognitive authoritarianism by acknowledging that the personality manifestations they were studying could in some instances merely reflect "surface resentment" with a "more or less rational" basis in learning.[31] Subsequent extensions of the cognitive explanation, for example, by Hyman and Sheatsley, have stressed the lack of information available in lower-class subcultures and the lack of opportunity for lower-class individuals to acquire the desire and capacity to manipulate symbols—or, at least, the symbols with which public discourse is conducted—with any degree of sophistication. Such social settings, it is suggested, produce individuals who respond to the F-scale in much the same fashion as would be predicted by the ego-defensive theory of authoritarianism, but who do not show the pathology described in the theory. When the F-scale items that one must agree with in order to score "high" are fairly realistic descriptions of situational reality, "authoritarianism" is likely to reflect little more

---

[30] See, for example, Angus Campbell, et al., *The American Voter* (New York: Wiley, 1960), pp. 512–15. Also see the very interesting attempt by Thomas F. Pettigrew to demonstrate that the amount of personality-based (that is, ego-defensive) prejudice toward Negroes is the same in the American North, in the American South and in South Africa, and that the higher level of anti-Negro sentiment in the latter two areas is due to the cognitive learning which occurs in cultures where race prejudice is prevalent. "Personality and Sociocultural Factors in Intergroup Attitudes: A Cross-National Comparison," *Journal of Conflict Resolution*, 2 (1958), 29–42. The question of cognitive versus ego-defensive authoritarianism is complex, however, and a fuller discussion would engage us in technical matters connected with the instruments used to measure authoritarianism.

[31] *AP*, pp. 753–56.

than learning from one's exemplars and a realistic attempt to characterize one's environment.

The Authoritarian Personality, however, concentrates on elucidating the childhood antecedents of ego-defensive authoritarianism. The typical early determinants of this pattern come as no surprise in the light of the theory of underlying dynamics.

> When we consider the childhood situation . . . we find reports of a tendency toward rigid discipline on the part of the parents, with affection which is conditional rather than unconditional, i.e., dependent upon approved behavior on the part of the child. Related to this is a tendency . . . to base [family] interrelationships on rather clearly defined roles of dominance and submission. . . . Forced into a surface submission to parental authority, the child develops hostility and aggression which are poorly channelized. The displacement of a repressed antagonism toward authority may be one of the sources, and perhaps the principal source, of his antagonism toward outgroups.[32]

The authors derived these and similar conclusions about how ego-defensive authoritarianism arises in the socialization process partly from their subjects' retrospective reports of childhood experiences, but also from direct studies by Frenkel-Brunswik of ethnically prejudiced and unprejudiced children. The studies of children suggested that "warmer, closer and more affectionate interpersonal relationships prevail in the homes of the unprejudiced children" and that prejudice was associated with "strictness, rigidity, punitiveness, rejection vs. acceptance of the child."

> In the home with the orientation toward rigid conformity . . . maintenance of discipline is often based upon the expectation of quick learning of external rigid and superficial rules which are bound to be beyond the comprehension of the child. Family relationships are characterized by fearful subservience to the demands of the parents and by an early suppression of impulses not acceptable to the adults.

---

[32] *Ibid.,* p. 482.

Since the moral requirements in such a home
must appear to the child as overwhelming and at the
same time unintelligible, and the rewards meager, submission to them must be reinforced by fear of and pressure from external agencies. Due to the lack of a
genuine identification with the parents, the fearfully
conforming child does not make the important developmental step from mere social anxiety to real conscience.[33]

I have earlier noted that the authoritarian personality research grew out of an intellectual tradition that drew on both
Freudian psychology and Marxian sociology. In *The Authoritarian Personality*, it is the Freudian emphasis on early childhood
socialization that occupies most of the discussion of how authoritarianism develops; but occasionally a Marxian explanation of
the genesis of authoritarianism appears. In the final paragraph of
the volume, for example, the authors remark that "people are
continuously molded from above because they must be molded if
the overall economic pattern is to be maintained."[34] The point
being made here is evidently that of Fromm, who in *Escape from
Freedom* develops, *inter alia*, roughly the following sequence of
conceptualization and reasoning:

1. "Social character . . . internalizes external necessi-
ties and thus harnesses human energy for the task of a given
economic and social system";

2. the authoritarian social character (rather than Weber's Protestant Ethic) is the energy source responsible for
the development of Western capitalism; and

3. the family is, in effect, mainly a transmission belt
providing the system with the type of personality it
"requires."[35]

Apart from whatever merit there may be in Fromm's specific historical argument, we have here a further class of explanatory factors—overlapping the references to culture in the cognitive model—which may be introduced to explain the genesis of

---

[33] Else Frenkel-Brunswik, "Further Explorations by a Contributor to
'The Authoritarian Personality,'" in *SSMAP*, pp. 236–37.

[34] *AP*, p. 976.

[35] See especially the appendix to *Escape from Freedom, op. cit.*, on
"Character and the Social Process," pp. 277–99.

authoritarianism, namely, social structure and social role requirements. There is, of course, no incompatibility between theories
explaining authoritarianism in terms of family and other pri-
mary-circle socialization experiences and theories explaining it
in terms of social structure, whether or not the theories emphasize
the economic features of social organization. The relationship
between such explanations is clearly shown in the map on page
27 and in the summary version of it at the head of Chapter
Three: the kinds of causal factors that interest Fromm are in the
distal social environment (Panel I), and these do not affect the
individual directly, but rather are mediated through influences in
the individual's past and present immediate environments.[36]

In Chapter Five on aggregation, I shall resume discussion of
the authoritarianism typology in order to consider various problems of "linkage" involved in using such typologies in analyses
of political behavior. As we shall see, distinctions need to be
made which insure that the investigator will be cognizant of a
variety of complex connections, for example, those between the
deeper personality trends analyzed in the foregoing reconstruction and specific political attitudes, and those between personal
psychology (deeper personality trends plus attitudes) and behavior in specific stimulus situations. Most difficult of all are the
questions of linkage that arise in analyzing the degree to which
the individual psychological dispositions and types of disposi-

---

[36] The reader should note that my assertion is a definitional gloss on
M. Brewster Smith's map and is not a falsifiable proposition. Thus, I am not
saying that there is invariably a "two-step flow" of socializing influence from
the remote environment (although this is typically the case), but rather that
even when signals from the "distal environment" do impinge directly upon an
individual (as in communications through the mass media) these are usefully
conceived as part of the immediate environment (in Lewin's phrase "life-
space") of the individual. Since the map does not permit causal relationships
to flow directly from the distal environment panel to the personality panel—
even though it is well known that remote happenings can have substantial impacts on people who experience them only "indirectly"—we have to adopt this
reading of the immediate environment. Evidence of the effects of the socioeconomic organization of a society on its members' personality characteristics
is now becoming available from a study of personality differences between
farmers and herders in four East African tribes. Two preliminary reports are:
Walter Goldschmidt, "Theory and Strategy in the Study of Cultural Adaptability," *American Anthropologist*, 67 (1965), 402–8; and Robert B. Edgerton,
"'Cultural' vs. 'Ecological' Factors in the Expression of Values, Attitudes, and
Personality Characteristics," *American Anthropologist*, 67 (1965), 442–47.

tions in populations are aggregated into characteristics of the systems within which the populations are organized.

But first we may conclude the present illustrative discussion of the authoritarianism typology by briefly observing a number of ways in which a reconstruction such as the present one—by making explicit the variables and their hypothetical connections and by distinguishing different classes of empirical questions— provides the initial pointers for research.

III. RESEARCH IMPLICATIONS OF THE RECONSTRUCTION OF THE AUTHORITARIANISM TYPOLOGY

A variety of empirical inquiries—indeed a possible program of inquiry—is suggested by the kind of reconstruction I have set forth. Broadly speaking, the difficulties of the literature have resulted from promiscuous, atheoretical use of a handy but imperfect instrument. In part, the difficulties have been specific to the F-scale; and in part, they have resulted more generally from exclusive reliance on questionnaire items (especially deliberately ambiguous attitude items) as indicators of deeper dimensions of personality. There are intrinsic difficulties in believing that deep inner psychological patterns will be reliably tapped by positive or negative responses to items like the following from the F-scale:

> Obedience and respect for authority are the most important virtues children should learn.
> No sane, normal, decent person could ever think of hurting a close friend or relative.
> Most people don't realize how much our lives are controlled by plots hatched in secret by politicians.

Not the least of the difficulties presented by such a measuring instrument is the response-set problem. Apart from whatever power the instrument has to distinguish among individuals who vary in the ego-defensive need to be in superior-subordinate relationships, the instrument appears simultaneously to sort people in terms of the mundane variable "level of education." Lack of education evidently encourages one to agree with any oracular-sounding homily—in fact, with any questionnaire assertion at all. Consequently, people of low educational levels tend to score high on such a scale, independent of their deeper personality needs.[37]

This kind of methodological flaw has contributed to a situation in which, despite the many studies—including factor analyses of the clustering of F-scale items—the available documentation about the phenomenology of authoritarianism is still imperfect. Research is needed that uses a variety of indicators of the relevant variables. These indicators should be non-verbal, as well as verbal, so as to avoid the many problems that arise from the different ways in which people of different classes handle language. A research program might well begin by "working back" from the original theory of the phenomenology of authoritarianism in order to establish whether and to what degree that theory captures the actual symptomology of individuals in the real world. Such a program would have to focus not only on the basic authoritarian type, but also on subtypes and on non-authoritarian comparison groups.

There are a number of interesting precedents for the use of non-verbal indicators in phenomenological classifications. One of these is an early study by Eager and Smith[38] which drew upon observers' reports of the actual behavior of the individuals being scored; another is Jack and Jeanne Block's fascinating exercise in correlating anti-Semitic attitudes with a visual indicator of intolerance of ambiguity.[39] Of even greater diagnostic promise (and converging with the techniques recommended in the previous chapter for rigorous single-actor analyses), are M. Brewster Smith's recent efforts at personality assessment of Peace Corps volunteers. Smith and his associates worked with psychi-

---

[37] Thus a variety of studies found that F-scale scores were negatively related to level of education; but when the authors of *The American Voter* administered *reversed* F-scale items (i.e., items in which a negative [disagreement] answer was scored as "authoritarian"), they found lower-education respondents in a national sample ostensibly showing lower levels of authoritarianism than higher-education respondents. Also see the sources cited in notes 29 and 30 above.

[38] Eager and Smith, *op. cit.*

[39] The indicator used was the rapidity with which individuals reach "closure" in estimating the oscillations of a light in the autokinetic effect (a perceptual illusion in which a stationary dot of light appears to the viewer to be in motion). Block and Block, *op. cit.*

atrists' qualitative summaries of general appraisal interviews with volunteers-in-training, coding the summaries in terms of a comprehensive set of personality-theory categories. Coding was by a Q-sort technique applied blind. Volunteers who scored high on a version of the F-scale that had been corrected for response set differed sharply from those who had scored low, and in spite of the fact that neither the psychiatric interviews nor the Q-sort variables specifically focused on authoritarianism, the differences were highly congruent with the assertions of authoritarianism theory.[40]

At the dynamic level, the most challenging possibilities seem to be for devising research strategies that address themselves to establishing whether or under what conditions particular phenomenological patterns of response do or do not have roots in ego defense. As Daniel Katz has emphasized, one important reason why we need to be able to determine whether behavior patterns (including expressions of beliefs) result from various kinds of personality dynamics is so that we can predict the circumstances under which the behavior pattern will arise and those that might change it. Katz notes, for example, the theoretical expectation that beliefs based in straightforward cognitive learning will change in the face of new and more appropriate information. If the same beliefs are serving ego-defensive functions, an attempt to change them by providing additional information may in fact have precisely the opposite of the desired effect. Defensively-based attitudes are more likely to change in response to such stimuli as "authoritarian suggestion," or quasi-therapeutic procedures which give the individual insight into the emotional bases of his attitudes. These notions have been used by Katz and his associates in research reported in such papers as "The Measurement of Ego-Defense as Related to Attitude Change." In their research, instruments such as the paranoia scale of the Minnesota Multiphasic Personality Inventory were

---

[40] Smith, "An Analysis of Two Measures of 'Authoritarianism' Among Peace Corps Teachers," *op. cit.* James D. Barber is in the process of devising coding criteria for characterizing typical patterns in the political styles and behavior of American presidents on the basis of biographical data. His procedures parallel those used by Smith in analyzing the interviews with Peace Corps teachers and have the additional advantage of identifying specifically political phenomenological patterns.

used in order to classify subjects by level of ego defensiveness. Using attitude change techniques that are especially designed to penetrate moderate ego defenses, but that are too weak for strong ego defenders, the investigators were able correctly to predict that attitude change would occur in the middle ego defense category.[41]

Finally, when the task is that of establishing the genesis of personality types, the *least* satisfactory approach is to rely upon retrospective data—upon the subject's own report of his background experiences. It is somewhat more useful to make use of cross-sectional data, gathered more or less simultaneously from different individuals of varying ages, in order to reconstruct a developmental pattern. The ideal procedure, though most time-consuming and difficult, is to make longitudinal observations of individuals throughout the course of their development.

Apart from studies in which cross-sectional populations are followed for relatively short time periods, the longitudinal design is rarely feasible for the student of development of political types. Nevertheless, he should keep in mind the conception of longitudinal research design, if only so he can properly estimate the degree to which his own procedures fail to capture the information that a longitudinal study might yield. A particularly sophisticated model for the present purposes is the study by Kagan and Moss in which observations (including behavioral observations of young children in family settings) collected from birth through adolescence were coded for personality themes by one investigator and then an intensive personality assessment, in terms of the same categories, was carried out by the other investigator.

A study of this sort can, in principle, find firm empirical indicators of the subtle and elusive levels of personality function-

---

[41] The device used was a procedure designed to provide the individual with insight into his own defenses and how they had produced his attitudes. For the present purposes, which are illustrative, I shall ignore a number of thorny questions about whether Katz, *et al.*, were actually successful in measuring ego defensiveness and reducing defensive barriers to attitude change. Daniel Katz, *et al.*, "The Measurement of Ego-Defense as Related to Attitude Change," *Journal of Personality*, 25 (1957), 465–74. For a possible alternative explanation of the findings in this and related studies by Katz and his associates, see Susan Roth Sherman, "Demand Characteristics in an Experiment on Attitude Change," *Sociometry*, 30 (1967), 246–61.

ing that are so difficult to measure, but that figure prominently in some of our more venerable theories about personality and politics. Thus, for example, Kagan and Moss were able to identify and reliably observe such elusive mechanisms as denial and reaction-formation in an analysis of a young man who had been exceedingly timorous and dependent as a young child and who, as a pre-adolescent and adolescent, had adopted the directly antithetical mode of hyperactive, independent behavior. Among this individual's adult responses in psychological testing was an extraordinary inability to perceive dependency themes in projective test material, such as TAT cards flashed by tachistoscope on a screen. With measurements of this sort, it is possible that clinical psychological notions, such as the various mechanisms of defense, can be firmly documented and removed from the arcane preserve of the gifted therapist's intuitions.[42]

IV. SUMMARY AND CONCLUSIONS

The psychological analysis of political types, like the analysis of single actors, can be broken down into the three tasks of describing phenomenology and attempting to establish the psychological dynamics and developmental influences which account for the phenomenology. Again, the order in which I have discussed these analytic problems both recapitulates their importance in explanations of how a particular type of individual will behave in given situations and suggests the degree to which straightforward investigative procedures are likely to be available which will produce generally agreed-upon findings.

Generally speaking, the tools for arriving at agreed-upon findings are more advanced in the realm of typological analysis than in that of single-actor analysis. This is partially a result of past intellectual history: case studies of individuals have mainly been carried out by clinicians whose prime interest was treating individual patients and by historians working in literary tradi-

---

[42] Jerome Kagan and Howard A. Moss, *Birth to Maturity* (New York: Wiley, 1962), esp. pp. 72–74. For a study which promises to be a landmark in longitudinal analysis, see Jack Block and Norma Haan, *Ways of Personality Development: Continuity and Change from Adolescence to Adulthood* (New York: Appleton-Century-Crofts, forthcoming).

tions. Typological work, on the other hand, can draw on more than a half-century of effort by psychometricians to perfect the standards and procedures for satisfactory classification and explanation. But the special knottiness of single-actor diagnosis also is in part intrinsic to characterizations of idiosyncratic behavior and development, given the inevitable uncertainties of applying probabilistic general principles to the explanation of single instances.

CHAPTER FIVE

Aggregative Effects of Personality Characteristics on Political Systems

As we saw in Chapter One, analyses of single actors and of types of actors have aggregative implications. In speaking of "aggregation," I refer not merely to what has sometimes been called aggregate psychology—namely, statistical summaries of observations that have been performed on some collection of individuals. In the real world, individuals and types aggregate into formally or informally organized *collectivities*. These range from informal, face-to-face interaction patterns all the way through the organizations and political patterns in the international arena. And, as it is commonly if rather loosely put, collectivities are not merely the sum of the individuals they contain.

The traditional concerns of political science are with these collective, macro-phenomena. Micro-political studies of individual behavior and its social psychological antecedents ordinarily are conducted with a view to explaining the institutional patterns into which the individuals fit. Moreover, it seems obvious on the face of it that micro-data *should* contribute to the understanding of macro-phenomena—that, for example, our understanding of the French political system ought to be enhanced by an aggregative analysis of the psychological dispositions of Frenchmen and their political leaders. Yet when it comes to disciplined, soundly documented aggregative analyses, the following blunt statement by Smelser suggests the present level of advancement in the social sciences: "We do not at the present," Smelser asserts, "have the methodological capacity to argue causally from a mixture of aggregated states of individual members of a system to a global characteristic of a system."[1]

Typical approaches to the analysis of political aggregates either fail to take advantage of the possibility of employing evidence about the psychology of members of the aggregate, or they engage in psychological reductionism. In part it is the reductionist excesses of the past that account for the present lack of attention given by students of institutional processes to aggregation: there are too many horrible examples of the treatment of institutions as individuals writ large. This sort of treatment is found in much of the older writing of the Good King–Bad King historiographical persuasion. By and large, however, the treatment of institutions as extended shadows of Great Men is out of fashion, so much so that there is probably still considerable justice in Sidney Hook's 1942 allegation that the impact of individual actors on historical events has come to be insufficiently appreciated. As Hook put it,

> During the twentieth century the overwhelming majority of historians have been in unconscious thraldom to one or another variety of social determinism. . . . [They have thrown much light] . . . on the fabric of social life of past times and on the slow accumulation of social tensions which discharge themselves with volcanic fury during periods of revolution. Without impugning the validity of their findings one wonders whether they have done as much justice to the activity of the leading personalities during the critical periods of world history whose roots they have uncovered so well.[2]

Attempts to suggest the aggregative implications of psychological typologies have often been marred by the fallacy of merely

---

[1] Neil J. Smelser, "Personality and the Explanation of Political Phenomena at the Social-System Level: A Methodological Statement," *Journal of Social Issues*, 24:3 (1968), 123.

[2] Sidney Hook, *The Hero in History* (New York: Humanities Press, 1943), pp. 19–20. For recent statements on this that especially emphasize the impact of the leaders of authoritarian political systems, see Robert C. Tucker in *The Soviet Political Mind* (New York: Praeger, 1963), pp. 145–65, and "The Dictator and Totalitarianism," *World Politics*, 17 (1965), 55–83.

reducing historical processes and sociopolitical structures to personal psychology. I refer especially to the wartime and Cold-War national-character literature, in which one finds inferences being made from (often imperfect) evidence about early childhood socialization and personality development, directly and with insufficient qualification, to such complicated social and historical ostensible consequences as the rise of Nazism, Japanese militarism, or Soviet foreign policy. These exercises in psychologism often impress no one less than the psychoanalysts themselves. A psychoanalyst relates that soon after the attack on Pearl Harbor,

> a small group of noted social scientists, intent on studying the cultural roots of German National Socialism, invited a number of refugee scholars and interviewed them about their experiences and ideas on this subject. I was among those invited. I remember that I mentioned among the factors which seemed to me had disposed the German people for a nationalistic dictatorship, the failure of German nineteenth century liberalism, and the subsequent success of Prussian militarism, in bringing about the much-desired unification of Germany; this experience, I argued, had conditioned the German people to distrust the democratic process and to put their faith in strong-arm methods. I also mentioned the impact of rapid industrialization upon a society still almost feudal in its caste structure, without interceding commercialism and without a strong commercial class such as was already established in Anglo-Saxon countries at the outset of industrialization; such a situation seemed to make people more alert to the possibilities of power, rather than the potentialities of welfare, inherent in industry. I was then interrupted by my host, a noted anthropologist; this was not what I had been expected to contribute. As a psychoanalyst I should point out how Nazism had developed from the German form of child rearing. I replied that I did not think that there was any such relationship; in fact, political opinion did not seem to me to be determined in early childhood at all. This view was not accepted and I was told that the way the German mother holds her baby must be different from that of mothers in democracies. When we parted, it was

clear that my hosts felt that they had wasted their time.[3]

We can clarify why personality analyses are an insufficient, even though sometimes necessary, basis for making inferences about political systems by resuming discussion of the authoritarianism literature at the point where we left off in Chapter Four. Although there are numerous statements by contributors to *The Authoritarian Personality* that personality factors are neither "the major [n]or exclusive determinants of political or social movements,"[4] it is difficult to gainsay the critics who argue that reductionism is implicit in a number of the formulations in that work. For example, by labeling the personality trends summarized in the previous chapter "pre-fascist" and "potentially fascist," the authors tended to resolve by definition the complex empirical question of how deeper personality trends articulate with specifically political belief and with actual behavior. And their references to the "great . . . fascist potential"[5] in American society seemed to reflect equally unrealistic assumptions about the relationship between the distribution of psychological dispositions in a society and its overall political structure. What such locutions tend to miss is the *links* that need to be explicitly considered in examining the chains of causation that run—or fail to run—from underlying personality structure to social and political structure.

I. FROM PERSONALITY STRUCTURE TO POLITICAL STRUCTURE: PROBLEMS OF LINKAGE

In schematic form:

Personality structures $\neq$ political belief $\neq$ individual political action $\neq$ aggregate political structures and processes.

---

[3] Robert Waelder, *Basic Theory of Psychoanalysis* (New York: International Universities Press, 1960), pp. 53–54.

[4] Else Frenkel-Brunswik, "Further Explorations by a Contributor to 'The Authoritarian Personality,'" in Richard Christie and Marie Jahoda, eds., *Studies in the Scope and Method of "The Authoritarian Personality"* (Glencoe, Ill.: Free Press, 1954), p. 228.

[5] Theodor W. Adorno, Else Frenkel-Brunswik, Daniel J. Levinson, and R. Nevitt Sanford, *The Authoritarian Personality* (New York: Harper, 1950), p. 974.

By $\neq$, I mean "does not necessarily predict." I do not mean to imply an absence of empirical connection across these various links: if that seemed probable, the entire effort of this book would be misdirected. Rather, what needs to be emphasized is that the connections *are* empirical, that they need to be carefully examined, and that the relationships are neither necessarily strong nor positive, especially those that cross more than one of the links. These assertions need to be considered in further detail.

Personality Structures $\neq$ Belief System

As is often pointed out, persons with similar underlying personality characteristics are capable of holding different political beliefs, and those with similar beliefs may differ in underlying personality characteristics. The psychic elements of underlying personality and belief are capable of independent variation. This is true because there are normally a variety of alternative channels through which psychic needs can be expressed and also because, as a result of the political inattentiveness of most citizens, political orientations are often acquired haphazardly, without engaging deeper personality sources. The original authoritarian personality research was influenced not only by the intellectual traditions to which I referred in Chapter Four, but also by the political climate of the 1930's and 1940's, particularly the grim history of German national socialism and the presence in the United States of nativistic radical-right movements. This seems to have contributed to the lack of attention in the original research to the possibility—which subsequently was widely discussed—that authoritarian character traits may be manifested in other than rightist political beliefs.[6] A further aspect of the

---

[6] See Edward A. Shils' discussion of "left authoritarianism" in "Authoritarianism: 'Right' and 'Left,'" in Christie and Jahoda, eds., *op. cit.*, pp. 24–49. Also see the work of Rokeach, who has attempted to develop a content-free alternative to the various approaches to the question of authoritarianism by stressing the "structure" of people's beliefs: Milton Rokeach, "Political and Religious Dogmatism: An Alternative to the Authoritarian Personality," *Psychological Monographs*, No. 425 (Washington: American Psychological Association, 1956); and his *The Open and Closed Mind* (New York: Basic Books, 1960). One might say that the Marxian heritage of the original authoritarian research (by discouraging attention to authoritarianism on the left) hinders

failure in the original work to focus also on non right wing authoritarianism was a tendency to treat the ethnically prejudiced and politically conservative attitudes of many authoritarians as if these were part of the defining characteristics of the syndrome itself. For some purposes, it may be desirable to treat opinions as "an integral part of personality."[7] But in studying personality and politics, it is often essential to distinguish analytically between underlying psychic structure and belief, lest the question of the connections between them be settled in our definitions rather than in our research. The research, of course, may well show that authoritarian personality characteristics do "fit" best with right-wing authoritarian ideology; but, at best, the relationship is likely to be imperfect because of the possibility that, for some people, personality characteristics will find alternative political outlets or no political outlet at all.

UNDERLYING PERSONALITY STRUCTURES AND POLITICAL BELIEFS ≠ POLITICAL BEHAVIOR

The individual who possesses what Adorno and his associates referred to as a "potentially fascist" personality structure, then, does not necessarily hold "fascist" beliefs. Furthermore, the impact on action of both underlying personality structures *and* the content of belief is not necessarily as straightforward as the usage "potential fascist" implies. Action, of course, results not only from psychological predispositions, but also from the situations in which people find themselves, including the formal and informal roles they are called upon to perform. Consequently, predictions of behavior from psychological data alone are exceedingly poor procedure.

It has often been said that there is no "one-to-one correlation" between psychological dispositions and action. It is not as

---

awareness of the diversity of belief consistent with common psychological characteristics, whereas the Freudian heritage (by pointing to ego-defensive rather than cognitive explanations) hinders awareness of the diversity of psychological characteristics consistent with common beliefs. For a discussion in *The Authoritarian Personality* of a personality subtype quite like Shils' notion of left-wing authoritarianism, see the treatment of the "rigid low scorer" on pp. 771–73.

[7] M. Brewster Smith, Jerome Bruner, and Robert White, *Opinions and Personality* (New York: Wiley, 1956), p. 1.

often appreciated that the correlation can even be *negative;* in some circumstances, an individual's behavior may actually be the reverse of what would have been expected if merely his predispositions were taken into account. An example of this is to be found in work by Katz and Benjamin on the behavior of northern, white, college undergraduates toward their Negro co-workers. Presumably racially prejudiced "authoritarians were actually more deferential with Negroes than were non-authoritarians"—a finding which the investigators felt was "due to the authoritarian's fear of revealing anti-Negro attitudes in a potentially punitive environment."[8] Still further insight into the subtleties of personality-role relationships might have been obtained if the investigators had also examined whether authoritarians felt more strain in such situations than did non-authoritarians, or how each group would have responded if sufficient tension and frustration had been introduced to challenge the authoritarians' "inner controls" of "their hostile impulses."[9]

The need then is for analytic distinctions that prevent the automatic inference from psychological predispositions to behavior without taking account of situational factors. As Smith puts it in the discussion of the map I have referred to so often: "For long, there was a disciplinary quarrel between psychologists and sociologists about the relevance and importance of personal dispositions (primarily *attitudes*) versus situations in determining social behavior. To take this feature of our map [the causal

---

[8] Irwin Katz and Lawrence Benjamin, "Effects of White Authoritarianism in Biracial Work Groups," *Journal of Abnormal and Social Psychology,* 61 (1960), 448–56.

[9] See the remarks of Riesman and Glazer in response to criticisms of their psychological explanations of social phenomena in *The Lonely Crowd.* "Although we said in *The Lonely Crowd* that different kinds of character could be used for the same kinds of work within an institution, we emphasized the price paid by the character types that fitted badly, as against the release of energy provided by congruence of character and task." David Riesman and Nathan Glazer, *"The Lonely Crowd:* A Reconsideration in 1960," in Seymour M. Lipset and Leo Lowenthal, eds., *Culture and Social Character: The Work of David Riesman Reviewed* (New York: Free Press of Glencoe, 1961), p. 438. The same point (i.e., that behavior may be inconsistent with personality, but that some people may nevertheless undergo "distinctive burdens" in conforming to role requirements) is made by Reinhard Bendix in a widely quoted essay criticizing the various "psychiatric" explanations of social institutions. Reinhard Bendix, "Compliant Behavior and Individual Personality," *American Journal of Sociology,* 58 (1952), 292–303.

arrows in the figure relating behavior to both situation and personality] seriously is to regard the argument as silly and outmoded: both classes of determinants are jointly indispensable."[10]

PSYCHOLOGICAL PREDISPOSITIONS AND INDIVIDUAL POLITICAL ACTION ≠ AGGREGATE POLITICAL STRUCTURES AND PROCESSES

The major analytic problems, however, are at the next stage of linkage—that of moving on to accounts of how the behavior that results from the interaction of situational stimuli and psychological factors aggregates into larger systemic phenomena. Here, as the assertion by Smelser quoted at the beginning of the chapter suggests, there is no cut-and-dried formula for proceeding. A number of complementary strategies are available. I shall devote the remainder of the chapter to an inventory of what seem to be the principal possibilities.

II. STRATEGIES FOR THE ANALYSIS OF AGGREGATION

A prime requirement for making satisfactory inferences about the effects of the psychology of political actors on the systems they compose is that the analyst seek psychological data based on *direct observation* of the actors in the system, or of an appropriate sample of them. As Inkeles and Levinson point out,[11] it is unsatisfactory to rely wholly or principally on such indirect indicators of the actors' psychology as the reports of informants

---

[10] M. Brewster Smith, "A Map for the Analysis of Personality and Politics," *Journal of Social Issues*, 24:3 (1968), 18–19. Also see Alexander George's remarks on the usefulness of subdividing the concept "attitudes" in studying the interplay of perceptions of situational stimuli and predispositions as individuals engage in decision-making in: Alexander George, "Comments on 'Opinions, Personality, and Political Behavior,'" *American Political Science Review*, 52 (1958), 18–26.

[11] Alex Inkeles and Daniel J. Levinson, "National Character: The Study of Modal Personality and Sociocultural Systems," in Gardner Lindzey, ed., *Handbook of Social Psychology*, 2 (Cambridge, Mass.: Addison-Wesley, 1954), 977–1020. Inkeles and Levinson have brought this essay up to date in the second edition of the *Handbook of Social Psychology*, 4, Gardner Lindzey and Elliot Aronson, eds., (Reading, Mass.: Addison-Wesley, 1969), 418–506.

on cultural mores and child-rearing practices or the themes in such cultural artifacts as novels and films. These are the kinds of indicators employed in much of the older literature on "national character." There is a second requirement that can best be stated negatively: it is inappropriate to assume *a priori* that the actors' characteristics have any particular distribution. A social system may have the unimodal psychological distribution implied in such phrases as "*the* character of *the* French"; but it is more likely, even in simple systems, that there will be a variety of principal types, the number depending upon both the system and the basis of personality classification.[12] Finally, for many purposes it is crucial to do more than produce a psychological census of the members of the system to be analyzed; the analyst also must locate the members within the structure of the system and within its ongoing processes.

The following four complementary strategies for aggregation are addressed to meeting these requirements. They consist of (1) "building up" from direct observation of small-scale political processes, (2) using surveys to estimate the frequency of psychological attributes in populations and relating the frequencies to system characteristics, (3) modifying the frequency analyses to take account of "non-additivity," and (4) "working back" from systematic theoretical analyses of systems and the hypothetical psychological requirements for their functioning.

"BUILDING UP" FROM DIRECT OBSERVATION OF SMALL-SCALE POLITICAL PROCESSES

My frequent emphasis on the importance of self-consciously analyzing the behavioral consequences of personality in terms of the joint impact of the actor's personality and of his social situation may have left the impression that there is in fact available another, if less desirable, tack—that of studying actors within a social vacuum. Kuznets' remarks in an essay on micro-macro relations in economics are a useful corrective:

---

[12] See, for example, the work by Anthony F. C. Wallace on personality variation in an American Indian tribe: "Modal Personality among the Tuscarora Indians as Revealed by the Rorschach Test," *Bulletin of Bureau of American Ethnology*, No. 150 (1952). For a valuable literature review, see Milton Singer, "Culture and Personality Theory and Research," in Bert Kaplan, ed., *Studying Personality Cross-Culturally* (New York: Harper & Row, 1961), pp. 9–90.

The ever-present intellectual puzzle that confronts economic study is how to explain the social result in terms of individual actions. And the purpose of the long chain of connections, which runs from the individual to the firm to the industry to the region to the nation, and so on . . . is the better specification and analysis of the relation between the two termini of the chain.

One aspect of the way this basic task is resolved in economics should be noted. Clearly, there is no individual outside the framework of society, nor is there any society except as it is reflected in the patterns of behavior of its individual members. To conceive the task of explaining the social process as the result of individual actions—as if one could start with "nonsocial" individuals as the primary units, each a *tabula rasa*, and end up with a social result—is obviously to deal with what in essence is an insoluble assignment. And indeed, despite the impression that may be conveyed in some economic writing by references to Robinson Crusoe, no such fruitless task is ever attempted. Instead, the individual units are endowed with principles of action and conditions of operation that are already a product of the social framework within which the individuals operate, even if the assumptions thus made contain a far more generalized and hence less complicated formulation of *socially* conditioned patterns of behavior and of *socially* determined conditions of operation than a more realistic description would require. Thus, the maximization principles are not truly descriptions of innate and inescapable characteristics of human "nature" to be found regardless of the kind of society in which individuals operate. It is hardly an accident that economic theory and analysis, as we know them, evolved largely during the historical periods and in the societies in which the assumed principles and conditions of individual behavior bore some resemblance to the way the individual members of those societies operated in those historical times.[13]

Because of the inevitability of studying the psychology of actors in terms of their social context, accounts of individual political actors tend to extend automatically into aggregate ac-

---

[13] Simon Kuznets, "Parts and Wholes in Economics," in Daniel Lerner, ed., *Parts and Wholes* (New York: Free Press of Glencoe, 1963), pp. 52–53.

counts of institutional functioning, at least at the small-group level. In the case of leaders, of course, analyses of individuals and their interactions may clarify the control mechanisms of large systems. The George and George analyses of Wilson's dealings with Lloyd George and Clemenceau at Paris and of Wilson's relationship with Lodge during the confirmation fight take into account both the dispositions of the actors and the relationships among their roles. The first of these analyses provides the beginnings of a general account of some of the possible states of the social system of the international conference and the second is a contribution to the literature on executive-legislative relations. In this respect, we should also note the work of Nathan Leites, especially his codification of the psychological orientations governing the political behavior of French legislators and his complementary case study, with Melnik, exhibiting the play of the legislators' psychology in an actual decision-making process.[14]

At a lower societal level and by means of somewhat more mundane procedures, Hodgson, Levinson and Zaleznik[15] have made progress toward the systematic analysis of how personal psychology aggregates. They have conducted extensive field observations of the psychological aspects of behavior in organizational settings. Organizing their observations under the rubric of "the executive role constellation," these investigators provide a detailed account of the ways that individual patterns of role performance intersect among the three top executives of an organization (in this case a mental hospital). Possibilities for applying identical or similar analytic procedures to political groups are substantial. One ingenious effort that involves at least a close approximation of the observation of organizational functioning in a natural setting is reported by Barber in *Power in Committees*.[16] Barber enlisted the cooperation of a number of "real" political groups (town boards of finance) and used psy-

---

[14] Nathan Leites, *On the Game of Politics in France* (Stanford, Calif.: Stanford University Press, 1959); and Constantin Melnik and Nathan Leites, *The House without Windows: France Selects a President* (Evanston, Ill.: Row, Peterson, 1958).

[15] Richard C. Hodgson, Daniel J. Levinson, and Abraham Zaleznik, *The Executive Role Constellation* (Boston: Division of Research, Harvard University Graduate School of Business Administration, 1965).

[16] James D. Barber, *Power in Committees: An Experiment in the Governmental Process* (Chicago: Rand McNally, 1966).

chological data on their members to help explain variations in the ways the groups performed certain tasks under controlled conditions.

It is sometimes the case that only by satisfactorily locating political actors in their situational contexts is it possible to find the ways in which personality is linked to political involvement. In this respect, the work of Browning and Jacob[17] is of considerable significance. Browning and Jacob used McClelland TAT's (projective personality tests in which subjects tell fantasy stories about a series of pictures and the stories are coded, according to well-validated criteria, for levels of need for achievement, power, and affiliation). They administered these tests to matched samples of politicians and non-politicians in the northern city of "Eastport" and to samples of politicians in two Louisiana parishes, "Casino" and "Christian." The most striking impressions left by their findings, when considered independently of situational factors, were (1) the lack of aggregate motivational differences between the politicians and the businessmen and (2) the extreme heterogeneity of the politicians on the McClelland measures. However, once controls were introduced for situational factors, particularly the actual (as opposed to the formal) norms and expectations connected with various political offices in the three communities, distinct motivational profiles began to emerge. Politicians fitting into what might be described as a "hard-driving activist" syndrome, which Browning has identified operationally in terms of high scores in the needs for achievement and power and low scores in the need for affiliation, were found in some political contexts and not in others.[18]

In the Eastport political system, Browning and Jacob note that, on the one hand, "expectations are prevalent that it is possible to go to state legislative office or higher" and, on the other, alternative non-political options for achievement in business are limited. In Louisiana, "there is no consensus that the

---

[17] Rufus Browning and Herbert Jacob. "Power Motivation and the Political Personality," *Public Opinion Quarterly*, 28 (1964), 75–90.

[18] This syndrome is actually reported in a later paper by Browning: "The Interaction of Personality and Political System in Decisions to Run for Office: Some Data and a Simulation Technique," *Journal of Social Issues*, 24:3 (1968), 93–110. The earlier paper makes personality comparisons on a variable-by-variable basis. I am indebted to Professor Browning for clarifying these matters for me.

important decisions are to be made in the political process," and "opportunities for power and achievement abound in the commercial and industrial life of the area." Furthermore, the Eastport politicians are generally higher on the high-power-and-achievement, low-affiliation syndrome than are the politicians in Louisiana.

The same pattern of differences can be found *within* each of the communities if the occupants of offices that provide possibilities for power and achievement are compared with the occupants of offices, such as sinecures, which do not offer these possibilities. Browning and Jacob analyse situational variables with great subtlety, classifying offices in terms of actual community expectations rather than formal requirements. Thus, the office of Justice of the Peace is coded as high in power potential in Casino Parish, where this official plays an important role in the relations between gamblers and parish authorities; in Christian Parish, which has no gambling, this office is coded as low in power. In some instances, Browning and Jacob were also able to interview defeated candidates for the various offices. Since the defeated candidates were similar in personality to the imcumbents, the investigators' confidence was increased in the conclusion that the stimulus characteristics of the office have their effect at the stage of recruitment and pre-selection, rather than by changing the McClelland score of the imcumbent after he is installed.

In the course of locating actor motivations in situational contexts, Browning and Jacob in effect characterize situations (community contexts and roles) in terms both of actual practices ("Does a particular local political office lead to higher office in Community X?") and of what Smith (in Panel II of his map) calls "situational norms" ("What is the consensual expectation in Community X of the consequences of running for a particular office?"). Clearly, an actor's *own* expectations—which may not be consistent with community expectations, assuming that there *is* a community consensus—will also be a key intervening variable mediating between his motivational processes and the situation. Browning shows this in another report of certain Eastport findings that were not alluded to in the paper with Jacob. A group of active, striving businessmen who took a leading part in redevelopment in Eastport were found to have the same motivational pattern as the high-power-and-achievement, low-affiliation politicians; but the businessmen came from apolitical families and evidently did not acquire a set of expectations and values that would legitimize partisan politics as a motivational outlet.[19]

The gist of the "building up" strategy, then, is that individual psychological characteristics be observed and analyzed *in situ*. Typically, this will involve direct observations of processes of institutional functioning over what necessarily must be rather brief periods of time. Often, as in the Browning and Jacob research, it is necessary to begin by studying microscopic slices of the universe which would eventually have to be studied in order to achieve satisfactory understanding. The presumption, however, is that such limited, short-term analyses can be proliferated and made to dovetail and cumulate towards explanations of still larger aspects of system functioning.

Relating Frequencies of Psychological Characteristics to System Characteristics

Sample survey techniques now make it practical to obtain censuses of the psychological dispositions of the members of large social systems based on direct observation. Among the

---

[19] Browning, *op. cit.* The observations on the interplay of personality and situation in Browning and Jacob's work more than vindicate a strategy first proposed by Harold D. Lasswell in *Psychopathology and Politics* (Chicago: University of Chicago Press, 1930); paperback edition with "Afterthoughts: Thirty Years Later" (New York: Viking Press, 1960). The strategy is that of isolating "functionally comparable" processes and phenomena for study in order to eliminate the high degree of "noise" and heterogeneity one finds when one examines personality concomitants of roles that are formally, but not actually, similar (such as in the Justice-of-Peace office in the two Louisiana parishes). Browning and Jacob's careful isolation of comparable situational opportunities for the exercise of power is a counterpart of Lasswell's strategy in devising his "political type" construct. Individuals fitting into Laswell's "political" (or power-centered) type seek out situations that are comparable in that they permit the exercise of power. These situations may or may not be part of the formal political process. As Lasswell puts it, "the simple fact that a role is performed that is conventionally perceived as political . . . does not warrant classifying a person among the political personalities nor, conversely, does failure to play a conventionally recognized political role necessarily imply that the person is not power-oriented." He goes on to suggest that all social processes—not just those that are conventionally labeled "political"—need to be studied "if the political personalities, in the *functional* sense, are to be identified. The point is implied when . . . it is said that during the rapid growth phase of a private capitalistic economy the most power-centered persons engage in 'business.' " Harold D. Lasswell, "A Note on 'Types' of Political Personality: Nuclear, Co-Relational, Developmental," *Journal of Social Issues*, 24:3 (1968), 81–91. Quotation at p. 84.

difficulties of the early culture-and-personality research, especially the work on national character, was the reliance on unsatisfactory samples and, more often, on indirect personality indicators of the sort noted above. Commonly, a single national character type was inferred from various properties and products of a social system; then the character type was used to explain many of these same attributes of the system.

As we noted in Chapter One, students of electoral behavior have lately begun to develop survey-data-based theories relating the frequency of psychological characteristics in large populations to certain overall features of institutional functioning. The kinds of psychological characteristics they have worked with—the voter's sense of identification with a political party, his interest in politics, his disposition to vote—are not central to the psychic functioning of most individuals. In fact, as we saw, most political scientists would not label these as "personality" variables, although, by and large, psychologists would. But there is no basic obstacle to extending the survey approach to include observations of deeper psychological characteristics. In the voting literature, the best presently available examples of the use of survey data to explain system characteristics are the "surge and decline" thesis and the analysis of "politicization" in the French and American electorates by Converse and Dupeux.

"Surge and decline" is an attempt to deal with, among other things, an almost perfectly consistent system regularity in American politics—the loss of Congressional seats in the mid-term elections by the party that won the Presidency the previous election year. The most common explanation of this phenomenon presumes that members of the electorate pay a good bit of attention to politics: it is assumed that Presidential actions tend to antagonize voters, that consequently the Presidential "honeymoon" reaches an end, and that the President's party is then punished by the voters in the mid-term election.

The "surge and decline" explanation proceeds from different and somewhat more complex assumptions. The first step of the explanation is the observation that mid-term elections are evidently of much less interest to the electorate than are the presidential-year elections, since turnout at the polls is about 20 per cent less in the former than in the latter. Then, through survey measurement, an assessment is made of the characteristics of the electorate that appear at the polls under these two stimulus circumstances. The mid-term electorate is very heavily composed of politically interested party-identifiers who vote in all elections and who tend regularly to vote for the party of their standing commitment. In the presidential year, the electorate additionally includes many voters with less stable attachments to the parties and with much weaker political interest, the so-called "peripheral voters." These voters are drawn in by the excitement of the presidential campaign, and their vote tends to be one-sidedly for the candidate most favored by factors specific to that election—candidate attractiveness and such short-term issues as the present level of prosperity or the nation's current military commitments.

In giving lopsided support to the winner of a presidential election, the peripheral voters also enable the winning presidential candidate to carry in on his coattails a more than normal quota of Congressmen from his party. But when the mid-term elections come, this tide recedes to a normal vote based on the party identifications of the "core" electorate—the citizens who vote in all elections. The seats that the President's party won in the presidential year revert to the opposition party. We thus have a theory that explains presidential-party seat loss not in terms of the conscious actions of voters in the year that the loss occurred, but rather in terms of inadvertent behavior of the least politically involved segment of the electorate in the *previous* election year.[20]

The comparative analysis of French and American political orientations by Converse and Dupeux, like "surge and decline," introduces a new, data-based explanation for a political regularity that had previously been explained speculatively on the basis of erroneous psychological assumptions. The regularity is the

---

[20] Angus Campbell, *et al.*, *Elections and the Political Order* (New York: Wiley, 1966). Campbell's analysis of surge and decline is at pp. 40–62. For an independently arrived at similar analysis, see William A. Glaser, "Fluctuations in Turnout," in William N. McPhee and William A. Glaser, eds., *Public Opinion and Congressional Elections* (New York: Free Press of Glencoe, 1962), pp. 19–51. Glaser also conveniently reproduces examples of the standard efforts to explain this political regularity in terms of voter disenchantment with the incumbent president's party. As "obvious" as the surge-and-decline thesis may be, it is still not fully recognized in discussion of the American mid-term elections. For an ingenious application of surge-and-decline reasoning to the regular British phenomenon of loss of by-elections by the Government, see Anthony King, "Why All Governments Lose By-Elections," *New Society*, 11:286 (1968), 413–15.

high level of support by the French electorate for new parties—
"flash" parties, such as the Poujadists and the various Gaullist
parties. There is much more of this sort of electoral volatility in
France than in the United States.

Traditional explanations often have alluded to the rational-
ism of the Frenchman, his predilection to luxuriate in small
ideological distinctions. To abbreviate a longer and more complicated analysis, the Converse and Dupeux survey analysis points
to a quite different explanation: the fascination with ideological
distinctions in France evidently does not pervade the general
population, but rather is typical of a very slim stratum of political activists. What distinguishes the general population, among
other things, is an exceptionally low level of standing attachments to political parties. About 45 per cent of the French are
party identifiers, compared with perhaps 65 per cent of the
Norwegians and 75 per cent of the Americans. Thus, there is
evidently a much greater reservoir of uncommitted voters in
France than in the United States and, hence, a greater market for
new political parties.[21]

MODIFYING THE FREQUENCY ANALYSIS TO TAKE ACCOUNT OF "NON-ADDITIVITY"

The surge and decline and the French-American analyses
are concerned with gross rates of behavior. For the purposes of
these analyses, it is feasible to abstract a few very superficial
psychological characteristics from the many idiosyncrasies that
mark each voter—characteristics such as party identification and
degree of interest in politics. In all other respects, each individual is treated as identical—like individual molecules of gas in a
thermodynamics demonstration. However:

> People are not like molecules in a gas. Some are
> different from others and some have more effect upon

---

[21] See the chapter by Philip Converse and Georges Dupeux in Campbell,
et al., op. cit., pp. 269–91. For a summary and critique of recent work on
"structural" or "compositional" effects in which survey analyses are modified
to include data on group characteristics (generated by the original survey
data), see Arnold S. Tannenbaum and Jerald G. Bachman, "Structural versus
Individual Effects," *American Journal of Sociology,* 69 (1964), 585–95. Also
see James S. Coleman, "Relational Analysis: The Study of Social Organization
with Survey Methods," *Human Organization,* 17 (1958), 28–36.

society than others. It is still a good question whether without Lenin there would have been the October Revolution.[22]

Or, as Ackley puts it, "aggregation is a legitimate procedure when the behavior of the individual units subject to aggregation is basically similar."[23] Coleman's example of the possible deficiences of a micro-macro proposition relating group productivity to the members' feelings of attachment to the group helps pin down a critical way in which the "behavior of the individual units" in a political or social system may not have "basically similar" consequences. Coleman points out that we might study a group over time and find the members' feelings of closeness to the group had, on the average, increased. Yet, if just one person's attachment to the group decreased, group productivity might decrease because "this one person may be the group leader, who is crucial to group productivity or have some other key role in affecting productivity. His decreased cohesiveness could more than offset the increased cohesiveness of the others."[24]

Thus, the appropriateness of Herbert Hyman's[25] observation that we cannot simply add the characteristics of individuals in systems (e.g., the number of authoritarians in the system) in order to reach conclusions about the characteristics of the system as a whole (e.g., whether it is likely to have an authoritarian political structure). Rather, we need ways of "weighting the sums" to account for the greater impact of the dispositions of actors in key roles. Moreover, the consequences of harnessing personality needs to institutional roles may be complex. Coleman

---

[22] May Brodbeck, "Methodological Individualisms: Definition and Reduction," *Philosophy of Science*, 25 (1958), 21. This essay is generally interesting on the logic of science questions raised by "levels of analysis" and micromacro relationships. Also see Chapter Eleven on "The Reduction of Theories," in Ernest Nagel, *The Structure of Science* (New York: Harcourt, Brace and World, 1961).

[23] Gardner Ackley, *Macroeconomic Theory* (New York: Macmillan, 1961), p. 573.

[24] James S. Coleman, "Group and Individual Variables," in his *Introduction to Mathematical Sociology* (New York: Free Press of Glencoe, 1964), pp. 84–90.

[25] Herbert Hyman, "The Modification of a Personality-Centered Conceptual System When the Project is Translated from a National to a Cross-National Study," in Bjorn Christiansen, Herbert Hyman, and Ragnar Rommetveit, *Cross-National Social Research* (Oslo: International Seminar, Institute for Social Research, 1951, mimeograph).

points to the example of the group member whose "productivity contributes *negatively* to . . . group productivity (e.g., the harder he works, the more he gets in the way of others) . . . an increase in his cohesiveness may offset the increased productivity due to the increased cohesiveness of the others." Shils observes, with reference to the implicit assumption in *The Authoritarian Personality* that authoritarian characteristics in the population lead to authoritarian political practices, that: "More than one set of personality characteristics" is needed "to make a political movement. . . . Movements and institutions, even if they are authoritarian, require both more and less than authoritarian personality structures," and even "a liberal democratic society itself could probably not function satisfactorily with only 'democratic liberal personalities' to fill all its roles."[26]

"Working Back" from Theoretical Analyses of Systems and Their Psychological Requirements

"Building up" toward an aggregate analysis via observations of specific decision-making processes offers one approach to weighting for role incumbency. A complementary approach, especially appropriate for initial clarification of the problems of analyzing psychological effects on large systems, is that of model-building and simulation (both informal and formal). We can seek to make explicit our models of political systems and subsystems, stipulating the roles and their requirements in order to identify the key empirical problems of determining the fit between role and the personal dispositions of role incumbents.

A particularly challenging statement of the kinds of operations that might go into such an effort to "work back" from a model to an aggregative analysis that attempts to relate role requirements to personality dispositions was made by Lasswell in his essay of a number of years ago on "Democratic Character."[27] In essence, Lasswell's strategy is to specify the behavioral requirements of an ideal-typical "democratic community" and then, drawing upon the current state of knowledge about person-

---

[26] Edward Shils, in Christie and Jahoda, eds., *op. cit.*, pp. 45, 48

[27] Harold D. Lasswell, "Democratic Character " in *Political Writings of Harold D. Lasswell* (Glencoe, Ill.: Free Press, 1951), pp. 465–525. For an expansion on the summary here see my "Harold D. Lasswell's Concept of Democratic Character," *Journal of Politics*, 30 (1968), 696–709.

ality psychology, to theorize about the kinds of personality types necessary—and permissible—for its functioning. Using the model of the system as one base point and the personality hypotheses as another, the analyst is provided with a reasonably formal theory about the personality and social structural relations that are of analytic concern. He can then go on to advance hypotheses and make empirical observations about the requirements of roles in real-world political systems and the degree to which the role demands fit the personalities of the role incumbents.

One of the more useful aspects of Lasswell's strategy consists of working with a conception of personality (or character) "strength": this notion refers to the intensity and stability of the psychological determinants of action. Its use sensitizes the analyst to examine the degree to which social and political regularities are maintained by "external" sanctions and the degree to which they are maintained by the internalized motivations of the participants. In general, the stronger an actor's motives, the less the need for structural safeguards to insure that his behavior will follow predictable patterns.[28]

III. SUMMARY AND CONCLUSIONS

The intellectual operations necessary for systematic aggregation remain to be perfected. It would be unfortunate if psychological data on the members of political systems were not used, where appropriate, in explaining system regularities. Past reductionist tendencies in micro-macro analyses no doubt account for the present absence of well-developed procedures for analyzing aggregation.

In moving from analyses of underlying personality structure

---

[28] Lasswell's attempt to bring out the interdependence of motivational intensity and the need for external sanctions is paralleled in J. Milton Yinger, "Research Implications of a Field View of Personality," *American Journal of Sociology*, 68 (1963), 580–92. For work at a less lofty level than Lasswell's democratic character essay which employs explicit (and commendably precise) modeling of personality and role-relationships, see Rufus Browning, "The Interaction of Personality and Political System in Decisions to Run for Office," *op. cit.* On the general strategy of "working back," see Alex Inkeles, "Society, Social Structure, and Child Socialization," in John A. Clausen, ed., *Socialization and Society* (Boston: Little, Brown, 1968), pp. 73–129.

to analyses of the political and social structure, we need to be sensitive to the many links in the inferential chain—each of them a possible source of complications. Thus, deeper levels of personality are imperfectly associated with political belief; personality and belief have varying behavior consequences, depending upon situational stimuli; and the behavior of individuals and types aggregates in ways that are often not additive in any simple arithmetic fashion. But a number of complementary strategies can be pursued in moving toward acceptable procedures for aggregation, including: (1) "building up" from small-scale analyses of personality in social situations; (2) relating the frequency of psychological characteristics in populations to system regularities; (3) attempting to take account of the location of actors in social and political structures as well as of their psychological characteristics; and (4) "working back" from formalization of role requirements and the personality types that fit them.

CHAPTER SIX

Concluding Remarks

There is a cyclical quality to work on personality and politics. One can point to a number of flurries of interest in these issues: to bodies of writings that began to emerge, enlisted the enthusiasm of some investigators and readers, and then became discredited, largely because of the failure to develop firm, communicable standards of inquiry. Work in this area has, to an excessive degree, been "stimulating" and "suggestive," but "controversial" and "inconclusive." Yet the subject matter, and the intellectual and practical needs to come to grips with it, are so compelling that each new generation produces its own political-personality Quixotes: scholars, journalists, clinicians, and others who feel compelled to examine the personal roots of politics.

It might be argued that these efforts are doomed to rise and fall because of the "scientifically" intractable nature of the subject matter—that personality and politics will remain a sanctuary for the insightful spinner of perceptive tales, the political analyst who is content, in Freud's phrase, to "have merely written a psychoanalytic novel."[1] Novels are not to be deprecated, and personality-and-politics inquiry is centrally dependent—especially for its hypotheses—on empathy, creative imagination, and intuitive insight. But, as I have tried to suggest, there are strategies for demonstration as well as for discovery; and to the degree that the impact of personal dispositions on politics is important,

---

[1] Sigmund Freud, *Leonardo da Vinci and a Memory of His Childhood, Standard Edition of the Complete Psychological Works of Sigmund Freud,* 11 (London: Hogarth, 1957), p. 134 (originally published in 1910).

the need to demonstrate and not just speculate about the nature of that impact increases.

I. RECAPITULATION

Much of what students of personality and politics have done and need to do can be considered under three headings: the psychological analysis of single political actors, the analysis of types of political actors, and the analysis of aggregative effects of individuals and types of individuals on political processes and institutions. Typologies evolve out of the regularities—the recurrent similarities and differences—we observe in examining the psychology of individual political actors. Individual diagnosis, in turn, is aided by reference to the regularities that have been observed in the past and crystallized into typological formulations. This is especially the case when the typology is theoretically well developed, since such typologies are, in effect, summaries of the general propositions that cover certain kinds of individual cases. But neither individuals nor types are intrinsically interesting to most students of politics: their aggregative impact on institutional functioning is what matters.

In discussing individual, typological, and aggregative analysis, it has been recurrently helpful to turn to Smith's elucidation of the relationships among five classes of variables that concern students of political personality: (1) political behavior itself; (2) situational antecedents of behavior; (3) the different aspects of personality processes and dispositions (attitudes and underlying modes of psychic functioning adapted to the requirements of object appraisal, mediation of self-other relations, and ego defense); (4) social determinants of personality; and (5) the past and present features of larger political and social systems that determine many of the basic conditions of the immediate environments within which personality development and political behavior occur.

Smith's map formulation has considerable utility. By reminding us that the variables of political psychology can be sorted into these broad categories and of the relationships among the categories, the map serves to obviate a number of empty debates about which of the various classes of, in fact, complementary variables are "better suited" to explain behavior. Each of the four classes of variables that connect directly or indirectly with the political behavior panel of Smith's map has at one time or another been viewed in reductionist isolation as *the* appropriate source for the explanation of behavior. Thus, there have been debates over whether it is more appropriate to seek psychological or situational determinants of action. The map reminds us that we need to examine the interaction of both, although, depending upon the circumstance, one class of variables may better account for the variance than another, or one may be more practically manipulable than another. There have also been debates about whether "social characteristics," i.e., aspects of social background, are more important than personality in determining behavior. A more fruitful approach is to analyze the former as antecedents of the latter and to attempt to come to an understanding of the developmental processes through which social environment shapes personality. Finally, as in certain of Fromm's formulations that were briefly considered in Chapter Four, there sometimes have been debates about whether the formation of political personality patterns were best explained in terms of the larger (in Smith's terms, "distal") social environment or in terms of the immediate social environment. Is "the market economy," for example, more important than family socialization practices as a determinant of authoritarian personality patterns? Again, the opposition is a false one: remote environmental variables are best seen as being *mediated by* socialization practices in the immediate environment.

A further merit of the kind of expository aerial view provided by Smith's map is its contribution to contextual analysis— to theorizing and inquiry that attempts to specify the complex interplay among and within the five classes of variables. Multivariate analysis that is illuminated by sensitivity to the complex interplay of different classes of complementary variables is especially urgent in studies of personality and politics. The complexities are of the following sort: rarely do we find simple and direct relationships between some indicator of personality and political behavior—relationships that are present under all circumstances and in all populations. The strong relationships and the theoretically and practically important relationships are likely to take the form of interactions; that is, they are likely to be contingent upon some further circumstances. (This helps explain the weak and unstable correlations between measures of personality and political measures which were found in some of the early quantitative literature.)

Some of the contingencies under which the student of personality and politics should find it promising to look for relationships were specified in Chapter Two in the course of discussing the various standard reasons that have been advanced for not anticipating significant payoffs in the study of personality and politics: personal variability affects behavior in ambiguous and unstructured environments, in situations where sanctions are weak, when roles allow the actor some discretionary power, etc. It has been possible to point to examples, in the growing body of contextually conceived personality-and-politics inquiry, of investigations in which important relationships were observable only by searching for the appropriate contingent interactions.[2]

Another set of distinctions is that of phenomenology, dynamics, and genesis; these terms are useful for sorting out the different kinds of operations involved in the psychological diagnosis of political actors, and for ordering diagnostic operations in terms of both the directness of their bearing on explanations of political action and the degree to which they can be carried out in a more or less standardized fashion. Accounts of the phenomenology of a political actor—of the regularities in the ways that he presents himself to the observer—are the most immediately relevant supplement to situational data in predicting and explaining the actor's behavior. And these accounts, if they stay close enough to the texture of the observables, can be agreed upon by investigators with theoretical interests as diverse as learning-theory and psychoanalysis. The constructs used to characterize psychological dynamics—the inner trends accounting for the outer regularities—are more difficult to agree upon and are less immediately necessary for analyses of behavior. By and large, explana-

---

[2] For examples, see Daniel Katz, *et al.*, "The Measurement of Ego-Defense as Related to Attitude Change," *Journal of Personality*, 25 (1957), 465–74; Rufus Browning and Herbert Jacob, "Power Motivation and the Political Personality," *Public Opinion Quarterly*, 38 (1964), 75–90; and Browning, "The Interaction of Personality and Political System in Decisions to Run for Office: Some Data and a Simulation Technique," *Journal of Social Issues*, 24:3 (1968), 93–110.

tions of genesis pose even more difficult questions of validation, and these are most remote from the immediate nexus of behavior. In moving toward firm demonstrations of assertions about the phenomenology, dynamics, and genesis of the personalities of individuals and types, the basic problems are the standard ones of reliability (developing stable observational procedures) and validity (developing procedures that measure what they are alleged to measure). Again, the order of difficulty in proceeding parallels the immediacy of need for political analysis: reliability is easier to establish than validity, and the need for it often is more immediately pressing. As long as we have reliable measures, we can proceed to analyze behavior on the basis of a kind of atheoretical operationalism. Very shortly, however, we will want to know what it is we are observing, and, in general, personality-and-politics research has suffered from too little theoretical clarity about the tasks at hand. A good bit of clarity is gained simply by the exercise of stipulating phenomenology, dynamics, and genesis and indicating their interconnections—that is, by formally stating the explanatory argument.

The traditions for proceeding rigorously with analyses of phenomenology, dynamics, and genesis are best developed for typological studies; the development of more satisfactory standards for the psychological diagnosis of individual political actors is both needed and possible, however. When we move on from diagnosis of individuals and types to analysis of their effects, we need to employ our diagnostic techniques; but we also need to examine the several causal links in the chain that runs from underlying psychological dispositions, through attitudes, individual actions, and their aggregative consequences. The procedures for systematic analysis of aggregation are insufficiently developed; among the complementary strategies that seem promising are: (1) analyses of actors and their psychology in the context of the actual situations within which their political behavior occurs; (2) psychological censuses of individuals participating in the institutional processes one is attempting to explain; (3) modification of such censuses to take account of the differential impact of actors that results from the roles they perform; and (4) more or less formal theorizing designed to identify critical relationships between "role requirements" and the personalities of role incumbents.

II. THE EMPHASIS ON EGO DEFENSE

There has been a preoccupation throughout this analysis with mechanisms and processes of ego defense. Are there objective means of distinguishing political behavior that has its roots in the ego's need to defend itself against inner conflicts from political behavior that does not have such roots? As we have seen, the fact that political behavior is not rational, in the sense of employing the appropriate means to the actor's perceived ends, is an insufficient indicator that the behavior is based in ego defense. Irrationality may also be "cognitive": it may stem from imperfect information, from using°cultural stereotypes, from insufficient time to make the appropriate calculations, and from other non-defensive sources.[3] My suggestions have involved pointing to ways of "objectifying" the often implicit procedures used to make clinical diagnoses.

I remarked in Chapter One that anyone attempting to explicate, clarify, and, if possible, improve upon the methodological assumptions of the existing personality-and-politics literature would find himself called upon to grapple with the manifestation of depth psychology—that is, the various notions, such as "ego defense," that are in our conceptual arsenal thanks to Freud and his successors. But it would be disingenuous to suggest that this is the only reason for my preoccupation with ego-defensive processes and their indicators. Like most social scientists, I find much of the theoretical apparatus with which Freud explained his clinical findings—especially his metapsychology—ill-adapted to modern empirical inquiry. Nevertheless, although the controversial and confused standing of psychoanalytic personality theory precludes the general acceptance of some psychoanalytically inspired propositions, the ramshackle state of psychoanalytic thought does not preclude heuristic applications.

In particular, since agreement is fairly readily obtained on assertions about phenomenology, the controversial standing of psychoanalysis may not prevent students of politics from employ-

---

[3] Compare M. Brewster Smith's application of his map in his "Personality in Politics: A Conceptual Map, with Application to the Problem of Rationality," in Oliver Garceau, ed., *Political Research and Political Theory* (Cambridge, Mass.: Harvard University Press, 1968), pp. 77–101.

ing what may be its most useful export for their purposes: the clinical portrait in the psychoanalytic literature of the observable regularities in human functioning. For certain purposes—such as the analysis of Woodrow Wilson or of certain of the more puzzling sub-types of authoritarians—it may be desirable to have these intellectual sensitivities that enable us to see the political actor as:

a full-bodied individual living partly in a world of reality and partly in a world of make-believe, beset by conflicts and inner contradictions, yet capable of rational thought and action, moved by forces of which he has little knowledge and by aspirations which are beyond his reach, by turn confused and clearheaded, frustrated and satisfied, hopeful and despairing, selfish and altruistic; in short a complex human being.[4]

The preceding statement is from the conclusion of Hall and Lindzey's summary of Freudian personality theory. One is not obliged to adhere in detail to any of the psychoanalytic orthodoxies simply because he finds this general characterization congenial. What *is* important is to remain open to hypotheses about mental functioning which take account of the possibility that, for some analytic purposes, it is instructive to think in terms of a human animal who, in the course of his development, forms a personality of labyrinthine subtlety and complexity, within which conscious and unconscious elements are intricately intertwined. It is also instructive to assume that the ego must sometimes be understood not only in terms of its external, reality-testing activities, but also in terms of its needs to defend itself internally against impulse and conscience.[5] Beyond this, psychoanalytic and related personality theories should be used as sources of hypotheses rather than dogmatically.

"For some analytic purposes," it is necessary to analyze political actors in the foregoing terms. But for which purposes? In Chapter Two, I attempted to specify a number of circum-

---

[4] Calvin S. Hall and Gardner Lindzey, *Theories of Personality* (New York: Wiley, 1957), p. 72.

[5] This admonition, of course, needs to be stood on its head in comments directed to these old-school personality-and-politics analysts who conceive of behavior wholly in ego-defensive terms.

stances under which ego-defensive needs might be likely to manifest themselves in political behavior. At bottom, however, the problem of "psychopathology and politics"[6] which Lasswell opened up in 1930 is one that still needs empirical examination. We are just now beginning to get estimates (some of which are rather chilling) of the incidence in general populations of what, by various criteria, can be defined as psychopathology.[7] Further work needs to be done on the degree to which psychopathological needs actually receive political channeling. Chapter Two suggested some of the reasons for expecting complex and imperfect connections between any kind of personal variability (including ego-defensive manifestations) and political behavior: in general populations, politics may have too low a cathexis to serve as a conduit for psychological needs; in elite populations, situational exigencies and role requirements may "squeeze out" personal variability. Nevertheless, a cursory inspection of politics and political history reveals countless instances of behavior that seems geared to the private needs of the political actor as well as to the demands of external reality.

III. POLITICAL PERSONALITY AS A DEPENDENT VARIABLE: A NORMATIVE APPLICATION

The student of personality and politics can still profitably return to the ur-contribution to this literature, Lasswell's *Psychopathology and Politics*, a work that does not yield its full message to the casual reader. The author's mode of exposition and his propensity to use terms in specialized ways pose exegetical demands. For example, the two cryptic sentences with which Lasswell concludes his Preface provide the only clue to the major structural principle of the book, which begins with an extreme argument about the psychopathological basis of politics stated in the initial ten chapters, followed by three extraordinarily astringent

---

[6] Harold D. Lasswell, *Psychopathology and Politics* (Chicago: University of Chicago Press, 1930) ; paperback edition with "Afterthoughts: Thirty Years Later" (New York: Viking Press, 1960).

[7] See the sources cited in Jerome G. Manis, *et al.*, "Estimating the Prevalence of Mental Illness," *American Sociological Review*, 29 (1964), 84–89.

chapters dissecting the empirical assumptions of Chapters One through Ten.[8]

In the initial sequence of chapters, Lasswell furnishes: an exposition of the theory of mental functioning in pre-ego-psychology psychoanalysis; a classification—with supporting case histories—of types of political actors (*viz.*, the agitator, the administrator, and the theorist); and a schematic statement of the implications of his account of personality for the political process. The account of personality that Lasswell borrowed from early psychoanalysis was one in which behavior is explained substantially, if not entirely, in terms of needs to cope with unconscious inner conflicts. In such an account, the actor's own perceptions of his motivations are assumed in fact to be rationalizations. Lasswell succinctly illustrates his account by describing behavior under post-hypnotic suggestion: A man is hypnotized and instructed to open an umbrella after he emerges from the hypnotic trance. When he opens the umbrella, he is asked why he opened it. His answer—"to see if it was mine"—is not his "reason," (since he does not consciously know what motivates him), but rather is his rationalization.

To the degree that behavior generally has this quality of being driven by unconscious needs, Lasswell's famous schema of the sources of the behavior of Political Man (private needs displaced on public objects and rationalized in the public interest[9]) obtains. In the rarely discussed final chapters of *Psychopathology*, Lasswell shows that the empirical premise of his account—that behavior is heavily determined by unconscious sources—has not been satisfactorily documented, and he advances methodological and theoretical suggestions for further exploration.

The portion of *Psychopathology* which pushes to its logical

---

[8] This principle of exposition is indicated only by a seemingly casual assertion: "The first part of the book proceeds in a rather dogmatic fashion, and this no doubt tends to obscure the highly unsatisfactory nature of the materials and methods of contemporary psychopathology. The later chapters are given over to the critical and constructive discussion of these materials, and should fully indicate the highly provisional, though potentially significant, character of the whole." Lasswell, *op. cit.*, preface unpaginated.

[9] *Ibid.*, p. 75.

conclusions the premise that behavior is based on unconscious needs and that ostensible reasons for acting are rationalizations is the brilliant treatment of "the politics of prevention" in Chapter Ten. If it is true that "political movements derive their vitality from the displacement of private affects upon public objects,"[10] then we are provided with insight into "the well-known disproportionality between responses and immediate stimuli" in politics.

> Farmers do vote against the Republicans when the crops fail through adverse weather conditions, although reflection would tend to minimize the possibility that the party in power exercises much authority over the weather. Oversights in personal relations which seem very slight do actually give rise to huge affective reactions. The clue to the magnitude of this notorious disproportionality is to be found in the nature of the deeper (earlier) psychological structures of the individual.[11]

This analysis leads Lasswell to the conclusion that standard modes of conflict-resolution—for example, through force, debate, and bargaining and compromise—are doomed to perpetuate political conflicts rather than to settle them. He proposes, instead, a characteristically visionary (yet also characteristically thought-provoking) approach to conflict-resolution involving the investment of great collective resources in the study of the sources of conflict in order to "apply social energy to the abolition of recurrent sources of strain in society."[12]

---

[10] *Ibid.*, p. 173.

[11] *Ibid.*, p. 191.

[12] *Ibid.*, p. 197. Lasswell's treatment of *inter*personal conflict-resolving processes is analogous to his account earlier in the book (pp. 28–37) of psychoanalytic free association as a procedure for resolving *intra*personal conflict and thus eliminating the tendency for reasons to be rationalizations. Lasswell's argument parallels Daniel Katz's emphasis, discussed in Chapter Four, on the inappropriateness of such procedures as the provision of new information for changing attitudes that serve ego-defensive functions. For a summary of the work of Katz and others on the use of "insight" techniques—in effect, simplified equivalents of psychoanalytic free association—for changing ego-defensive attitudes, see Daniel Katz, "The Functional Approach to the Study of Attitudes," *Public Opinion Quarterly*, 24 (1960), 163–204.

It is in connection with proposing how the politics of prevention would be enforced—how societies would come to conduct politics as a process of eliminating rather than perpetuating chronic sources of conflict—that Lasswell suggests a way in which the analysis of personality and politics can be turned to the persisting normative concerns of political studies.[13] In addition to reflecting on the impact of personality on politics, we can also, as Fromm realized, explore the impact of political and other social institutions and practices on personality. By treating political personality as a dependent variable, it is possible to begin turning political analysis to the ends of political evaluation. While well-documented accounts of the human consequences of political practices are not compelling in the sense that satisfactory scientific explanations compel acceptance, they *are* likely to be psychologically persuasive.

> The politics of prevention will insist upon a rigorous audit of the human consequences of prevailing political practices. How does politics affect politicians? One way to consider the human value of social action is to see what that form of social action does to the actors. When a judge has been on the bench thirty years, what manner of man has he become? When an agitator has been agitating for thirty years, what has happened to him? How do different kinds of political administrators compare with doctors, musicians, and scientists? Such a set of inquiries would presuppose that we were able to ascertain the traits with which the various individuals begin to practice their role in society. Were we able to show what certain lines of human endeavor did to the same reactive type, we would lay the foundation for a profound change in society's esteem for various occupations.[14]

> [The practitioners of a preventive politics would] gradually win respect in society among puzzled people

[13] On the prospects for applying empirical knowledge to the traditional problems of evaluation, see Robert A. Dahl, "The Evaluation of Political Systems," in Ithiel de Sola Pool, ed., *Contemporary Political Science: Toward Empirical Theory* (New York: McGraw-Hill, 1967), pp. 166–81.

[14] Lasswell, *op. cit.*, p. 198.

who feel their responsibilities and who respect objective findings.[15]

IV. EPILOGUE

I conclude by descending from the flight of fancy. The small population of students of personality and politics has as yet not contributed enough that is well established on the impact of personality on politics—much less on the impact of politics on personality.

It would simply perpetuate the standard difficulties of personality-and-politics writings to suggest that by employing the magic bag of tricks of the psychologist, the political scientist will immediately unravel the mysteries of his subject-matter, be they empirical or normative. What I have presented is not a set of how-to-do-it instructions designed to produce forthwith a comprehensive corpus of reliable, valid, and theoretically interesting observations about the influence of personality, in the various senses of the term, on politics. A good bit of solid effort by a larger component of investigators than is presently engaged in working on these issues will be necessary if we are to begin to chart the terrain with something like the completeness of, say, the present state of knowledge about voting behavior. I have suggested a number of reasons why our present cartography is inadequate. An additional one is in the elusiveness of the phenomena that concern students of personality and politics; the objects of analysis are complicated and difficult to observe. The ambiguities of our theories and vocabulary make them difficult even to think about clearly.

My operating assumption is not that perfection in personality-and-politics study is needed, but rather that improvement is possible. Work that escapes the classical difficulties of such inquiries is already appearing. My further and more fundamental assumption is that the rather tedious task of clarifying strategies of analysis and demonstration is important because, as I attempted to demonstrate in Chapter One, the effects of the psychological variables that mediate between stimulus and response

---

[15] *Ibid.*, p. 203.

in politics can be exceedingly great. Thus, it was illuminating to look at the Cuban Missile Crisis as a vivid example of an infinitely larger set of instances. On that occasion, with nuclear war in the balance, decisions had to be made by American decision-makers about which stimuli would produce which Soviet responses. The decisions necessarily entailed assumptions about the psychology of the Soviet leadership—the ways in which alternative stimuli were likely to be processed with what behavioral consequences. The option of not presenting the Soviet leadership with a stimulus was nonexistent, since even inaction is a stimulus; and, in a sense, the option of making no assumptions about the psychology of the Soviet leadership, "since our knowledge of these matters is so uncertain," did not exist. Whenever actions are taken with a view to producing reactions from one's counterparts, psychological assumptions are being made, whether or not self-consciously.

It may be that we can limp along for further millennia without clarifying our assumptions about personality and politics and without devoting major intellectual resources to testing the assumptions against reality; but the possible consequences of continuing to muddle through may be too grim to contemplate. As one reflects on political history and contemporary politics, the phrase "living partly in a world of reality and partly in a world of make-believe—yet capable of rational thought and actions" does not seem far from the mark as a characterization of *homo politicus*. Even if the probability were very slight that psychological inquiry into politics might encourage governing practices that were more firmly located in the world of reality, the risks would seem to warrant more substantial colonies of investigators on the borders between psychology—including personality psychology—and political science.

A Bibliographical Note

These bibliographical observations are divided into five sections. The first suggests some general introductions to the study of personality. The second lists methodological and theoretical investigations that relate the study of politics to the study of personality. Section three includes studies of the personalities of individual political actors. Section four points to some of the many typologies of personality that have been suggested, especially typological studies of political actors. The fifth section is concerned with analyses of "aggregation"—ranging from small groups through institutions, nations, and international relations —in which personality investigation has played a part. In short, the first two sections of this bibliography deal with the issues Greenstein raises in his initial two chapters and with background issues that underlie his entire essay. The final three sections parallel his Chapters Three through Five.

Since the total corpus of writings involving psychology and politics is far too large to cover here, these observations are necessarily highly selective. They do not attempt to include all of the good work on political psychology and have doubtless overlooked some particularly valuable studies. Moreover, some not-so-good work that has illustrative or historical value is included. The selectivity of the suggestions is especially great in the general-background suggestions of the first section. The writings noted in that section are simply a few of the works which the bibliographer, a political scientist, has found personally useful as background to his reading in the personality-and-politics literature.

The division of the personality-and-politics literature into studies of individuals, typologies, and aggregation has drawbacks as well as advantages. This classificatory scheme does not draw together works from categories that cut across the classifications —studies of ideology and personality, for example, which may be drawn from investigations of individuals, of types of individuals with certain traits, or of aggregations. To remedy this, I have grouped clusters of articles which treat a single subject—such as ideology and personality—in one place, in this case under "Typologies," though some of the articles might better be placed under "Individuals" or "Aggregation" because of the approach used. As Greenstein indicates, "any actual contribution to the literature may in fact contain more than one of the three modes of analyses."

In drawing together a large proportion of the investigations referred to by Greenstein in the body of the book and in the chapter footnotes and to indicate further readings in several areas, *I have frequently used Greenstein's own words in describing the particular utility of one of his references.* Since this is meant to be more a compilation of convenience than an original contribution (although I have registered my own judgments), I have avoided the cumbersome procedure of using quotation marks and giving page references when I draw on Greenstein's remarks on the literature.

I. GENERAL BACKGROUND: INTRODUCTIONS TO THE STUDY OF PERSONALITY

Among the best introductions to the range of personality theories and approaches is Calvin S. Hall and Gardner Lindzey, *Theories of Personality* (New York: Wiley, 1957). Hall and Lindzey consider the principal psychoanalytic theorists (Freud, Adler, Jung, Fromm, Sullivan); non-psychoanalytic theorists, such as Murray, Lewin, and Allport; and academic approaches, such as learning theory. Ruth L. Munroe lowers her lens on the psychoanalytic theorists—whose approaches she compares and criticizes—in her *Schools of Psychoanalytic Thought* (New York: Dryden Press, 1955). For clinical psychiatric approaches, see Silvano Arieti, ed., *American Handbook of Psychiatry* (New

York: Basic Books, 1959), especially Volume 1, and Frederick C. Redlich and Daniel X. Freedman, *The Theory and Practice of Psychiatry* (New York: Basic Books, 1966).

Psychoanalytic concepts and hypotheses have had a place in the personality-and-politics literature far out of proportion to the attention they receive in general psychology or even in personality psychology. In part, at least, this may be a consequence of the tendency of investigators to turn to personality analyses only when they are faced with the need to account for seemingly "irrational" or "inexplicable" behavior. Psychoanalysis, of course, even in its modern ego-psychology variants, is *par excellence* an approach specialized to unravelling and explicating such behavior. The basic theoretical text that applies psychoanalytic theory to psychopathology is Otto Fenichel, *The Psychoanalytic Theory of Neurosis* (New York: Norton, 1945). This book is still of great value, although the fact that nothing written subsequently can really replace it must imply something about the likelihood that a genuinely cumulative scholarship on these matters will emerge from the psychoanalytic fraternity.

Two highly divergent thinkers whose work is of the greatest interest to political psychologists are Erik H. Erikson and Jean Piaget. Erikson's *Identity and the Life Cycle* (New York: International Universities Press, 1959) is an incisive path into his thinking. Piaget's work has not penetrated the social sciences to the degree that the work of Erikson and other post-Freudians has; but his formulations are of considerable potential relevance to the student of politics, especially his book with Barbel Inhelder, *The Growth of Logical Thinking, from Childhood to Adolescence* (New York: Basic Books, 1958). Attempts to present systematic expositions of Piaget's prolific writings include John H. Flavell's *The Developmental Psychology of Jean Piaget* (Princeton, N.J.: Van Nostrand, 1963).

Perhaps the most convenient comprehensive source to the many mansions in contemporary psychology—including personality studies—is the monumental seven-volume series edited by Sigmund Koch, *Psychology: A Study of a Science*. This set of essays and reviews, published by McGraw-Hill, was set in motion by the American Psychological Association in the early 1950's and appeared in the early 1960's. Of particular interest to the student of personality and politics are Volumes 2, 3, 5, and 6.

Also see Gardner Lindzey and Elliot Aronson, eds., *Handbook of Social Psychology*, 1–5 (Reading, Mass.: Addison-Wesley, 1968–1969).

One convenient way into the vast periodical literature relevant to personality-and-politics inquiry is through the reader edited by Neil J. Smelser and William T. Smelser, *Personality and Social Systems* (New York: Wiley, 1963), which also has an instructive analytic introduction. Among the sources for finding one's way through the periodical literature are: the current and cumulated *Index Medicus*, published by the U.S. Department of Health, Education, and Welfare (the listings under "politics" include many articles on psychology and politics); *Psychological Abstracts* and the *Cumulated Index to the Psychological Abstracts, 1927–1960* (Boston: G. K. Hall and Co.), both of which list a wealth of relevant articles under "politics," "government," "law," "social power," "voting," and the like; the *Social Sciences and Humanities Index* (New York: H. W. Wilson Co.), which gives relevant references under "social psychology," "psychology and history," and other headings; the *Public Affairs Information Service Annual Cumulated Bulletin* (New York: Public Affairs Information Service, Inc.), which includes listings for "political psychology," "psychiatry and law," "psychological warfare," and so forth; the *Readers' Guide to Periodical Literature* (New York: H. W. Wilson Co.), which catalogues articles on personality and politics from popular periodicals. Excellent bibliographical articles on the full range of issues that concern psychologists are to be found in the *Annual Review of Psychology* (Stanford, Calif.: Annual Reviews, Inc.).

Relevant work by anthropologists is best located in the *Index to Current Periodicals Received in the Library of the Royal Anthropological Institute* (London: Royal Anthropological Institute), under "cultural anthropology, ethnography," and in the *International Bibliography of the Social Sciences, International Bibliography of Social and Cultural Anthropology* (Chicago: Aldine Publishing Company), under "culture and personality," "national character," and other specific listings. Work by sociologists can be found in *Sociological Abstracts* under such headings as: "personality (and culture)," "social psychiatry," and "social anthropology."

The psychoanalytic literature has been indexed by Alexander Grinstein in *The Index of Psychoanalytic Writings* (New York: International Universities Press, 1956–65). Grinstein produced an elaborate and intelligently organized nine-volume work that includes two volumes of subject index. Volume 5 gives some fifty-four references under "political" and "politics"; Volume 9 gives thirty more. Also see "international" in the subject indices, and other specific subject references. Grinstein undertook the work as a revision and updating of John Rickman's *Index Psychoanalyticus 1893–1926* (London: L. and V. Woolf at the Hogarth Press and the Institute of Psychoanalysis, 1928). Rickman's index is in one volume and does not give subject listings.

Finally, a number of very useful bibliographies for virtually every aspect of the study of personality and politics may be found appended to the relevant articles in the *International Encyclopedia of the Social Sciences* (New York: Crowell-Collier and Macmillan, 1968), referred to hereafter as *IESS*. Volume 17 provides indexes to the contributors, articles, and subject matter.

II. THEORETICAL AND METHODOLOGICAL ISSUES IN PERSONALITY AND POLITICS

Three related issues account for the bulk of methodological and theoretical writings on personality and politics. The narrowest issue is how and whether research methods can be improved; the second issue is the broader question of the scientific status of data culled by psychiatric and psychoanalytic techniques; and the third issue is how important individual personality is to political behavior in any case. Regarding this third issue, Daniel J. Levinson has characterized the extremes as the "mirage" and "sponge" theories:

> I have used the term "mirage" theory for the view, frequently held or implied in the psychoanalytic literature, that ideologies, role-conceptions, and behavior are merely epiphenomena or by-products of unconscious fantasies and defenses. Similarly, the term "sponge" theory characterizes the view, commonly forwarded in the sociological literature, in which man is merely a passive, mechanical absorber of the prevailing structural demands. [From "Role, Personality, and Social

Structure in the Organizational Setting," *Journal of Abnormal and Social Psychology*, 58 (1959), 170–80, reprinted in Smelser and Smelser, *Personality and Social Systems*.]

Particularly instructive articles in this controversy include: Reinhard Bendix, "Compliant Behavior and Individual Personality," *The American Journal of Sociology*, 58 (1952), 292–303, and Dennis H. Wrong, "The Over-Socialized Concept of Man in Modern Sociology," *American Sociological Review*, 26 (1961), 183–93, both reprinted in Smelser and Smelser, *op. cit.* Bendix's essay is a critique of "psychologizing" in social analysis; Wrong's is an attack on much sociological writing for the opposite shortcoming—insufficient psychological depth. Also see the several articles cited by Greenstein in Chapter Two in connection with his discussion of "actor dispensability."

Levinson has attempted to lay out a middle ground between sponge and mirage in "The Relevance of Personality for Political Participation," *Public Opinion Quarterly*, 22 (1958), 3–10, a companion piece to the article quoted above. Urie Bronfenbrenner implicitly takes the sponge position in "Personality and Participation: The Case of the Vanishing Variables," *Journal of Social Issues*, 16 (1960), 54–63, an analysis that Greenstein has commented upon in Chapter Two above. Chapter Two derives from an earlier article by Greenstein, "The Impact of Personality on Politics: An Attempt to Clear Away Underbrush," *American Political Science Review*, 61 (1967), 629–41. Bronfenbrenner's article may be compared with David Horton Smith, "A Psychological Model of Individual Participation in Voluntary Organizations: Applications to Some Chilean Data," *American Journal of Sociology*, 72 (1966), 249–66. Theodore Abel attacks both over-simplified sponge theories and the use of psychological data in social analysis more generally in "Is a Psychiatric Interpretation of the German Enigma Necessary?" *American Sociological Review*, 10 (1945), 457–64. M. Brewster Smith has an incisive discussion of the relationships among situational, social-background and larger social-system variables and the ways they interact with personality process and dispositions: see his "A Map for the Analysis of Personality and Politics," *Journal of Social Issues*, 24:3 (1968), 15–28. Greenstein discusses and reproduces Smith's map in Chapter One, above. Also see Smith's application of his map to the problem of rationality in Oliver Garceau, ed., *Political Research and Political Theory: Essays in Honor of V. O. Key, Jr.* (Cambridge, Mass.: Harvard University Press, 1968), pp. 77–101.

For the argument (summarized by Greenstein on pp. 13–14 above) that usefulness of data typically collected by psychologists for social analysis is reduced by formal analytic conventions of psychology, see Richard A. Littman, "Psychology: The Socially Indifferent Science," *American Psychologist*, 16 (1961), 232–36. Two discussions by psychoanalysts of the bearing of psychological data on explanation of social phenomena are Heinz Hartmann, "The Applications of Psychoanalytic Concepts to Social Science," *Essays on Ego Psychology* (New York: International Universities Press, 1964), and Harry Stack Sullivan, "A Note on the Implications of Psychiatry, the Study of Interpersonal Relations, for Investigations in the Social Sciences," *American Journal of Sociology*, 42 (1937), 848–61.

An excellent introduction to the literature on socialization emphasizing both sociological and psychological perspectives is John A. Clausen, ed., *Socialization and Society* (Boston: Little, Brown, 1968). Other investigators who have addressed themselves to the relationship between psychology and the study of society in general or political phenomena in particular include: Alex Inkeles, "Sociology and Psychology," in Sigmund Koch, ed., *Psychology: A Study of a Science*, 6 (New York: McGraw-Hill, 1963), 318–87; Harold D. Lasswell, "What Psychiatrists and Political Scientists Can Learn from Each Other," *Psychiatry*, 1 (1938), 33–39; and Hans H. Gerth and C. Wright Mills, *Character and Social Structure* (New York: Harcourt, Brace & World, 1953). Also see Karl Popper, *The Open Society and Its Enemies*, 2 (New York: Harper Torchbook Edition, 1963), 97ff., in which Popper argues that sociology is an autonomous discipline because psychological evidence is so frequently of limited relevance; Richard Lichtman's rejoinder in his "Karl Popper's Defense of the Autonomy of Sociology," *Social Research*, 32 (1965), 1–25; and Arnold Rogow, "Psychiatry as a Political Science," *Psychiatric Quarterly*, 40 (1966), 319–32. Hendrik M. Ruitenbeck has edited a collection entitled *Psychoanalysis and Social Science* (New York: Dutton Paperback, 1962) which reprints an intriguing article by Harold Lasswell, "The Impact of Psychoanalytic Thinking on the Social Sciences," and other contributions by Talcott Parsons, Heinz Hartmann, Erik H. Erikson, and Kai T. Erikson. There is a massive two-volume reader by J. K. Zawodney, ed., *Guide to the Study of International Relations* (San Francisco: Chandler, 1966), Volume 1 subtitled "Conflict" and Volume 2, "Integration." It includes approximately 184 articles, many bearing on personality and politics. The collection is very uneven but includes some valuable articles.

The scientific status of psychoanalytic theory is a continuing source of debate. A careful investigation that seeks to clarify the empirical issues is Peter Madison's, *Freud's Concept of Repression and Defense: Its Theoretical and Observational Language* (Minneapolis: University of Minnesota Press, 1961). Also see B. A. Farrell's "Can Psychoanalysis Be Refuted?" *Inquiry*, 1 (1961), 16–36, which argues that psychoanalysis is not a closed system, but rather can be subdivided into theories of instincts (dynamics), development, psychic structure, mental economics or defense, and symptom formation. Each of these theories, Farrell suggests, can be investigated empirically and confirmed or disconfirmed in some sense. In addition, see Michael Martin's "Mr. Farrell and the Refutability of Psychoanalysis" in the same issue of *Inquiry*, to which Farrell replied in kind. Two other contributions by Farrell are: "The Status of Psychoanalytic Theory," *Inquiry*, 7 (1964), 104–23; and a symposium in which he participated with J. O. Wisdom and P. M. Turquet, "The Criteria for a Psycho-Analytic Interpretation," *The Aristotelian Society*, Supplementary Volume 36 (1962), 77–144. In the former article Farrell distinguishes Freudian theory from Freudian clinical method and attempts to specify the status of the theory: "a provisional story; an approximation of the truth." In the latter Farrell, with Wisdom and Turquet, engage in an especially instructive discussion of a psychoanalytic interpretation. The transcript of the interview between the analyst and his patient is presented to the reader; then the three men participate in a discussion of the status of an interpretation made during the psychoanalytic session. Farrell suggests that to assert an interpretation in the analytic setting is practicably impossible to confirm or deny does not mean that the same is true of interpretations made outside of the dyadic context. This observation has apparent import for sensitive psychobiographical work in the social sciences.

These somewhat fugitive papers, in which Farrell and others attempt to clarify the standing of psychoanalytic theories, evidence and procedures, flow out of contemporary British philosophical interests in conceptual clarification. In this mode, also see: A. C. MacIntyre, *The Unconscious: A Conceptual Study* (London: Routledge and Kegan Paul, 1958); Richard S. Peters, *The Concept of Motivation* (London: Routledge and Kegan Paul; New York: Humanities Press, 1958); and Gilbert Ryle, *The Concept of Mind* (London: Hutchinson, 1949). A handy compendium reprinting work by Farrell, Ryle, and others is Donald F. Gustafson, ed., *Essays in Philosophical Psychology* (New York: Doubleday Anchor, 1964).

For a plea from a clinician for research that is designed to perfect standards of clinical inquiry, see Jules D. Holzberg, "The Clinical and Scientific Methods: Synthesis or Antithesis?" *Journal of Projective Techniques*, 21 (1957), 227–42. Thomas M. French and Erika Fromm have suggested ways of increasing the reliability of even such an intricate investigative mode as psychodynamic dream interpretation; see their *Dream Interpretation* (New York: Basic Books, 1964). Bjorn Christiansen, "The Scientific Status of Psychoanalytic Clinical Evidence," *Inquiry*, 7 (1964), 47–79, reviews some of the efforts toward greater precision and reliability in psychoanalytic investigations. He points out that, while clinical evidence has intrinsic limitations, current investigations are not knocking against these upper limits. Also, a collection edited by Sidney Hook, *Psychoanalysis: Scientific Method and Philosophy* (New York: New York University Press, 1959), includes a number of critiques of the epistemological underpinnings of psychoanalysis.

Finally, for general treatments of the problems of studying personality and politics, see Robert E. Lane's article on "Political Personality" in *IESS* and the various contributions to the special July, 1968, number of *The Journal of Social Issues* (24:3) on "Personality and Politics: Theoretical and Methodological Issues" (a number of which are cited in the remainder of this essay), along with Greenstein's introduction to that number: "The Need for Systematic Inquiry into Personality and Politics: Introduction and Overview," pp. 1–14.

III. ANALYSIS OF THE PERSONALITIES OF INDIVIDUAL POLITICAL ACTORS

Two psychobiographical case studies of politicians—if Luther may be called a politician—especially stand out: Erik Erikson's artful, evocative analysis of *Young Man Luther* (New York: Norton, 1958); and the more systematic and directly reasoned work of Alexander and Juliette L. George, *Woodrow Wilson and Colonel House: A Personality Study* (New York: John Day, 1956); paperback edition with new preface (New York: Dover, 1964). For an extended consideration of the Georges' volume, see Bernard Brodie, "A Psychoanalytic Interpretation of Woodrow Wilson," *World Politics*, 9 (1957), 413–22, reprinted in Bruce Mazlish, ed., *Psychoanalysis and History* (Englewood Cliffs, N.J.: Prentice-Hall, 1963), pp. 115–23.

Other recent full-scale psychobiographies include: Lewis J. Edinger, *Kurt Schumacher: A Study in Personality and Political Behavior* (Stanford, Calif.: Stanford University Press, 1965); Arnold Rogow, *James Forrestal: A Study of Personality, Politics, and Policy* (New York: Macmillan, 1963); E. Victor Wolfenstein, *The Revolutionary Personality: Lenin, Trotsky, and Gandhi* (Princeton, N.J.: Princeton University Press, 1967); and Betty Glad, *Charles Evans Hughes and the Illusions of Innocence* (Urbana: University of Illinois Press, 1966).

A questionable psychobiography of Whittaker Chambers and Alger Hiss has been written by Meyer A. Zeligs, *Friendship and Fratricide* (New York: Viking, 1967). Zeligs worked with fascinating, if often unreliable, materials; one misses almost completely the studied sense of balance and impartiality conveyed by the Georges. Equally questionable is a psychobiography that appeared at the same time as Zeligs' book, originally written in the 1930's by Sigmund Freud and William C. Bullitt, *Thomas Woodrow Wilson, Twenty-Eighth President of the United States: A Psychological Study* (Boston: Houghton Mifflin, 1967). The question of how much of this study Freud was actually responsible for has been widely discussed. A number of reviews of both the Zeligs and the Freud-Bullitt volumes bring out the dangers and possibilities of psychobiography. For example, refer to: Meyer Shapiro, "Dangerous Acquaintances," *New York Review of Books*, February 23, 1967, pp. 5–9; "Brotherly Hatred," *The*

Times Literary Supplement (London), November 9, 1967, p. 1057; Ernest van den Haag, "Psychoanalysis and Fantasy," *National Review*, March 21, 1967, pp. 295ff.; and Erik Erikson and Richard Hofstadter, "The Strange Case of Freud, Bullitt, and Wilson," *New York Review of Books*, February 9, 1967, pp. 3–8. The Freud-Bullitt volume is worth comparing with the analysis Freud originally published in 1911 of an eminent German jurist, Daniel Paul Schreber, "Psycho-Analytic Notes Upon an Autobiographical Account of a Case of Paranoia (Dementia Paranoides)," *Standard Edition of the Complete Psychological Works of Sigmund Freud*, 12 (London: Hogarth, 1958), 3–82. The later work shows little of the sensitivity of Freud's earlier commentary.

A vast number of brief psychobiographical sketches of various political personages has been published. For a sampling of such studies, see: Karl Abraham, "Amenhotep IV (Ikhnaton): A Psychoanalytic Contribution to the Understanding of his Personality and the Monotheistic Cult of Aton," *Psychoanalytic Quarterly*, 4 (1935), 537–69; Sebastian de Grazia, "Mahatma Gandhi: The Son of His Mother," *Political Quarterly*, 19 (1948), 336–48; Erik Erikson, "Gandhi's Autobiography: The Leader as Child," *American Scholar*, 35 (1966), 632–46; Erik Erikson, "On the Nature of Psycho-Historical Evidence: In Search of Gandhi," *Daedalus*, 97 (1968), 695–730; Bernice Engle and Thomas M. French, "Some Psychodynamic Reflections Upon the Life and Writing of Solon," *Psychoanalytic Quarterly*, 20 (1951), 253–74; Charles Kligerman, "The Character of Jean Jacques Rousseau," *Psychoanalytic Quarterly*, 20 (1951), 237–52; A. W. Levi, "The 'Mental Crisis' of John Stuart Mill," *Psychoanalytic Review*, 32 (1945), 86–101; John Durham, "The Influence of John Stuart Mill's Mental Crisis on his Thoughts," *American Imago*, 20 (1963), 369–84; Philip Weisman, "Why Booth Killed Lincoln: A Psychoanalytic Study of a Historical Tragedy," *Psychoanalysis and the Social Sciences*, 5 (1958), 99–115; and Edwin A. Weinstein, "Denial of Presidential Disability: A Case Study of Woodrow Wilson," *Psychiatry*, 30 (1967), 376–91. The last cited article by Weinstein is a clinical-organic analysis of Wilson's illness; it gives some indication of how subtle clinical-organic psychobiographical studies can become. Another interesting study of this kind is Edward J.

Kempf, "Abraham Lincoln's Organic and Emotional Neurosis," which appears in a mixed bag of *Psychological Studies of Famous Americans: The Civil War Era*, Norman Kiell, ed., (New York: Twayne Publishers, 1964), pp. 67–87. A summary of early psychological studies of public figures is contained in F. Fearing's "Psychological Studies of Historical Personalities," *Psychological Bulletin*, 24 (1927), 521–39.

The second of the Erikson articles cited in the previous paragraph also raises important methodological questions about psychological diagnosis of political and other historical figures. Such issues also arise in: L. Pierce Clark, "Unconscious Motives Underlying the Personalities of Great Statesmen and Their Relation to Epoch-Making Events: A Psychologic Study of Abraham Lincoln," *Psychoanalytic Review*, 8 (1921), 1–21; George Devereux, "Charismatic Leadership and Crisis," *Psychoanalysis and the Social Sciences*, 4 (1955), 145–57; and Erwin C. Hargrove, Jr., *The Tragic Hero in Politics: Theodore Roosevelt, David Lloyd George, and Fiorello LaGuardia* (unpublished Ph.D. dissertation, Yale University, 1963).

A small number of articles link individual and aggregative analysis by attempting to assess the connection between the psychological state of the leader and his relationship to his nation at that particular historical point. See especially Robert C. Tucker, "The Dictator and Totalitarianism," *World Politics*, 17 (1965), 555–83. Also see Gustav Bychowski, "Dictatorship and Paranoia," *Psychoanalysis and the Social Sciences*, 4 (1955), 127–34.

Several essays have been written on the general methodological problems of psychological analyses of single individuals. One of the best is B. A. Farrell's introduction to the English paperback edition of Freud's *Leonardo* (Harmondsworth: Penguin edition, 1963). Lewis J. Edinger has a suggestive two-part article entitled "Political Science and Political Biography," *Journal of Politics*, 26 (1964), 423–39 and 648–76. A number of the articles in Bruce Mazlish, ed., *Psychoanalysis and History* (Englewood Cliffs, N.J.: Prentice-Hall, 1963), are useful, as are the following: John A. Garraty, *The Nature of Biography* (New York: Knopf, 1957); J. A. Garraty, "The Inter-relations of Psychology and Biography," *Psychological Bulletin*, 51 (1954), 569–82; Richard L. Bushman, "On the Uses of Psychology:

Conflict and Conciliation in Benjamin Franklin," *History and Theory*, 5 (1966), 225–40; Edward Hitschmann, "Some Psychoanalytic Aspects of Biography," *International Journal of Psycho-Analysis*, 37 (1956), 265–69; Robert R. Holt, "Clinical Judgment as a Disciplined Inquiry," *Journal of Nervous and Mental Disease*, 133 (1961), 369–82; R. R. Holt, "Individuality and Generalization in the Psychology of Personality," *Journal of Personality*, 30 (1962), 377–404; Leon Edel, "The Biographer and Psychoanalysis," *International Journal of Psycho-Analysis*, 42 (1961), 458–66; and Alfred L. Baldwin, "Personal Structure Analysis: A Statistical Method for Investigating the Single Personality," *Journal of Abnormal and Social Psychology*, 37 (1942), 163–83. Also see: A. F. Davies, "Criteria for the Political Life History," *Historical Studies of Australia and New Zealand*, 13:49 (1967), 76–85; Betty Glad, "The Role of Psychoanalytic Biography in Political Science," paper delivered at the 1968 Annual Meeting of the American Political Science Association; and two important early contributions by John Dollard, *Criteria for the Life History* (New Haven, Conn.: Yale University Press, 1935), and by Gordon W. Allport, *The Use of Personal Documents in Psychological Science*, (New York: Social Science Research Council Bulletin 49, 1942).

A number of excellent articles have been written by Alexander George on a range of problems encountered in psychological biography. See Alexander L. George and Juliette L. George, "Woodrow Wilson: Personality and Political Behavior," paper presented at the 1956 Annual Meeting of the American Political Science Association, and the following articles by Alexander George: "Some Dynamic Uses of Psychology in Political Biography," (unpublished paper, 1960); and "Power as a Compensatory Value for Political Leaders," *Journal of Social Issues*, 24:3 (1968), 29–50.

Standing somewhere between the psychological biographies and the investigations of typologies and aggregation is A. F. Davies, *Private Politics: A Study of Five Political Outlooks* (Melbourne: Melbourne University Press, 1966). This interesting attempt to apply psychoanalytic insights to extensive interviews of five middle-level Australian politicians is well worth referring to. See also Fred I. Greenstein, "Art and Science in the Political Life History: A Review of A. F. Davies' *Private Poli-*

tics," *Politics: The Journal of the Australasian Political Science Association*, 2 (1967), 176–80.

IV. ANALYSIS OF THE PERSONALITIES OF TYPES OF POLITICAL ACTORS

To some extent all studies of personality and politics must use taxonomies. This section notes a number of general discussions of the problems of typology and indicates investigations that have generated typologies that are particularly useful to political psychology. Two excellent general essays on typologies are: Edward A. Tiryakian, "Typologies," *IESS*, and Carl G. Hempel, "Typological Methods in the Natural and the Social Sciences" in his *Aspects of Scientific Explanation* (New York: Free Press of Glencoe, 1965), pp. 156–71. Also see John C. McKinney, *Constructive Typology and Social Theory* (New York: Appleton-Century-Crofts, 1966); and Paul F. Lazarsfeld and Allen Barton, "Qualitative Measurement in the Social Sciences: Classification, Typologies, and Indices," in Daniel Lerner and Harold D. Lasswell, eds., *The Policy Sciences* (Stanford, Calif.: Stanford University Press, 1951), pp. 155–92.

A seminal demonstration of the possibilities of typologies in the study of personality and politics was produced by Harold D. Lasswell in his 1930 study, *Psychopathology and Politics*, especially Chapter IV, "The Criteria of Political Types." This work was reprinted in 1951 by The Free Press in *The Political Writings of Harold D. Lasswell*. It was again reprinted in a 1960 Viking Press Compass Book paperback, which inexplicably dropped two appendixes to the original work, but added Lasswell's "Afterthoughts: Thirty Years Later." Lasswell expands on his 1930 formulation of nuclear, co-relational, and developmental types in a "Note on 'Types': Nuclear, Co-Relational, and Developmental," *Journal of Social Issues*, 24:3 (1968), 81–91. In Chapter III, "The Political Personality," of Lasswell's *Power and Personality* (New York: Norton, 1948) he drew a portrait of the political man who accentuates power because he expects power to help him overcome low estimates of himself. (This book was issued in a paperback edition by Viking in 1962 which was also devoid of an appendix from the original.) Later in the book,

Chapter VII, Lasswell turned to the formation of "Democratic Personality," a construct he elucidated in 1951 in the concluding section of *The Political Writings of Harold D. Lasswell,* entitled "Democratic Character," pp. 465–525.

Without saying much about the immense field of psychoanalytic types, it is worth noting that psychoanalysts have been concerned with the typological implications of their work from the start. See Sigmund Freud's very brief essay of 1931, "Libidinal Types," in Volume 2 of *Standard Edition* (1961), 215–20. A brief statement of Jung's approach is available in his "A Psychological Theory of Types," in *Modern Man in Search of a Soul* (New York: Harvest paperback edition, 1960). Also see Jung, *Psychological Types: or the Psychology of Individuation* (London: Routledge, 1959; originally published, 1933).

The work that has generated the most widely used typology of political psychology is Theodor W. Adorno, Else Frenkel-Brunswik, Daniel J. Levinson, and R. Nevitt Sanford, *The Authoritarian Personality* (New York: Harper, 1950), hereafter cited as *AP.* A review of the massive literature that the *AP* inspired is available in John P. Kirscht and Ronald C. Dillehay, *Dimensions of Authoritarianism* (Lexington: University of Kentucky Press, 1967). Also see Richard Christie and Peggy Cook, "A Guide to the Published Literature Relating to *The Authoritarian Personality* through 1956," *Journal of Psychology,* 45 (1958), 171–99.

Precursors of the *AP* research include Erich Fromm and Wilhelm Reich, who first sketched the theory of authoritarianism. Reich contributed *The Mass Psychology of Fascism* (New York: Orgone Press, 1946, 3d ed. revised and expanded; originally published, 1933). Fromm's first statement was in an essay in Max Horkheimer's collection *Studien über Autorität und Familie* (Paris: Alcan, 1936). In 1941, Fromm published his influential *Escape from Freedom* (New York: Holt, 1941), setting out his conception of authoritarianism more fully. Two years later, A. H. Maslow published "Authoritarian Character Structure," *Journal of Social Psychology,* 18 (1943), 401–11, an essay which the authors of the *AP* acknowledge. The formative influences more generally for the *AP* were the national-character literature of the 1930's and 1940's and the attitude-correlations studies then popular. Representative studies of "fascist attitudes" include: Ross Stagner, "Fascist Attitudes: Their Determining Conditions," *The Journal of Social Psychology*, 7 (1936), 438–54; and Allen L. Edwards, "Unlabeled Fascist Attitudes," *Journal of Abnormal and Social Psychology*, 36 (1941), 575–82. Representative national-character studies include: Fromm's work; Ruth F. Benedict, *The Chrysanthemum and the Sword* (Boston: Houghton Mifflin, 1946); Henry V. Dicks, "Personality Traits and National Socialist Ideology," *Human Relations*, 3 (1950), 111–54; and H. V. Dicks, "Observations on Contemporary Russian Behaviour," *Human Relations*, 5 (1952), 111–75.

Not an influence, but a product of the same historical period, is the work of the Nazi psychologist E. R. Jaensch, "Der Gegentypus," *Beiheft zur Zeitschrift für angewandte Psychologie und Charakterkunde*, Beiheft 75 (1938). Jaensch presented a typology remarkably similar to that of the *AP*. He praised the authoritarian type and excoriated the deviant "anti-type" whose personality was incongruent with Nazism.

A valuable overview and defense of the work reported in the *AP* is provided by *AP* co-author Nevitt Sanford, "The Approach of the Authoritarian Personality," in J. L. McCary, ed., *Psychology of Personality* (New York: Grove Press, 1959). The best collection of critiques is in Richard Christie and Marie Jahoda, eds., *Studies in the Scope and Method of "The Authoritarian Personality"* (Glencoe, Ill.: Free Press, 1954). This collection includes Edward A. Shils, "Authoritarianism: 'Right' and 'Left' " and Herbert H. Hyman and Paul B. Sheatsley, " 'The Authoritarian Personality'—A Methodological Critique." Also useful are: Nathan Glazer, "New Light on 'The Authoritarian Personality,' " *Commentary*, 17 (1954); M. Brewster Smith, "Review of *The Authoritarian Personality*," *Journal of Abnormal and Social Psychology*, 45 (1950), 775–79; and Daniel J. Levinson, "Political Personality: Conservatism and Radicalism," *IESS*.

Two of the major controversies arising from the *AP* have been the controversy over "ego-defensive" versus "cognitive" authoritarianism, discussed by Greenstein in Chapter Four above, and the controversy over systematic errors attributable to "response-set." Four key articles on response-set and authoritarianism are reprinted in Chapter Six of Martha T. Mednick and

Sarnoff A. Mednick, *Research in Personality* (New York: Holt, Rinehart and Winston, 1963). The question of distinguishing "cognitive" from "ego-defensive" authoritarianism has been treated variously by Angus Campbell, *et al.*, *The American Voter* (New York: Wiley, 1960), pp. 212–15; and by Thomas F. Pettigrew, "Personality and Sociocultural Factors in Intergroup Attitudes: A Cross-National Comparison," *Journal of Conflict Resolution*, 2 (1958), 29–42. "Working-class authoritarianism" is treated by Seymour Martin Lipset, *Political Man: The Social Bases of Politics* (Garden City, N.Y.: Doubleday, 1960), and by S. M. Miller and Frank Riessman, "Working Class Authoritarianism: A Critique of Lipset," *British Journal of Sociology*, 12 (1961), 263–76.

Other interesting authoritarianism studies include: Herbert C. Schulberg, "Insight, Authoritarianism, and Tendency to Agree," *Journal of Nervous and Mental Disease*, 135 (1962), 481–88; Irwin Katz and Lawrence Benjamin, "Effects of White Authoritarianism in Biracial Work Groups," *Journal of Abnormal and Social Psychology*, 61 (1960), 448–56; M. Brewster Smith, "An Analysis of Two Measures of 'Authoritarianism' Among Peace Corps Teachers, *Journal of Personality*, 33 (1965), 513–35; Joan Eager and M. Brewster Smith, "A Note on the Validity of Sanford's Authoritarian-Equalitarian Scale," *Journal of Abnormal and Social Psychology*, 47 (1952), 265–67; Jack Block and Jeanne Block, "An Investigation of the Relationship Between Intolerance of Ambiguity and Ethnocentrism," *Journal of Personality*, 19 (1951), 303–11; and Daniel J. Levinson, "Authoritarian Personality and Foreign Policy," *Journal of Conflict Resolution*, 1 (1957), 37–47. See Herbert J. McClosky, "Conservatism and Personality," *American Political Science Review*, 52 (1958), 27–45, for a carefully designed typological study addressed to issues that arise in the authoritarianism literature, but not directly a part of that literature. See also Greenstein's "Personality and Political Socialization: The Theories of Authoritarian and Democratic Character," *Annals of the American Academy of Political and Social Science*, 361 (1965), 81–95, which provides the basis for much of Chapters Four and Five of the present volume.

Several other typologies of political psychology are closely related to that of the *AP*, particularly the "dogmatism" categorization of Milton Rokeach, *The Open and Closed Mind: Investigations into the Nature of Belief Systems and Personality Systems* (New York: Basic Books, 1960). Rokeach suggests that a high level of "dogmatism" is characteristic of personalities found at both extremes of the political spectrum. Using Rokeach's measures on Italian deputies, Gordon J. DiRenzo got results contrary to those Rokeach's hypotheses would have led one to expect; see DiRenzo, *Personality, Power, and Politics* (Notre Dame, Ind.: University of Notre Dame Press, 1967). Hans J. Eysenck has proposed a related "tough-mindedness" syndrome which, like dogmatism, is hypothetically high in both Communists and Fascists. His views have been challenged, notably by Richard Christie, "Eysenck's Treatment of the Personality of Communists," *Psychological Bulletin*, 53 (1956), 411–30; and also by Rokeach and Charles Hanley, "Eysenck's Tender-mindedness Dimension: A Critique," *Psychological Bulletin*, 53 (1956), 169–76. Eysenck replies in *"The Psychology of Politics:* A Reply," *Psychological Bulletin*, 53 (1956), 177–82. Other psychologically relevant categorizations include those presented by: Morris Rosenberg, "Misanthropy and Political Ideology," *American Sociological Review*, 21 (1956), 690–95; and Richard F. Christie and F. Geis, *Studies in Machiavellianism* (New York: Academic Press, forthcoming).

Another typological work that has had a major impact, although in a more diffuse way than *The Authoritarian Personality*, is David Riesman's *The Lonely Crowd* (New Haven, Conn.: Yale University Press, 1950). Influenced by Erich Fromm's views, Riesman produced a categorization of character types—the tradition directed, the inner directed, and the other directed orientations—as well as various subtypes, including such political types as the indifferent, the moralizer, and the inside dopester. Riesman's typology is discussed by Robert Lane in "Political Character and Political Analysis," *Psychiatry*, 16 (1953), 387–98. A variety of aspects of Riesman's work are critically considered in Seymour Martin Lipset and Leo Lowenthal, eds., *Culture and Social Character: The Work of David Riesman Reviewed* (New York: Free Press of Glencoe, 1961). The essays in this book which raise issues especially concerning psychological types include: Talcott Parsons and Winston White, "The Link Between Character and Society," pp. 89–135; Robert Gutman and Dennis Wrong, "David Riesman's Typology of Character," pp. 295–315; and Elaine Graham Sofer, "Inner-Direction, Other-Direction, and Autonomy: A Study of College Students," pp. 316–48.

A bold and interesting typology of political psychology has been suggested by James D. Barber in *The Lawmakers* (New Haven, Conn.: Yale University Press, 1965). Barber found that his sample of freshman Connecticut legislators could be grouped into four categories arranged along the axes of willingness-to-return-to-the-legislature (measuring commitment) and level-of-activity. High in activity and low in willingness-to-return he labeled the Advertiser; low in activity and high in willingness-to-return, the Spectator; low in activity and low in willingness-to-return, the Reluctant; and high in activity and high in willingness-to-return, the Lawmaker. Drawing on Lasswell, Barber describes those in the first three categories as appearing to suffer from deficiencies of self-esteem. "Their low self-estimates seem to be linked in significant ways to their political participation" (p. 217). Only the Lawmakers, Barber contends, seem to have resources of self-esteem deep enough so that one must explain why they took the unusual step of running for the legislature in a different way. "Like Riesman's autonomous man, Lawmakers are freed to deviate from the common path because they are in possession of powerful techniques for dealing directly with the accompanying strains" (p. 224).

Robert E. Lane also deals with the psychological roots of political participation in *Political Life* (Glencoe, Ill.: The Free Press, 1959) and in *Political Ideology* (New York: Free Press of Glencoe, 1962), the latter of which uses case studies. While Lasswell had earlier stressed the possible pathological roots of political involvement, Lane in *Political Life* argued that, for the most part, pathological psychic processes were too preoccupying to leave an individual with much energy for political participation. Lane sees the energetic political participant as a fundamentally psychologically-healthy man. The change in stress in political psychology from participation as arising from pathology to participation as arising from neurosis-free energies parallels in an interesting way the rise and coronation of post-Freudian ego psychology, which is much more likely to stress the strengths and resources of the human ego than did earlier Freudian theory.

When read closely, Lane and Lasswell's views are not at all irreconcilable on the question of who participates in politics. But the difference in emphasis has prompted a fascinating study by Brent M. Rutherford, "Psychopathology, Decision-Making, and Political Involvement," *Journal of Conflict Resolution*, 10 (1966), 387–407. Rutherford sought to discover what the characteristics were of patients in Elgin State Mental Hospital who had the energy and motivation to function in the leadership councils. He found that manic-depressives and schizophrenic-paranoid patients were vastly over-represented in the leadership. Says Rutherford, "The Elgin findings support Lasswell's formulation of political man as a displacer and externalizer" (p. 405). Manic and paranoid trends in personlity have long been reported among the political figures studied (and among a few who have been treated); what Rutherford's findings do is to help advance the question of who participates in politics to that of the specification of hypotheses about what kinds of psychological disturbances do not hinder or even increase political participation and under what circumstances.

Another approach to the question of the roots of belief systems is to examine the beliefs of mental patients in hope of learning about variation in the normal range by studying deviant cases. This has been done by Marguerite Hertz in "Mental Patients and Civil Rights: A Study of Opinions of Mental Patients on Social and Political Issues," *Journal of Health and Human Behavior*, 1 (1960), 251–58. Hertz found mental patients held views similar to those of hospital employees on most issues. They differed in perceiving the international situation as less dangerous than did the control group of employees. They were more willing to adopt any measures to avoid war, more certain that the United States could defend itself, than were the comparison group of employees. Thus, they seem to lend support to Lane's position that most psychically disturbed people are too drained by their inner conflicts to have much taste for outer conflicts. (Their more pacific positions may also be held to support R. D. Laing's contention in *The Politics of Experience* [New York: Pantheon, 1967] that the schizophrenic may be someone unable to suppress sane instincts to conform with the expectations of an abnormal society.) On the other hand, the patients in Hertz's study were more willing to use drastic defenses (germ and chemical warfare) if the United States were attacked. Perhaps this relates to their own need to use massive and regressive defenses in their relationships with their environment.

Others who have addressed themselves to whether politicians are more or less likely than other citizens to be neurotic include John B. McConaughy, "Certain Personality Factors of State Legislators in South Carolina," *American Political Science Review*, 44 (1950), 897–903, although problems of sampling and scale validity make these data difficult to assess. In an important theoretical article, "The Dictator and Tolalitarianism," *op. cit.*, Robert C. Tucker criticizes "the theory of organizational rejection of aberrant personalities from leadership positions." Stalin and Hitler, Tucker points out, moved up outside the established bureaucracies, seizing control with revolutionary organizations from without. Though Tucker does not extend the argument, it is apparent that elected politicians and presidential aides in the United States are frequently recruited outside the bureaucracies. It is not clear, moreover, that the individual who has worked up through a bureaucracy is less likely to possess the type of disturbance with paranoid or compulsive components that can leave largely intact the surface appearance of competent intellectual functioning.

A broad approach to the question "who participates in politics and why?" has been taken in various studies on political motivation. Notable among these studies is Gabriel Almond's *The Appeals of Communism* (Princeton, N.J.: Princeton University Press, 1954) in which the different kinds of motives for joining the Communist Party in France, Italy, Britain and the United States are explored. The tenth chapter is based on psychiatric data. Other psychological studies of participation include: Bernard Hennessy, "Politicals and Apoliticals: Some Measurements of Personality Traits," *Midwest Journal of Political Science*, 3 (1959), 336–55; Gardner Murphy, "The Internalization of Social Controls," in Morroe Berger, *et al.*, *Freedom and Control in Modern Society* (New York: Van Nostrand, 1954), pp. 3–17; and Herbert McClosky and John H. Schaar, "Psychological Dimensions of Anomy," *American Sociological Review*, 30 (1965), 14–40. Also see Edward L. McDill and Jeanne C. Ridley, "Status, Anomia, Political Alienation and Political Participation," *American Journal of Sociology*, 68 (1962), 205–13;

and Paul H. Mussen and Anne B. Wyszynski, "Personality and Political Participation," *Human Relations*, 5 (1952), 65–82.

There is a growing literature on why students get involved in politics, both on campus and in the wider community. *The Journal of Social Issues* devoted its Number 3 of Volume 23 (1967) to the subject. Particularly useful in this number are: an empirical study by Richard Flacks, "The Liberated Generation: An Exploration of the Roots of Student Protest," pp. 52–75; and a theoretical essay by Kenneth Keniston, "The Sources of Student Dissent," pp. 108–37. Keniston, like Barber (*The Lawmakers*) and Lane (*Political Ideology*), finds the sources of his subjects' dissent and activity in unusually healthy personality constellations—a subject he explores in *Young Radicals: Notes on Committed Youth* (New York: Harcourt, Brace & World, 1968).

The cognitive elements in personality and their political relevance constitute an important realm of typological inquiry, as much of the research cited previously suggests—the literature on authoritarianism, dogmatism (Rokeach), tough-mindedness (Eysenck), misanthropy (Rosenberg), Machiavellianism (Christie and Geis). Here I wish to note some other cognitively-oriented research that did not come out in those connections. Two of the most significant studies of the roles of such cognitive functions as opinions, attitudes, and ideology in personality are: Robert Lane, *Political Ideology, op. cit.*; and M. Brewster Smith, Jerome Bruner, and Robert White, *Opinions and Personality* (New York: Wiley, 1956). Also see Paul Schilder, "The Analysis of Ideologies as a Psycho-Therapeutic Method, Especially in Group Treatment," *American Journal of Psychiatry*, 93 (1936), 601–17.

A sub-category of ideological studies might be called the "images-and-reactions" studies. In these the symbolic-ideological meanings of politics and the affect attached to these symbols are explored. The principal work in this mode is Murray Edelman's *The Symbolic Uses of Politics* (Urbana: University of Illinois Press, 1964). The reports of reactions to the death of presidents provide further examples of this kind of investigation. These include: Sebastian de Grazia's early study, "A Note on the Psychological Position of the Chief Executive," *Psychiatry*, 8 (1945), 267–72; Richard Sterba, "Report on Some Emotional

Reactions to President Roosevelt's Death," *Psychoanalytic Review*, 33 (1946), 393–98; Harold Orlansky, "Reactions to the Death of President Roosevelt," *Journal of Social Psychology*, 26 (1947), 235–66; Paul B. Sheatsley and Jacob J. Feldman, "The Assassination of President Kennedy: A Preliminary Report on Public Reactions and Behavior," *Public Opinion Quarterly*, 28 (1964), 189–215; and David Kirschner, "Some Reactions of Patients in Psychotherapy to the Death of the President," *Psychoanalytic Review*, 51 (1964), 125–28. The reactions of children in psychotherapy to the death of President Kennedy are reported in Martha Wolfenstein and Gilbert Kliman, eds., *Children and the Death of a President: Multi-Disciplinary Studies* (New York: Doubleday, 1965). See also Augusta Alpert, "A Brief Communication on Children's Reactions to the Assassination of the President," *Psychoanalytic Study of the Child*, 19 (1964), 313–20; and John J. Sherwood, "Authoritarianism, Moral Realism, and President Kennedy's Death," *British Journal of Clinical Psychology*, 5 (1966), 264–69. Greenstein has proposed a research strategy for bringing some order into the reports of practicing psychoanalysts on their patients' reactions to political events: see "Private Disorder and the Public Order: A Proposal for Collaboration Between Psychoanalysts and Political Scientists," *Psychoanalytic Quarterly*, 37 (1968), 261–81. Also see his "Popular Images of the President," *American Journal of Psychiatry*, 122 (1965), 523–29.

Another approach to the role of political cognitions in personality is to ask not so much *what* the common man believes (Lane) or *how* his affective life is tied to his political cognitions (the "reactions" literature), but to ask "of what use to a man are his opinions?" This question of what function an opinion serves for the man who holds it has led to some of the most fruitful recent writings on opinion and attitude. The sentence quoted above is the opening question on the first page of Smith, *et al.*, *Opinions and Personality, op. cit.*, in which the usefulness of opinions about Russia is analyzed in detail in the cases of three men, and more summarily in the cases of seven others. The authors note that "a framework for the study of attitude change bearing a striking resemblance to ours [Smith, *et al.*] has recently been presented by Irving Sarnoff and Daniel Katz," in "The Motivational Bases of Attitude Change," *Journal of Abnor-*

mal and Social Psychology, 49 (1954), 115–24. Katz and Sarnoff developed a research program in which they assumed that
attitudes can be useful (*a*) as ways of giving structure and
meaning to the individual's world, (*b*) "as instrumental means
toward achieving goals external to the individual, as in the case
of the worker who favors the political party he perceives as
committed to his welfare, and (*c*) as defenses for the ego of the
individual" (from Daniel Katz, Charles McClintock, and Irving
Sarnoff, "The Measurement of Ego Defense as Related to Attitude Change," *Journal of Personality,* 25 [1957], 465–74; here,
at 465). They outlined other findings in "Ego-Defense and
Attitude Change," *Human Relations,* 9 (1956), 27–45. Katz
summarized his views in "The Functional Approach to the
Study of Attitudes," *Public Opinion Quarterly,* 24 (1960), 163–
204.

This functional approach to attitudes and opinions has been
ably extended to the conflicts that political actors face in decision-making by Irving L. Janis, "Decisional Conflicts: A Theoretical Analysis," *Journal of Conflict Resolution,* 3 (1959),
6–27; and in a companion piece that treats the sources of decisional conflict and the different types of resolutions more
broadly: "Motivational Factors in the Resolution of Decisional
Conflicts," *Nebraska Symposium on Motivation,* 7 (1959),
198–231. The literature on personality and attitudes is far too
broad to do justice to it here. However, a few studies that might
prove particularly rewarding are: Eugenia Hanfmann and Jacob
W. Getzels, "Interpersonal Attitudes of Former Soviet Citizens,
as Studied by a Semi-Projective Method," *Psychological Monographs,* 69 (1955), 1–37; Herbert McClosky, "Personality and
Attitude Correlates of Foreign Policy Orientation," in James N.
Rosenau, ed., *Domestic Sources of Foreign Policy* (New York:
Free Press of Glencoe, 1967), pp. 51–109; Llewellyn Queener,
"The Development of Internationalist Attitudes," a three-part
series in Volumes 29–30 (1949) of *Journal of Social Psychology,* 221–35 and 237–52 in Volume 29, 105–26 in Volume 30;
and Ross Stagner, "Studies of Aggressive Attitudes: I. Measurement and Interrelation of Selected Attitudes," and "Studies of
Aggressive Attitudes: II. Changes from Peace to War," *Journal
of Social Psychology,* 20 (1944), 109–20 and 121–28 respectively. A valuable review of recent findings, as well as an interest-

ing report of an imaginatively unorthodox empirical study, is
contained in Bjorn Christiansen, *Attitudes toward Foreign Affairs as a Function of Personality* (Oslo: Oslo University Press,
1959).

V. AGGREGATIVE EFFECTS OF PERSONALITY
CHARACTERISTICS

The obstacles in moving from analysis of the impact of an
individual personality on politics to analysis of the impact of
aggregated personalities on political systems are immense. These
obstacles are by no means restricted to the personality-and-politics field. Greenstein discusses the difficulties and some possible
strategies for overcoming them in Chapter Five above and in
"Personality and Politics: Problems of Evidence, Inference, and
Conceptualization," *American Behavioral Scientist*, 10 (1967),
38–53. See also J. David Singer, "Man and World Politics: The
Psychological Interface," and Neil J. Smelser, "Personality and
the Explanation of Political Phenomena at the Social-System
Level," both in *Journal of Social Issues*, 24:3 (1968), 127–156
and 111–125 respectively.

There are, Greenstein suggests, four strategies for aggregat-
ing. The first is building up from direct observation of small-scale
political processes, an example of which is provided by Richard
C. Hodgson, Daniel J. Levinson, and Abraham Zaleznik, *The
Executive Role Constellation* (Boston: Division of Research,
Harvard University Graduate School of Business Administration,
1965). Other examples include: Robert Rubenstein and Harold
D. Lasswell, *The Sharing of Power in a Psychiatric Hospital*
(New Haven, Conn.: Yale University Press, 1966); and Erving
Goffman, *Asylums: Essays on the Social Situation of Mental
Patients and Other Inmates* (New York: Anchor, 1961). In more
general terms, this strategy of aggregating by "building up"
often involves observing the relationships within small groups.
To this task, the enormous literature on small-group research is
pertinent. Particularly useful references are: A. Paul Hare,
Handbook of Small Group Research (New York: Free Press of
Glencoe, 1962); Theodore M. Mills, *The Sociology of Small
Groups* (Englewood Cliffs, N.J.: Prentice-Hall, 1967); and

Philip E. Slater, *Microcosm: Structural, Psychological, and Religious Evolution in Groups* (New York: Wiley, 1966).

A second strategy for aggregation, Greenstein suggests, is using surveys to estimate the frequency of psychological attributes in populations and relating the frequencies to system characteristics. Modern survey techniques, Greenstein points out, now make it possible to obtain systematic "censuses" of the psychological disposition of populations of very large social systems. Indicative of the kinds of personality research possibilities that survey techniques open up are some of the more sophisticated voting studies. Philip E. Converse and Georges Dupeux have produced one of the most psychologically-intriguing investigations: "Politicization of the Electorate in France and the United States," *Public Opinion Quarterly*, 26 (1962), 1–23, reprinted in Campbell, *et al.*, *Elections and the Political Order* (New York: Wiley, 1966), pp. 269–91. The ground has been broken for censuses of personality characteristics of large populations by such monumental works as Leo Srole, *et al.*, *Mental Health in the Metropolis: The Midtown Manhattan Study* (New York: McGraw-Hill, 1962). Obtaining the census is, however monumental the task, one of the least of difficulties, since one still must specify the links between personality and political actions and between these individual actions and aggregate processes.

The third strategy that Greenstein identifies for aggregating involves modifying the frequency analysis to take account of nonadditivity. See, for example, Hayward R. Alker, "The Long Road to International Relations Theory: Problems of Statistical Nonadditivity," *World Politics*, 18 (1966), 623–55. Clear analyses of the difficulties of identifying the causal impact of different components in an aggregation are presented by Hubert M. Blalock in *Causal Inference in Nonexperimental Research* (Chapel Hill: University of North Carolina Press, 1967), and A. H. Yee and N. L. Gage, "Techniques for Estimating the Source and Direction of Causal Influence in Panel Data," *Psychological Bulletin*, 70 (1968), 115–26.

The fourth strategy for aggregation which Greenstein identifies is working back from theoretical analyses of systems and their psychological requirements. This means beginning with a model of how a system functions and then formulating hypotheses about the types of personality that theoretically would make it function best. In his "Harold D. Lasswell's Concept of Democratic Character," *Journal of Politics,* 30 (1958), 696–709, Greenstein treats at length an important example of this kind of theorizing, Harold D. Lasswell's essay on "Democratic Character," which was published in *The Political Writings of Harold D. Lasswell, op. cit.*

Some combination of the second, third, and fourth strategies that Greenstein identifies—taking population censuses, taking structural effects into account, and working backward from the requirements of an ideal-typical social system—underlies the approach of many of the studies of national character. The national-character literature is a particularly uneven and difficult one. During the 1940's, national-character work burgeoned. Most studies relied upon impressions of social institutions and cultural artifacts to infer character structure, which was then dissected in terms of Freudian mechanisms. Some of the better-known works of the decade are: Ruth F. Benedict, *The Chrysanthemum and the Sword, op. cit.;* Geoffrey Gorer, *The American People* (New York: Norton, 1948); Geoffrey Gorer and John Rickman, *The People of Great Russia* (London: Cresset Press, 1949); F. L. K. Hsu, *Under the Ancestors' Shadow* (New York: Columbia University Press, 1948); Abraham Kardiner, *et al., The Psychological Frontiers of Society* (New York: Columbia University Press, 1945); and Margaret Mead, *And Keep Your Powder Dry* (New York: William Morrow, 1942).

The methodology of these studies came under severe criticism during the 1950's. A sustained effort at constructive criticism is Alex Inkeles and Daniel J. Levinson, "National Character: The Study of Modal Personality and Sociocultural Systems," in Gardner Lindzey, ed., *Handbook of Social Psychology,* 2 (Cambridge, Mass.: Addison-Wesley, 1954), 977–1020; a later version of this article noting some of the subsequent literature is in Volume 4 of the revised *Handbook,* Lindzey and Aronson, eds., *op. cit.,* 418–506. In the 1950's and 1960's, national-character studies became less popular, frequently more narrow in objectives, and sometimes more sophisticated. See, for example, *The Annals of the American Academy of Political and Social Science,* 370 (1967), "National Character in the Perspective of the Social Sciences," ed. Don Martindale. Such studies as David McClelland, *et al.,* "Obligations to Self and Society in the United States and Germany," *Journal of Abnormal and Social Psychology*, 56 (1958), 245–55, David McClelland, *The Achieving Society* (New York: Free Press of Glencoe, 1961), and Lucian Pye, *Politics, Personality and Nation-Building: Burma's Search for Identity* (New Haven, Conn.: Yale University Press, 1962), showed how national-character studies, by narrowing their scope and sharpening their procedures, could become both more deserving of confidence and more susceptible to detailed evaluation. An excellent review of Lucian Pye's work, cited above, is Clifford Geertz, "A Study of National Character," *Economic Development and Cultural Change*, 12 (1964), 205–9. (Geertz points out a danger inherent in the use of Eriksonian "identity" analysis: circularity may be introduced by treatments of personal identity as the "carrier" of cultural freight. But culture, Geertz reminds us, entails more than the content of personal identities. Culture takes external, palpable form in enduring institutions. Geertz suggests that Pye ignores the physical mainstays of Burmese culture and that Pye's arguments become circular because culture is that which is internalized and that which is internalized is culture. For a very useful inventory of national-character studies, see H. C. J. Duijker and N. H. Frijda, *National Character and National Stereotypes* (Amsterdam: North-Holland Publishing, 1960).

Some attempts have been made to combine individual and group data in systematic quantitative analyses of aggregation, especially in the studies of "structural" or "compositional" effects. See a review and critique of this literature by Arnold S. Tannenbaum and Jerald G. Bachman, "Structural vs. Individual Effects," *American Journal of Sociology*, 69 (1964), 585–95; and Peter M. Blau's pioneering "Structural Effects," *American Sociological Review*, 25 (1960), 178–93. See also James S. Coleman, "Relational Analysis: The Study of Social Organization with Survey Methods," *Human Organization*, 17 (1958), 28–36.

The problems of relating different "levels of analysis" to one another are considered in a logic-of-science context by May Brodbeck, "Methodological Individualisms: Definition and Reduction," *Philosophy of Science*, 25 (1958), 1–22; and by Ernest Nagel, *The Structure of Science* (New York: Harcourt, Brace & World, 1961), Chapter 11. Shifting from abstract conceptualization to concrete inquiry, the following political study makes use of personality and structural data: Rufus Browning and Herbert Jacob, "Power Motivation and the Political Personality," *Public Opinion Quarterly*, 28 (1964), 75–90. Other disparate treatments of the relationships between social structure and personality include: Hans H. Gerth and C. Wright Mills, *Character and Social Structure*, *op. cit.*, which includes a chapter (ch. 14) emphasizing the part political actors take in shaping their own roles and environments; Alex Inkeles, "Personality and Social Structure," in Robert K. Merton, *et al.*, eds., *Sociology Today* (New York: Basic Books, 1959), pp. 249–76; A. Inkeles and Daniel J. Levinson, "The Personal System and the Sociocultural System in Large-Scale Organizations," *Sociometry*, 26 (1963), 217–29; Bert Kaplan, "Personality and Social Structure," in Joseph B. Gittler, ed., *Review of Sociology* (New York: Wiley, 1957), pp. 87–126; George A. Kelly, "Man's Construction of His Alternatives," in Gardner Lindzey, ed., *Assessment of Human Motives* (New York: Grove Press, 1958), pp. 49–50; and Robert K. Merton, "Bureaucratic Structure and Personality," *Social Forces*, 18 (1940), 560–68.

The causes of war and the conditions of peace have been a continuing source of interest to those who employ the concepts of psychological analysis. Freud turned to the problem in 1915 with "Thoughts for the Time on War and Death," *Standard Edition*, *op. cit.*, 14 (1957), 275–300, and with a preface to an early collection of psychoanalytic writings: "Introduction to Psycho-Analysis of the War Neuroses," *ibid.*, 17 (1955), 207–10. In 1932, he wrote a now famous open letter to Albert Einstein: "Why War?" *ibid.*, 22 (1964), 197–215. Some of the classic studies of the psychology of war and peace are reprinted in Leo Bramsen and George W. Goethals, eds., *War: Studies from Psychology, Sociology, Anthropology* (New York: Basic Books, 1964).

Representative treatments of the psychological sources of war and international tension include, starting chronologically with work of the 1930's: Irene Titus Malamud, "A Psychological Approach to the Study of Social Crises," *American Journal of Sociology*, 43 (1938), 578–92, which analyzes psychological mechanisms in the Russian Revolution; Thomas M. French, "social Conflict and Psychic Conflict," *American Journal of Sociol-

ogy, 44 (1939), 922–31; Franz Alexander, "A World without Psychic Frustration," *American Journal of Sociology*, 49 (1944), 465–69; Ranyard West, *Conscience and Society: A Study of the Psychological Prerequisites of Law and Order* (New York: Emerson, 1945); Talcott Parsons, "Certain Primary Sources and Patterns of Aggression in the Social Structure of the Western World," *Psychiatry*, 10 (1947), 167–81, reprinted in his *Essays in Sociological Theory* (rev. ed.; New York: Free Press of Glencoe, 1954), pp. 298–322; Tom H. Pear, ed., *Psychological Factors of Peace and War* (New York: Philosophical Library, 1951); Frederick S. Dunn, *War and the Minds of Men* (New York: Harper and Brothers, 1950); Otto Klineberg, *Tensions Affecting International Understanding* (New York: Social Science Research Council Bulletin 62, 1950); Kenneth N. Waltz, *Man, the State, and War* (New York: Columbia University Press, 1959); Werner Levi, "On the Causes of War and the Conditions of Peace," *Journal of Conflict Resolution*, 4 (1960), 411–20; Otto Klineberg, *The Human Dimension in International Relations* (New York: Holt, Rinehart and Winston, 1965); Herbert C. Kelman, ed., *International Behavior: A Social-Psychological Analysis* (New York: Holt, Rinehart and Winston, 1965); Judd Marmor, "Nationalism, Internationalism, and Emotional Maturity," *International Journal of Social Psychiatry*, 12 (1966), 217–20; and Edward D. Hoedemaker, "Distrust and Aggression: An Interpersonal-International Analogy," *Journal of Conflict Resolution*, 12 (1968), 69–81. The Group for the Advancement of Psychiatry has published a number of studies by its committee on social issues, notably "Psychiatric Aspects of the Prevention of Nuclear War," Report 57 (1964). For reasons for ignoring psychological factors in international relations—in the interest of economical explanation—see Sidney Verba, "Assumptions of Rationality and Non-Rationality in Models of the International System," *World Politics*, 14 (1961), 93–117.

Other investigators have approached the psychological study of international relations in their more peaceful aspect. An example is Theodore Caplow and Kurt Finsterbush, "France and Other Countries: A Study of International Interaction," *Journal of Conflict Resolution*, 12 (1968), 1–15, which treats similarities between interaction within a small group of nations and within a small group of individuals, using methods drawn from the study of primary groups. Relevant theoretical analyses include: Hadley Cantril, *Human Nature and Political Systems* (New Brunswick, N.J.: Rutgers University Press, 1961); Hermann Weilenmann, "The Interlocking of Nation and Personality Structure," in Karl W. Deutsch and William J. Foltz, eds., *Nation-Building* (New York: Atherton Press, 1963), pp. 33–55; and G. M. Gilbert, ed., *Psychological Approaches to Intergroup and International Understanding* (Austin: Hogg Foundation for Mental Hygiene, University of Texas, 1956).

Finally, questions of aggregation arise in the various psychological works that offer what Greenstein refers to as "sweeping macro-formulations about politics and society." See, for example, the Ranyard West volume referred to two paragraphs above; Erich Fromm, *Escape from Freedom, op. cit.;* Herbert Marcuse, *Eros and Civilization* (rev. ed.; Boston: Beacon Press, 1966); Norman O. Brown, *Life Against Death* (Middletown, Conn.: Wesleyan University Press, 1959); Franz Alexander, *Our Age of Unreason* (rev. ed.; Philadelphia: Lippincott, 1951); R. E. Money-Kyrle, *Psychoanalysis and Politics* (New York: Norton, 1951); Alexander Mitscherlich, *Society without the Father* (London: Tavistock Publications, 1969), a translation of *Auf dem Weg Zur Vaterlosen Gesellschaft* (Munich: Piper, 1963).

Author Index

Abel, Theodore, 19n, 159
Abraham, Karl, 164
Ackerman, Nathaniel, 61
Ackley, Gardner, 15n, 137
Adler, Alfred, 155
Adorno, Theodor W., 15n, 58n, 97, 102–3, 110, 123n, 125, 168
Alexander, Franz, 4n, 183, 184
Alker, Hayward R., 179
Allport, Gordon, 3, 69n, 155, 166
Almond, Gabriel, 174
Alpert, Augusta, 176
Arieti, Silvano, 155
Aronson, Elliot, 127n, 167, 180

Bachman, Jerald G., 136n, 181
Baker, Ray Stannard, 80, 82–83
Baldwin, Alfred L., 166
Barber, James D., 15, 21–23, 77n, 95, 116n, 130, 172, 175
Barton, Allen, 95, 167
Bendix, Reinhard, 19n, 33n, 126n
Benedict, Ruth, 4, 15n, 99n, 169, 180
Benjamin, Lawrence, 126, 170
Berelson, Bernard, 59n
Berger, Morroe, 174
Blalock, Hubert M., 38n, 179
Blau, Peter M., 181
Block, Jack, 101n, 115, 118n, 170
Block, Jeanne, 101n, 115, 170
Bramsen, Leon, 16n, 182
Brennan, Donald G., 10n
Brodbeck, May, 137n, 181
Brodie, Bernard F., 10–11, 69, 80–81, 163
Bronfenbrenner, Urie, 37–39, 159
Brown, Norman O., 4, 184
Browning, Rufus P., 24, 131–33, 139n, 144n, 182

Bruner, Jerome, 14, 19, 25, 29, 68, 125n, 175
Budner, Stanley, 50, 51
Bullitt, William C., 72, 82n, 163–64
Bullock, Alan, 44n
Bushman, Richard L., 72n, 165
Bychowski, Gustav, 161

Campbell, Angus, 25n, 39n, 110n, 170
Cantril, Hadley, 184
Caplow, Theodore, 183
Carlyle, Thomas, 41
Chambers, Whittaker, 72, 163
Chomsky, Noam, 65n
Christiansen, Bjorn, 89, 137n, 162, 178
Christie, Richard F., 15nn, 33n, 39n, 47n, 48n, 50n, 53n, 56nn, 97n, 101, 106n, 123n, 124n, 138n, 168, 169, 171, 175
Clark, L. Pierce, 18n, 165
Clausen, John A., 139n, 160
Coleman, James S., 136n, 137–38, 181
Converse, Philip E., 25n, 135–36, 179
Cook, Peggy, 97n, 168
Crain, Robert L., 46n

Dahl, Robert A., 151n
Davies, A. F., 14n, 72n, 166
Davies, James, 7n
DeGrazia, Sebastian, 164, 175
Denney, Reuel, 15n, 104n
DeSola Pool, Ithiel, 161n
Deutsch, Karl W., 184
Devereux, George, 165

185

188

AUTHOR INDEX

Subject Index

Library of Congress Cataloging-in-Publication Data

Greenstein, Fred I.
Personality and politics.

Reprint. Originally published: New York :
Norton, 1975, c1969. (The Norton library ; N767)
Bibliography: p.   Includes indexes.
1. Political psychology. 2. Personality. 3. Inference. I. Title.
JA74.5.G74   1987   320′.01′9   87-2427
ISBN 0-691-07731-2 (alk. paper)
ISBN 0-691-02260-7 (pbk.)